Lobbying: Business, Law and Public Policy

Why and How 12,000 People Spend $3+ Billion Impacting Our Government

Lobbying: Business, Law and Public Policy

Why and How 12,000 People Spend $3+ Billion Impacting Our Government

Mark Fagan

VANDEPLAS PUBLISHING, LLC
UNITED STATES OF AMERICA

Lobbying: Business, Law and Public Policy,

Why and How 12,000 People Spend $3+ Billion Impacting Our Government

Fagan, Mark

Published by:

Vandeplas Publishing, LLC – February 2015

801 International Parkway, 5th Floor
Lake Mary, FL. 32746
USA

www.vandeplaspublishing.com

ISBN 978-1-60042-238-6

Dedication

To the three outstanding advocates in my life - Janet, Miriam, and Abigail
- Mark

Acknowledgements

I owe the motivation for this book to my students at Harvard Kennedy School who continually push me to refine my own understand of lobbying. I thank my colleague Professor Tamar Frankel for introducing me to the law and ethics of lobbying and encouraging me to examine the business and policy aspects of advocacy. The book would not have been possible without the continual stream of insights and energy of Christina Marin. She was my sounding board, cheerleader, and substantive editor. Thanks also to Larry DiCara for his improvements to the book. Any remaining errors or inaccuracies are my sole responsibility. A final thank you to the cartoon artists who make the book much more fun to read – Emily Abramovich, Bujar Kapexhiu, Nick Nazzaro and Rachel Prouty.

Contents

Preface

Mention the words "lobbying" and/or "lobbyist" to a friend or colleague and you will likely get a strong response. Some people view lobbying as nothing more than the practice of buying influence, power and legislation. To others, lobbying plays a vital part of our policy-making process, enabling us to exercise one of our most treasured constitutional rights – the right to petition the government. In reality, both positions have merit and that is what makes lobbying such an interesting practice. Lobbying is a multibillion-dollar industry that impacts all aspects of public policy at the highest level of government. At the same time, it is also the avenue by which the average citizen meets with their government representative to request action.

Lobbying is inherently a multi-disciplinary topic. Effective lobbying requires understanding the political and policy-making process. It is also a function of understanding human psychology as well as creating and executing impactful strategies. Many lobbyists have a legal background, which enables them to draft and/or dissect legislation and make meaningful recommendations. Lastly, lobbying requires business acumen, drawing on skills such as networking, consulting and public relations. While these disciplines can be looked at separately, it is putting them together that unlocks the real value of lobbying.

This book is United States centric for several reasons. The lobbying profession is most developed in the United States in terms of size, scale, and codification. The transparency that results from years of refining lobbying regulations opens a wider window to the people, policies and strategies that make the industry robust. Because lobbying has a long and well-documented history in the United States, there is comparatively more scholarship and written material on the topic. Finally, many other nations look to the United States as they both develop and regulate lobbying in their own geography.

The goal of this book is to take the mystery and hyperbole out of lobbying and explain the business, law and public policy aspects of this critical function; one that is not going away. This goal is achieved not only by reading the text but also completing the *Challenges* in each chapter. There is a growing body of literature that indicates active learning is the most effective learning. Therefore, throughout the book there are *Learning by Doing* sections which provide an opportunity to apply the concepts detailed in the book. The theme of these sections is hydraulic fracturing, a topic that provides fertile ground for lobbyists for four reasons. First, fracking is a new process that offers great promise (e.g. low cost fuel and energy independence) but also raises important environmental concerns. Second, it is largely unregulated today but legislation is likely at the state and federal level. Third, people are passionate on the topic on both sides – there is not an obvious right answer. Finally, lobbyists are already shaping the discussion and will continue to do so. Investing the time to complete these exercises will pay dividends.

The motivation for writing this book is to provide a manual of instruction for the lobbying profession. While there are texts for journalists, lawyers, businessmen, and nonprofit leaders; an all-encompassing, introductory handbook for the study of lobbying is largely absent in academic environments across the United States. The effort is successful if by the last page of the book the reader understands and appreciates (1) the history and rationale of lobbying from King Solomon to the present day; (2) the business of lobbying; (3) the laws, regulations and ethics that accompany lobbying; (4) the art and science of effective lobbying; and (5) the differences in lobbying worldwide.

One way the reader can measure the impact of the book is to complete the following short lobbying survey before reading the book and then after. I trust the factual questions can be answered with greater confidence at the end of the book. As to the attitude questions, the answers may or may not change, but they should have a stronger rationale at the last page.

Lobbying Attitude Survey

	Strongly Disagree	Disagree	Agree	Strongly Agree
1. Lobbying adds great value to the democratic process	O	O	O	O
2. The average citizen gains from the activities of lobbyists.	O	O	O	O
3. Lobbying is about money, money is about power, power corrupts; ergo lobbying corrupts.	O	O	O	O
4. Disclosure based regulation of lobbying is sufficient to prevent corruption.	O	O	O	O
5. The lobbyists who have the best resources (money, access, people) win.	O	O	O	O
6. Lobbying is more about whom you know than what you know.	O	O	O	O
7. Lobbyists have more influence on lawmakers' decisions than voting constituents.	O	O	O	O
8. Lobbying grows in lockstep with government spending.	O	O	O	O
9. Lobbying is predominantly a United States-based concept.	O	O	O	O
10. I can see myself being a lobbyist in the future.	O	O	O	O

Chapter 1: History of Lobbying

The starting point for any new exploration is a definition: What is the definition of lobbying? As with most terms, there are many definitions. The Oxford English Dictionary defines lobbying as "a group of people seeking to influence politicians or public officials on a particular issue."[1] BusinessDictionary.com's definition is: "The act of attempting to influence business and government leaders to create legislation or conduct an activity that will help a particular organization."[2] From the legal world, one definition of lobbying is "any personal solicitation of a member of the legislative body during a session thereof, by private interview, or letter or message, or other means and appliances not addressed solely to the judgment, to favor or oppose, or to vote for or against any bill...."[3] The academic and practitioner communities offer the following: (1) "...a deliberate attempt to effect or resist change in the law through direct communications with public policymakers..."[4] (2) "...all direct attempts to influence government officials and employees in Congress and at the very highest levels of the Executive Branch while excluding other types of government actors and to influence the public."[5] (3) "...[an interest group is] any nonparty organization that regularly tries to influence government policy."[6]

Each of the definitions is unique and reflects a particular viewpoint. Looking across them, however, there are common themes. The word "influence" is used in most of the definitions. The targets of influence are government officials and policymakers. There are also concepts that are not reflected broadly but are nevertheless important. For example, the phrase "effect or resist change." Here the author introduces the idea that lobbying can be directed not only at changing policy but also maintaining the status quo. In the last quote the term "regularly" highlights that lobbying is often a sustained activity. While several of the definitions focus on legislation, one also highlights the importance of lobbying at the executive branch. Lobbying regulators is often as important as lobbying legislators.

Based on the areas of commonality and some of the unique aspects of these definitions, four overall themes emerge (Exhibit 1-1). The first is that lobbying is <u>active</u>. It is organized, strategic, and direct. Second, lobbying is about <u>influence</u>, which is achieved through education, persuasion, contacts and money. Third, lobbying targets <u>government policymakers</u> including legislators, their staffs, regulators, and/or administrators. Finally, lobbying is about <u>impact</u> – making change or protecting the status quo.

```
┌─────────────────────────────────────────────────────────────┐
│                         Exhibit 1-1                          │
│                  Lobbying Definition Redux                    │
│  ┌───┬─────────────────────────────────────────────────────┐ │
│  │ L │                                                     │ │
│  │ O │         **Active**: Strategic and direct            │ │
│  │ B ├─────────────────────────────────────────────────────┤ │
│  │ B │                                                     │ │
│  │ Y │        **Influence**: Make a difference             │ │
│  │   ├─────────────────────────────────────────────────────┤ │
│  │ I │                                                     │ │
│  │ N │      **Government Policymakers**: All                │ │
│  │   ├─────────────────────────────────────────────────────┤ │
│  │ G │                                                     │ │
│  │   │          **Impact**: Get results                    │ │
│  └───┴─────────────────────────────────────────────────────┘ │
└─────────────────────────────────────────────────────────────┘
```

Exhibit 1-1
Lobbying Definition Redux

LOBBYING	
	Active: Strategic and direct
	Influence: Make a difference
	Government Policymakers: All
	Impact: Get results

Origins of Lobbying

Lobbying is not a new concept. The term dates back to the mid-1800s. Urban legend has it that 'lobbying' described the petitioners waiting for President Grant at the Willard Hotel. Supposedly, Grant complained about the annoying lobbyists getting in the way of his cigar and drink. There are, however, references to the term lobbyist 30 years earlier and as far back as the 1600s in Europe when it was used to refer to the lobbies of Parliament.[7]

While the term itself may be hundreds of years old, the concept of petitioning the government has existed for thousands of years (Exhibit 1-2). The idea can be traced back to the Old Testament where people came to petition King Solomon and later, to The Magna Carta, which protected an individual's ability to petition. In the United States, the concept is rooted in the Bodies of Liberties adopted to rule the Massachusetts Bay colony in 1630 and came to form a central part of the United States Constitution. The First Amendment reads: "Congress shall make no law respecting the establishment of religion, or prohibiting the free exercise thereof; or abridging the freedom of speech, or of the press; or the right of the people peaceably to assemble, and to petition the government for redress of grievances." Looking back at the definition of lobbying, three elements of the First Amendment are used by lobbyists: assembly, free speech, and the right to petition.

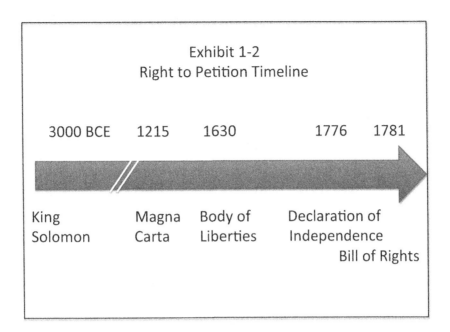

Exhibit 1-2
Right to Petition Timeline

3000 BCE	1215	1630	1776	1781
King Solomon	Magna Carta	Body of Liberties	Declaration of Independence	
				Bill of Rights

The right to petition the government is clearly well-established and deeply rooted. However, this is only half of the lobbying story. The other half, a counterbalance, is the prohibition on buying legislation. After the outbreak of the Civil War, the Province Tool Company sought to sell its rifles to the United States government. The company retained a lobbyist, Norris, to go to Washington and advocate on its behalf. Norris and Tool Company entered into a contract that called for Tool Company to pay Norris the difference between the sale price to the government and $17 for each rifle sold. Norris, leveraging his lobbying skills, succeeded in selling 25,000 rifles to the war department for $20 each. Thus, Norris was entitled to a $75,000 payment from Tool Company; a great deal of money in the 1860s. The company refused to pay claiming that Norris was not the reason the sale was made. Norris sued the company claiming breach of contract.

The case went to the Supreme Court where the majority ruled against Norris. Their rationale was that the structure of the contract and its associated activities were counter to sound public policy since they had a potentially corrupting influence on the decision-makers.

"It has been asserted in cases relating to agreements for compensation to procure legislation. These have been uniformly declared invalid, and the decisions have not turned upon the question, whether improper influences were contemplated or used, but on the corrupting tendency of the agreements. Legislation should be prompted solely from considerations of the public good... Whatever tends to divert the attention of legislators from their high duties, to mislead their judgments, or to substitute other motives for their conduct then the advancement of the public interests, must necessarily and directly tend to impair the integrity of our public institutions."[8]

More than 150 years after this decision, the basic prohibition on "buying" legislation remains in force.

Lobbying therefore is pulled in opposite directions. The right to petition, one of our strongest rights, is juxtaposed with the prohibition on buying legislation. This tension is one reason why lobbying is so controversial.

Lobbyists Circa 1850
The controversy surrounding lobbying is not new. Former Senate Majority Leader Robert Byrd delivered a speech in 1987 entitled "Lobbyists." He quotes the following from an 1869 newspaper article: "Winding in and out the long, devious basement passage, crawling through the corridors, trailing its slimy length from gallery to committee room, at last it lies stretched at full weight on the floor of Congress – this dazzling reptile, this huge, scaly serpent of the lobby."[9] There was a solid basis for this characterization of lobbyists. At the time, lobbying was evolving from an individual petitioning on his or her own behalf to a third party professional doing the lobbying on behalf of others, as in the case of Tool Company. The country was learning that public policy was being shaped in no small part by "hired gun" lobbyists and many were skeptical.

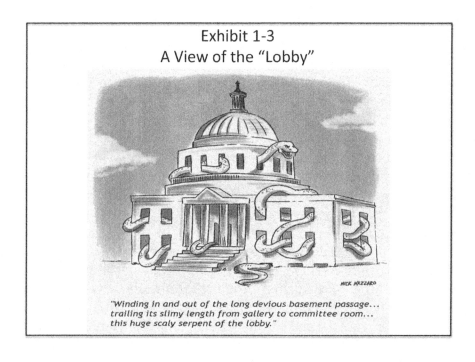

Exhibit 1-3
A View of the "Lobby"

NICK NAZZARO

"Winding in and out of the long devious basement passage...
trailing its slimy length from gallery to committee room...
this huge scaly serpent of the lobby."

This new breed of lobbyist was typified by Samuel Ward, King of the Lobby. Ward came to Washington in the 1850s after a series of business successes and failures. With some mentoring from Thurlow Weed and leveraging his own business savvy, he was able to successfully settle some Paraguayan claims. Over the next 30 years, he became one of the most powerful lobbyists in Washington. His own explanation of lobbying is instructive: "This business of lobbying, so-called, is as precarious as fishing in the Hebrides. You get all ready, your boats go out – suddenly there comes a storm, and away you are driven... Everyone who knows anything about Washington, knows that 10 times, [no], 50 times, more measures are lost then are carried; but once in a while a pleasant little windfall of this kind recompenses us, who are toiling here, for the disappointments. I am not ashamed – I do not say I am proud, but I am not ashamed – of the occupation. It is a useful one."[10] In his description, he highlights the difficulty in successfully influencing the passage of legislation. He also introduces the idea that lobbying is "useful."

> **Notable Quote**
> Uncle Sam [Ward], the one man who knows everybody worth knowing.
> - Vanity Fair

> **Notable Quote**
> To reach the heart or get the vote, the surest way is down the throat.
> Colt Lobbyist
> (Byrd 1987)

In his case, the usefulness or value-added was in bringing people together over fine wine and food so that they could exchange information and influence. Senator Byrd describes these dinners as an opportunity to "educate legislators."[11] The setting he created was certainly conducive to conversation. As Catherine Jacob describes in her biography of Sam Ward: "No delicacy, claimed one reporter, was too costly or rare for Sam Ward's table. He shopped for his own terrapin and canvas backed ducks, imported his own teas and blended his own coffee. With painstaking care, Sam filled annotated menus for 15-course meals many with wines..."[12] Jacob goes on to write: "Sam's motto was that the shortest distance between a pending bill and a congressman's "aye" was through his stomach."[13]

The success of lobbyists like Ward encouraged others to join his ranks. During the latter half of the 1800s the number of lobbyists in Washington increased dramatically. The prevalence of lobbyists attending House sessions became enough of a concern that in 1876 the House required lobbyists to register with the Clerk. In 1879, lobbyists were restricted from the Press Gallery after complaints that they were using the gallery to access the chamber, thus pushing out the real press. The increase in the number of lobbyists was fostered by stories of success and by the growing professionalism of those who lobbied. While wining and dining legislators remained important, the facts, figures and arguments that lobbyists could provide were also seen as essential to the passage or defeat of legislation.

The Lobbyist Circa 2000

For more than 100 years, lobbying continued to grow and become increasingly professional. Today, more than 12,000 individuals are federally registered lobbyists. Lobbying expenditures at the federal level exceed $3 billion annually. Despite the growth, the new Kings of the Lobby have many characteristics and use processes similar to those of Sam Ward.

Consider Gerald Cassidy, the founder of one of Washington's largest and most prestigious lobbying firms, Cassidy & Associates. Cassidy rose from humble origins. Early in his career he served as a legal aid lawyer helping migrants on hunger issues. Through a chance encounter with Senator George McGovern he landed a job working for the Senate Select Committee on Nutrition and Human Needs. The experience introduced him to Washington – people, process and opportunity. After leaving the Committee, he and a colleague Kenneth Schlosberg created a firm to help clients navigate in Washington.

One of their first clients, Jean Mayer, was a nutritionist who had recently become president of Tufts University. Mayer sought to create a nutrition school at the university to expand the school's notoriety. Cassidy and Scholsberg devised a strategy to do so that would revolutionize individual project funding – they invented the earmark. An earmark bypasses the historic two-part process of securing funds for a project by hardwiring (and legally binding) funds to a specific project in the first part of the process. The concept only had value if it could be executed. Here Cassidy leveraged a relationship with the House member whose district included Tufts. The member was the powerful Speaker of the House, Tip O'Neil. Cassidy carefully orchestrated a lobbying campaign that included education and then relationship building between Mayer and Congressional leaders. The strategy worked and Tufts received $27 million to create the Friedman School of Nutrition Science and Policy in 1981.

With the Tufts success as a calling card, Cassidy's firm began a three decade expansion leveraging the earmark concept for universities, hospitals, corporations and local governments. During this time, he built strong relationships with some of the most powerful decision makers in Washington. Success clearly fosters relationships: Everyone wants to be associated with a winner. There is, however, another aspect of Cassidy's relationship building – campaign contributions. He and his wife have donated more than $1 million to campaigns. Members of his firm have contributed more than $5 million.[14]

A comparison of Ward and Cassidy shows numerous similarities. Both understood how to meet client expectations in the Washington environment. They leveraged their networks and built a reputation for getting things done. Lastly, wining and dining influential policy makers was also a key strategy. Yet, there are some important differences. Ward was dominantly a facilitator, bringing interested parties together but not directly making the case. Cassidy was an advocate, taking positions and supporting them with policy makers. Also, Ward's influence centered more on leveraging personal relationships. Cassidy used an innovation in the legislative process to meet client expectations. Finally, campaign contributions are now a requirement for relationships between lobbyist and legislators. With the cost of a House campaign exceeding $1 million and a Senate race nearly $10 million, legislators pay attention to those who "pay" in the form of direct contributions and/or fundraising.[15]

Scandals and Response

Throughout the 200-plus years of lobbying history, lobbying has not been able to disassociate itself from scandal, perhaps because 'what's right' versus 'what's wrong' is not well defined. Sam Ward, notwithstanding his lobbying by facilitation, was embroiled in many controversies. A newspaper charged him with distributing money to the media and federal officials in support of a subsidy for the Pacific Mail Steamship Company and lavishly entertaining decision makers. He was also questioned by a congressional committee. Rather than dodge the issue, he responded directly: "There is nothing in the world as excellent as entertainments of a refined order. Talleyrand says that diplomacy is assisted by good dinners..."[16] He felt the same was true for lobbying.

Major scandals seem to erupt every 10 or 20 years. The Credit Mobilier in 1872, in which Representative Oakes Ames distributed stock in a railroad company to other members of Congress was one such controversy. Ames sought his colleagues' support on railroad legislation. He viewed his actions in giving away stock as simply a way of making more friends in Congress. He openly testified to his activities before a congressional committee. However, his congressional colleagues likely, spurred by the media, saw things differently and he was censured.[17] In 1935, Congress debated legislation that would break up utility holding companies. A lobbyist for the Associated Gas and Electric Company adopted a novel approach to influence legislators. He decided to have constituents send telegrams supporting the status quo to influential legislators; however, rather than bother constituents he dictated and sent the telegrams himself! One legislator received 816 such telegrams.[18]

Fast forward to the 2000's and meet Jack Abramoff. Abramoff was a high profile and very well-connected lobbyist who plead guilty to fraud, conspiracy and tax evasion and was sentenced to six years in prison. He was active in Republican politics from college on. After a stint as Chair of the College Republicans, he went on to become a very successful lobbyist. His core relationship was with Texas Republican Representative Tom Delay. Through that relationship, he built a network among the republican elite. During the Bush Administration, he had access and influence that reached to the highest levels. Abramoff practiced Sam Ward-style entertainment; wining and dining lobbyees at his co-owned posh restaurant, Signatures, and sharing his skyboxes with policy makers at major league sporting events to curry favor.

He added a 21st Century twist – travel to desirable destinations. He hosted and paid for golfing outings to Scotland for members of Congress including Tom Delay, Bob Ney, and Tom Feeney. Abramoff's lobbying extended to the executive branch, too. He also took David Safavian, a top procurement officer in the Bush Administration, for a golfing junket at the same time he was seeking to do business with the General Services Administration. The gifts and travel accepted by legislators and members of the administration actually had a high price – many of Abramoff's guests were found guilty of ethics violations and breaking the law (Exhibit 1-4). For example, Representative Bob Ney was sentenced to two and a half years in prison after pleading guilty and acknowledging he took bribes from Abramoff. Tom Delay was twice reprimanded by the House Ethics Committee. Numerous Congressional staffers were also convicted in conjunction with Abramoff.

> Notable Quote
>
> I was involved deeply in a system of bribery — legalized bribery for the most part… [that] still to a large part exists today.
>
> - Abramoff
> (Abramoff 2011)

Abramoff himself was sentenced to prison as a result of his lobbying efforts for American Indian tribes. On behalf of one of his initial clients, a Choctaw Indian group from Mississippi, he successfully lobbied to defeat legislation that would have taxed Indian casinos. The victory enabled him to build a large lobbying practice supporting the interests of Indian tribes' casino operations. However, he also lobbied on behalf of interests opposing his clients' positions to ensure his clients would continue to need his services. After his time in prison, Abramoff wrote a biography in which he was highly critical of lobbying.

```
Exhibit 1-4
Some of Abramoff's Casualties


House Member:                 1 yr. prison      Favors for gifts
Deputy Interior Secretary     10 mo. prison     Obstructing justice
Chief Procurement Officer     1 yr. prison      Lying to investigators
Justice Department Official   1 mo. halfway     Conflict of interest
Member Chief of Staff         100 hrs service   Conspiring to corrupt
Member Chief of Staff         2 yrs. probation  Conspiracy
Member Chief of Staff         5 yrs. probation  Conspiracy to defraud
Lobbyist                      20 mo. prison     Bribery
Lobbyist                      4 yrs. Prison     Mail fraud, conspiracy,
                                                tax evasion
```

The typical response to scandals is regulation. While there have been calls for reforms and regulations since the 1800s, the only significant reform in the country's early years was the requirement to register with the Clerk of the House. In 1938, Congress passed legislation to limit the influence of foreign entities, concerned about the rising power of the Nazis. Six years later, Congressmen took a first swing at enacting legislation to directly regulate lobbying. The legislation was poorly drafted and was eviscerated by court challenges. It was not until 1995 (The Lobbying Disclosure Act) that the United States adopted meaningful lobbying regulation. The philosophical foundation of the regulation was registration and disclosure. The shared belief was that, paraphrasing Justice Louis D. Brandeis, sunlight would be an effective disinfectant. Notwithstanding the 1995 Act, scandals (such as the one involving Abramoff) surfaced only ten years later.

Explanations of Lobbying's Longevity
What accounts for the continued growth of lobbying despite the scandals? It very often works. Cassidy was able to secure earmarked funds for Tufts School of Nutrition Science and Policy. Subsequently, he was able to secure federal funding for a veterinary school at Tufts. Abramoff was able to prevent legislation that would have taxed American Indian gambling revenues. Furthermore, lobbying continues to have high paybacks. The *Boston Sunday Globe* ran a front-page story in 2013 highlighting the astronomical returns from lobbying investments. The article titled, "Tax Lobbyists Help Businesses Reap Windfalls," highlights the tax benefits Whirlpool and other companies have achieved through their lobbying efforts. "By investing just $1.8 million over two

years in payments for Washington lobbyists, Whirlpool secured the renewal of lucrative energy tax credits for making high–efficiency appliances that it estimates will be worth a combined $120 million for 2012 and 2013. Such breaks have helped the company keep its total tax expenses below zero in recent years. The return on that lobbying investment? About 6,700 percent. These are the sort of returns that have attracted growing swarms of corporate tax lobbyists to the capital over the last decades..."[19]

Three models offer insight into how lobbying yields such benefits (Exhibit 1-5). First is exchange – I do for you and you do for me. The following quote from Senator Daniel Webster typifies the exchange model circa 1820: "Since I have arrived here, I have had an application to be concerned, professionally, against the bank, which I have declined, of course, although I believe my retainer has not been renewed, or refreshed, as usual. If it be wished that my relation to the bank should be continued, it may be well to send me the usual retainer."[20] A recent example is Abramoff's funding travel for congressional members and staff in exchange for favorable action of legislation of interest to Abramoff's clients. The core implication of this model is that those with the resources – money, access, time, membership, expertise – will significantly dominate policy making.

While intuitively appealing, a more careful consideration raises questions about the exchange model. First, what is the currency of exchange? Funds for reelection would seem logical but analytical studies show little consistent connection. A detailed study of farm bill appropriations showed that the lobbying expenditures did not appear to be a credible driving factor.[21] A second concern is the extensive evidence that lobbyists spend much of their time with those who support their position.[22] If lobbyists were seeking an exchange, they should be spending time with the opposition or at least the undecided. Third, a 2013 study by Frank R. Baumgartner of the University of North Carolina found that money does not buy outcomes. He analyzed the resources of various special interest groups and found that the most resourced won only 45 to 56 percent of the time.[23] There must be more than just exchange to explain lobbying.

A second model is education. President John F. Kennedy captured this model when he said, "Lobbyists are, in many cases, expert technicians and capable of explaining complex and difficult subjects in a clear, understandable fashion...the lobbyists who speak for the various economic, commercial and other functional interests of this country serve a very useful purpose and have assumed an important role in the legislative process."[24] Visit the websites of major lobbying firms and you will read about their role in educating members and staff about the complex issues of the day. For example, the Patton Boggs website states: "Our understanding of the complexities of federal agencies, rulemaking processes, and regulatory frameworks is augmented by our knowledge of specific industry sectors those agencies regulate, enabling us to provide expert advice on the impact of proposed or pending policy changes, potential impact of those changes and how best to plan for pending regulatory changes well in advance of their realization."[25] This also explains why public interest groups provide legislators and administrators with extensive policy analysis. Their goal is to influence policy makers through education. While this model is attractive, it also has limitations. It does not answer the question why lobbyists are needed. Why can't legislators have their own information-gathering staff or do their own fact-finding? Moreover, the education/persuasion model does not resolve the finding that lobbyists tend to spend much of their time educating supporters. If lobbying is really about educating, wouldn't more time be spent educating those 'in the dark'?

A third model offered by Hall and Deardorff is that lobbying is a legislative subsidy. They write: "[Lobbying] is an attempt to subsidize the legislative resources of members who already support the cause of the group. In short, lobbying operates on the legislator's budget line, not on his or her utility function. It is akin more to a gift than a trade."[26] This model has intuitive appeal. Legislators have limited resources and immense needs for information and insight. They seek to influence multiple issues but do not have the expertise to act on multiple fronts without assistance. Lobbyists fill this gap. The lobbyists are most influential when they support a receptive audience – those who agree with their client's position. Hall and Deardorff provide a strong theoretical framework for the subsidy model. The practical implications of their model are (1) lobbyists focus on their allies and the stronger the supporter the more the focus (i.e. subsidy); (2) lobbyists avoid their opponents; and (3) uncommitted policy makers receive little attention from lobbyists.[27]

Exhibit 1-5
Models of Lobbying

Model #1: Exchange
You scratch my back...I scratch yours

Model #2: Education/Persuasion
Policy issues are complex...I am here to help

Model #3: Legislative Subsidy
Overworked and understaffed?...Let me help

Reflect on the three models and you are likely to conclude that each has merit but also some limitations. Thus, it is likely that the successful lobbyist today leverages all three models in meeting their clients' objectives. (Exhibit 1-6)

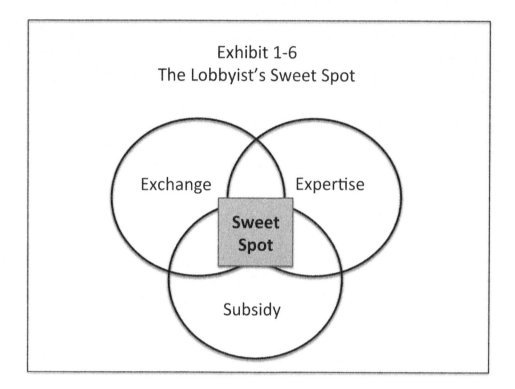

Exhibit 1-6
The Lobbyist's Sweet Spot

Exchange

Expertise

Sweet Spot

Subsidy

Challenge: What Went Wrong?

Samuel Colt was the inventor and manufacturer of the first firearm that could shoot multiple bullets using a mechanical rotating cylinder. He received a patent for his "revolver" in Great Britain in 1835 and in the United States in 1839. His revolver allowed for six shots without reloading, compared to the more common single- or double-loading firearms. With these patents in hand, Colt began to compete for sales of his firearms to the United States military. His initial attempt was not a great success. He was only able to get a contract for 500 units. Colt's response to this disappointment was twofold. First, he went about improving the quality of his firearms. Second, he launched a lobbying campaign in Washington to influence the government's procurement offices. He enlisted powerful politicians and military officers to advocate on his behalf. The team included influential, well-respected, and motivated individuals. Of the dozen "lobbyists", two were members of Congress. His team lobbied key Congressional leaders using the Sam Ward approach – it wined and dined them. He also distributed custom-made revolvers to family members of Congressmen. One commentator remarked: "Colt had given out enough pistols to arm a platoon of Congressman." In 1840, his lobbying efforts paid off, he was awarded a large government contract for his firearms.

Colt realized that his patent would expire in the early part of the 1850s and, with it, his lucrative government contracts. He resolved to introduce legislation that would add seven to ten years to his patent. He again leveraged his lobbying savvy. A congressional committee did recommend the extension. Legislative action, however, was stalled by allegations of bribery and fraud. An investigation was held "to inquire whether money had been offered to members, or other illegal or improper means used, to induce members in securing the passage or defeat of a bill to extend Colt's patent for seven years." While the investigation did not reveal a "smoking gun" (pun intended), the inquiry was sufficient to kill the legislation.

Colt had a demonstrated track record of success lobbying Congress. He had money, prestige, and a skilled team of lobbyists; yet, he was unable to achieve his objective. What might have gone wrong? What could he have done differently to achieve his desired outcome?

The Growth Trajectory

Notwithstanding the uncertainty about which model is driving lobbying outcomes and the endless scandals, lobbying continues on a growth trajectory. Between 1998 and 2012, federal lobbying expenditures rose from $1.4 billion to $3.3 billion.[28] What accounts for the rapid growth? The obvious answer is the expansion of federal government's policy making and spending pulls advocates to Washington who seek a portion of the largess or desire to influence policy outcomes. The federal government's reach is much broader today than any time in the past. From healthcare to consumer protection to foreign aid, congress and regulators are impacting private actions thus inducing interest group action. Government spending has increased dramatically in recent years, from just over $1.5 trillion in 1998 to about $3 trillion in 2012. Exhibit 1-7 shows the growth in lobbying expenditures, which grew proportionally to federal outlays. Government spending, however, is only part of the story. Government involvement in non-spending issues has also grown substantially. One example of this is the government's role in intellectual property protection in the digital age. Lobbyists are just as active on these issues as they are on those associated with government spending.

> **Fun Fact**
> There are 22 lobbyists for each member of Congress.
> (OpenSecrets)

> **Food For Thought**
> Why are lobbying expenditures and the federal budget so tightly linked?

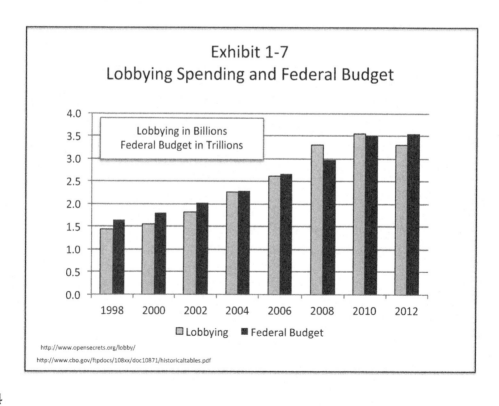

Exhibit 1-7
Lobbying Spending and Federal Budget

Lobbying in Billions
Federal Budget in Trillions

Lobbying   Federal Budget

http://www.opensecrets.org/lobby/
http://www.cbo.gov/ftpdocs/108xx/doc10871/historicaltables.pdf

Beyond the <u>pull</u> argument described above, there are also active social organizations that <u>push</u> their agenda (and their lobbyists) to the Capital. Civil rights, gender equality, environmental protection are but a few of the interest groups that have been formed to change federal policy. Organizations created to advance these agendas push their way onto the Congressional and regulatory scenes. The logic of the push model is that as new groups are formed they go to Washington seeking to have their voices heard.

The push versus pull question has been analytically answered by Leech, Baumgartner, Pira and Semanko. Using databases of lobbying activity and Congressional hearings, the group found a strong relationship between government activity and advocates being drawn to Washington. Their research leads to the following conclusion: "Government activity acts like a magnet, pulling groups of all kinds to become active. More so than direct federal spending or the number of business firms in various areas of the economy, government attention, as measured by congressional hearings, draws groups to Washington."[29] It is this magnet that has created the multi-billion dollar lobbying industry detailed in the next chapter.

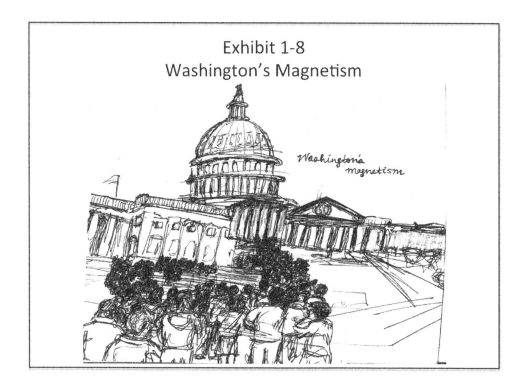

Exhibit 1-8
Washington's Magnetism

History Highlights

- Lobbying is about actively influencing government policymakers to make change or protect the status quo.
- The term "lobbying/lobbyist" is hundreds of years old but the concept of petitioning the government dates back to biblical times.
- The legal foundation for lobbying is the First Amendment right to free speech, assembly and petition but there is a counterbalance and that is the prohibition on buying legislation.
- Lobbying has long been controversial. Its poor repute is due – at least in part – to Sam Ward-style, wining and dining lobbying.
- Scandals have plagued the profession. Legislators have responded to these scandals by passing bills aimed at preventing corruption while protecting First Amendment rights through registration and disclosure.
- All three models of lobbying (exchange, education/persuasion, and legislative subsidy) are used by successful lobbyists today.
- Lobbying has been a growth industry; revenues now top $3 billion annually.
- The growth results from government involvement pulling interest groups to Washington and business and social groups pushing their agenda to the capital.

Learning by Doing

The history of lobbying demonstrates that new areas of activity generate new government involvement which in turn fosters lobbying. Hydraulic fracturing to extract natural gas and oil is in the early stages of this evolutionary process. Hydraulic fracturing is a technique for extracting natural gas and oil from micro-pores in some shale rock formations. Exhibit 1-9 contrasts this process with traditional gas and oil extraction. Traditional extraction is accomplished by drilling a vertical well directly into a pool of gas or oil. The lower pressure at the surface compared to the higher pressure in the pool propels the fuel upward. Once the bulk of the fuel is extracted, a mix of water and chemicals is injected in the well to recover the remaining product. Over the past 100 years, the easily-accessible pools of gas and oil have been tapped out, which is why fracturing has become an important process.

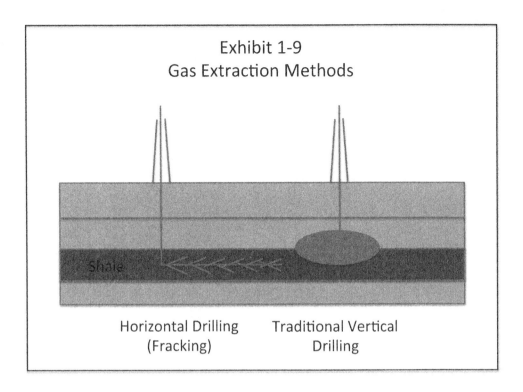

Exhibit 1-9
Gas Extraction Methods

Shale

Horizontal Drilling (Fracking)   Traditional Vertical Drilling

Geologists have long understood that gas and oil was trapped in pores of some shale formations. However, it was not economical to extract this gas as it required the rock to be fractured to loosen the gas and oil. In the past ten years, technology improvements have made tapping shale gas and oil cost effective. The first enabler was refined horizontal drilling. In contrast to traditional vertical drilling, the well is drilled vertically, the drill is turned horizontally 90 degrees and then run for a mile or more. A mix of high pressure water, sand and chemicals are injected into the well to fracture the shale allowing the freed gas and oil to move up the well to the surface. A second innovation was improvements in geologic information about shale formations to identify the most promising drilling locations.

Three geologic areas are the current focus of fracking. The Barrnett Field in central Texas, one of the largest reserves of onshore gas in the country, has been extracting gas from shale for more than ten years. The Marcellus Formation extends from West Virginia through Pennsylvania to New York. While extensive fracking is taking place in Pennsylvania on the Marcellus Formation, there is a drilling moratorium in New York as the state assesses the benefits, costs and risks of fracking. The value of the gas and oil in the Marcellus region is estimated at more than $200 billion. A third area is the Bakkan Formation in Montana and North Dakota. The primary product here is oil, an estimated two billion barrels. The reserves in these location and others are substantial. Exhibit 1-10 shows the expected gas production from fracking in the coming years.

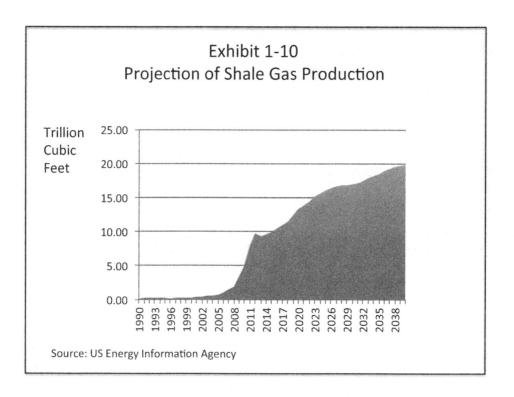

Exhibit 1-10
Projection of Shale Gas Production

Trillion Cubic Feet

Source: US Energy Information Agency

Fracking has changed the energy dynamics in the United States. The growing supply of gas from fracking has put significant downward pressure on gas prices. Cheap gas has changed the energy economics for several sectors. There has been a dramatic shift to gas for producing electricity, thus displacing coal. The share of electricity produced from gas has increased by 10-15 percentage points in recent years at coal's expense. After years of shifting plastics production offshore, companies are again opening United States capacity because more affordable gas makes domestic manufacturing attractive.

Hydraulic fracturing has been controversial. Many environmentalists contend that the process is contaminating ground water. There have been incidences of well water burning as it comes out of the tap, allegedly as a result of fracking. There are also reports of increased seismic activity also blamed on fracking. Other environmentalists are in support of fracking because they see the process as a way to substitute lower carbon emitting gas for higher carbon coal to generate electricity. Landowners with the opportunity to earn revenues from fracking are also supportive of drilling.

Fracturing is fertile ground for lobbyists for four reasons. First, fracking is a new process that offers great promise (e.g. low cost fuel and energy independence) but also raises important environmental concerns. Second, it is largely unregulated today but legislation is likely to occur at the state and federal level. Third, people are passionate on the topic on both sides – there is not an obvious right answer. Finally, lobbyists are already shaping the discussion and will continue to do so.

Your task at the end of each chapter is to apply the general concepts described in the text to lobby on hydraulic fracturing. In the next chapter, you will create a business plan for a lobbying firm focused on fracking. Subsequent activities will include registering as a lobbyist and preparing your quarterly disclosure forms, developing a lobbying campaign, targeting policy makers, and honing your pitch.

Bibliography for Chapter 1

Abramoff, Jack, "Capital Punishment: The Hard Truth About Washington Corruption From America's Most Notorious Lobbyist." WND Books, 2011.

Baumgartner, Frank R. "Converting Expectations: New Empirical Evidence on Congressional Lobbying and Public Policy." *University of North Carolina at Chapel Hill* (2013)

Byrd, Robert. "United States Senate." Government. *Lobbyists*, September 28, 1987. http://www.senate.gov/legislative/common/briefing/Byrd_History_Lobbying.htm.

"Corporations Record Huge Returns from Tax Lobbying, as Gridlock in Congress Stalls Reform - The Boston Globe." *BostonGlobe.com*. Accessed July 19, 2013. http://www.bostonglobe.com/news/politics/2013/03/16/corporations-record-huge-returns-from-tax-lobbying-gridlock-congress-stalls-reform/omgZvDPa37DNlSqi0G95YK/story.html.

"DC Mythbusting: 'Lobbyist' Coined at Willard Hotel." *We Love DC*. Accessed July 18, 2013. http://www.welovedc.com/2009/06/09/dc-mythbusting-lobbyist-coined-at-willard-hotel/.

"Government Relations and Lobbying." *Patton Boggs*. Accessed July 18, 2013. http://www.pattonboggs.com/practice/government-relations-and-lobbying.

Hall, Richard L., and Alan V. Deardorff. "Lobbying as Legislative Subsidy." *American Political Science Review* 100, no. 01 (2006): 69–84. doi:10.1017/S0003055406062010.

Jacob, Kathryn Allamong. "King of the Lobby." *Smithsonian* 32, no. 2 (May 2001): 122–131.

Kollman, Ken. *Outside Lobbying: Public Opinion and Interest Group Strategies*. Princeton, N.J.: Princeton University Press, 1998.

Leech, Beth L., Frank R. Baumgartner, Timothy M. La Pira, and Nicholas A. Semanko. "Drawing Lobbyists to Washington: Government Activity and the Demand for Advocacy." *Political Research Quarterly* 58, no. 1 (March 1, 2005): 19–30. doi:10.1177/106591290505800102.

"Lobby." *Oxford Dictionaries*. Oxford University Press, 2013. http://oxforddictionaries.com/us/definition/american_english/lobby.

"Lobbying Database." *OpenSecrets.org*. Accessed July 18, 2013. http://www.opensecrets.org/lobby/.

Mayer, Lloyd Hitoshi. *What Is This "Lobbying" That We Are So Worried About?* SSRN Scholarly Paper. Rochester, NY: Social Science Research Network, January 1, 2008. http://papers.ssrn.com/abstract=1012334.

Ostas, Daniel T., and Philosophy Documentation Center. "The Law and Ethics of K Street." Edited by Denis G. Arnold. *Business Ethics Quarterly* 17, no. 1 (2007): 33–63. doi:10.5840/beq200717113.

"To Keep the Lobbyist Within Bounds." *The New York Times Magazine*, February 19, 1956. Congressional Record, March 2, 1956, vol. 102, pp. 38023.

"Tool Company V. Norris - 69 U.S. 45 (1864)." *Justia US Supreme Court Center*. Accessed July 18, 2013. http://supreme.justia.com/cases/federal/us/69/45/case.html.

"WGBH American Experience . Transcontinental Railroad | PBS." *American Experience*. Accessed July 18, 2013. http://www.pbs.org/wgbh/americanexperience/features/general-article/tcrr-scandal/.

"What Is Lobbying?" *The Law Dictionary*. Accessed July 18, 2013. http://thelawdictionary.org/lobbying/.

"What Is Lobbying? Definition and Meaning." *BusinessDictionary.com*. Accessed July 18, 2013. http://www.businessdictionary.com/definition/lobbying.html#ixzz2Tz3y4A3l.

Chapter 2: The Lobbying Industry

Lobbying is big business. More than 12,000 registered lobbyists spend more than $3 billion per year to influence public policy through direct communications with government officials. (Billions more are spent supporting political campaigns, grassroots lobbying – mobilizing citizens to contact their legislators to influence policy– and general public relations.) These figures are only for lobbying the Federal

> **Fun Fact**
> 2011/2012 Spending
> Federal elections: $7B
> Lobbying: $6.6B
> (openSecrets, Federal Elections Commission)

government. Lobbying also takes place at the state and local level. While the magnitude of spending in these jurisdictions is not readily available, estimates are that the spending across the 50 states is in the hundreds of millions of dollars. The number of lobbyists at the state and local level is likely to exceed 40,000. (Exhibit 2-1)

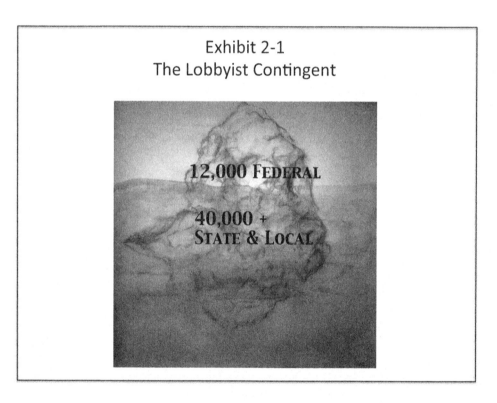

Exhibit 2-1
The Lobbyist Contingent

12,000 FEDERAL

40,000 +
STATE & LOCAL

This chapter examines the lobbying industry – its growth, principle actors, and economics. It considers what information sources are available to evaluate the industry and concludes by exploring how lobbyists lobby on behalf of their own industry.

Industry Growth

The industry has seen steady, sizable growth for several decades, owing to the expansion of government actions as explained in Chapter 1. Not only has the number of lobbyists grown and their spending increased, but also the number of issues they address has multiplied. The federal government established 76 issue categories in conjunction with mandated disclosure. The categories range from the obvious (agriculture, defense, health, taxation) to the obscure (animals, District of Columbia, trucking, sports). The lobbying activity associated with each issue varies widely as shown in Exhibit 2-2. Issues that impact a large portion of the population -- including healthcare, Medicaid/Medicare, and transportation -- see extensive lobbying. Issues that have widespread impact in the business community, such as taxes and trade, are also focal points for lobbying. Industries that are both well-resourced and subject to regulation are very active; environment, banking and telecommunication are examples. Finally, areas of high government spending such as federal budget/appropriations and defense see extensive lobbying activity. Those issues that cut across multiple areas (e.g. healthcare, taxation) are the most active.

Exhibit 2-2
Issues Profile

	Mass Impact	Business Focus	Government Spending	Resourced & Regulated
Fed. Budget			✓	
Taxation	✓	✓		✓
Defense			✓	
Health	✓	✓	✓	✓
Environment	✓		✓	✓
Trade		✓		
Transportation			✓	
Medicare/aid			✓	✓
Education	✓		✓	
Agriculture			✓	
Banking		✓		✓

Author analysis of data from: Drawing Lobbyists to Washington, Leech et al

Areas of limited lobbying are also important to understand. One set of less active issues are those where stakeholders have limited resources (people, funding, political clout). Welfare, unemployment, arts/entertainment, and animals are examples. Other issues see limited lobbying because they are episodic concerns; disaster planning and immigration fall into this category. Others yet, are narrowly focused with limited (but often passionate) appeal such as firearms, veteran affairs, and the postal service.

Baumgartner and Leech analyzed lobbying activity (as measured by the number of lobbying reports filed on the issue) across a sample of issues. Their work reveals a great deal of concentration in lobbying activity. Ten percent of the issues account for 50 percent of lobbying contacts. The top 20 percent of issues are the focus of 66 percent of lobbying reports. The other end of the spectrum is equally important. The bottom 10 percent of issues accounts for less than one percent of lobbying contacts. Exhibit 2-3 shows the resulting distribution. The implication of this is that a few high profile issues dominate the lobbying stage; however, there are many other issues where only one or two groups are engaged in influencing public policy. Question to Ponder: At which end of the spectrum is lobbying likely to have the largest impact?

> **Food For Thought**
>
> Why do so many issues have minimal interest? What are the implications?

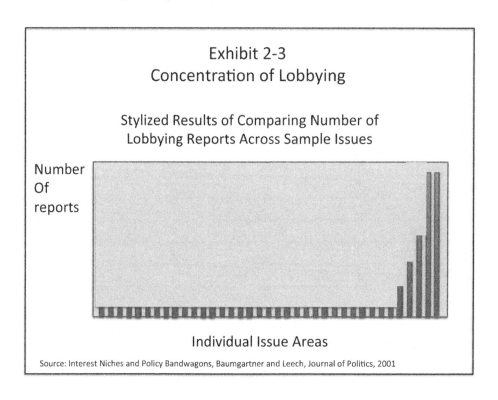

Exhibit 2-3
Concentration of Lobbying

Stylized Results of Comparing Number of
Lobbying Reports Across Sample Issues

Number
Of
reports

Individual Issue Areas

Source: Interest Niches and Policy Bandwagons, Baumgartner and Leech, Journal of Politics, 2001

A final observation about the issues that are lobbied is the general stability of focus on issues. Year in and year out, federal budget/appropriations, healthcare, taxation, transportation, energy/nuclear power and defense top the list of lobbying clients. (Exhibit 2-4)

Exhibit 2-4
Stability of Focal Issue Areas

Issue Area	Ranking (lobbying clients)					
	2007	2008	2009	2010	2011	2012
Budget/Appropriation	1	1	1	1	1	1
Health	3	3	2	2	2	2
Taxes	4	4	4	4	3	3
Transportation	5	5	6	6	4	4
Defense	2	2	3	3	5	5
Energy/Nuclear Power	6	6	5	5	6	6
Environment/Superfund	9	8	7	7	7	7
Education	7	7	8	8	8	8

Source: Author analysis of OpenSecrets data.

The Principle Actors – Organizations that Lobby

The top spenders for lobbying are largely businesses and trade organizations. Data from the Center for Responsive Politics detailed in the OpenSecrets database shows the US Chamber of Commerce dominates the spending, writing checks for $136 million in 2012. The National Association of Realtors spent $41 million in that year. (Unless otherwise noted the data in this section comes from OpenSecrets.) The next 18 organizations each spent more than $13 million. (Exhibit 2-5) The interests represented by these top spenders are centered on healthcare, defense, telecommunications and energy. Several trade organizations are also major lobbyists. The American Medical Association, the National Cable and Telecommunications Association, and American Association of Retired Persons (AARP) are perennial major spenders for lobbying activities.

```
┌─────────────────────────────────────────────────────────┐
│                      Exhibit 2-5                        │
│             Big Spenders on Lobbying (2012)             │
│                                                         │
│                 (millions of dollars)                   │
│    US Chamber of Commerce                    $136       │
│    National Association of Realtors           41        │
│    Blue Cross/Blue Shield                     22        │
│    General Electric                           21        │
│    American Hospital Association              19        │
│    National Cable and Telecom Assoc.         18        │
│    Pharmaceuticals Research and Mfg. Assoc.  18        │
│    Google                                     18        │
│    Northrop Grumman                           17        │
│    AT&T                                        17        │
│    American Medical Assoc.                    16        │
│    Boeing                                     15        │
│                                                         │
│    OpenSecrets database, Center for Responsive Politics │
└─────────────────────────────────────────────────────────┘
```

The US Chamber of Commerce has spent the most on lobbying of any organization for the past several years. The organization's lobbying spending was modest in the late 1990s and early 2000. However, since 2007, their spending has tripled, peaking in 2010 at more than $150 million. The increase in spending is a function of augmenting the voice of the Chamber in policy making. The majority of expenditures support lobbying with internal Chamber staff. The organization includes approximately 100 federally registered lobbyists. The

> **Fun Fact**
> US Chamber Lobbying Spend
> (millions of dollars)
> 2000 - $18
> 2004 - $53
> 2008 - $92
> 2012 - $136
> (OpenSecrets)

chamber's lobbying efforts address a wide array of issues. Finance, banking, government issues, intellectual property, law enforcement, and trade are focal areas. The lobbying is done predominantly at the House and Senate; however, the Chamber is also active at the US Trade Representative's Office and at the Securities and Exchange Commission. The Chamber advocated on dozens of bills in 2012. Examples include Arbitration Fairness Act of 2011, Protecting Access to Health Care Act, Lawsuit Abuse Reduction Act of 2011, Furthering Asbestos Claim Transparency Act of 2012, and Sunshine in Litigation Act of 2011.

The Chamber has become a powerful force in policymaking in Washington. With 500 employees and a $250 million budget, they have the resources to influence policy outcomes that support the Chamber's business members' objectives. The

Chamber has a well-defined and structured policymaking process that identifies emerging issues, defines the organization's positions and supports the associated analysis and communications. Equally important are the policy issues that are off the table such as those that benefit a particular company or industry and issues involving price setting. One reason the Chamber's influence has grown in recent years is that it is able to be more aggressive in public than its individual members. In the words of the advocacy group Public Citizen: "The Donohue [the current CEO] Chamber is in full-attack mode. From their point of view, they've been very aggressive in advancing the interests of their constituents. From our point of view, they have very aggressively expanded the corporate grip over policy making in Washington, D.C."[30] One example of the aggressive public stance is the Chamber's participation in the 2012 election cycle. The group spent millions in support of pro-business (i.e. those who support the Chamber's policies) candidates; 38 Republicans and two Democrats in the House versus 12 Republicans and no Democrats in the Senate. The efforts were not very successful but that has not deterred the Chamber's leadership; they are doing a *post mortem* to understand what went wrong and what they need to do better in the future.

The lobbying practices of General Electric (GE) are representative of many large corporations. The firm generally spends $20 million a year on lobbying. The majority of these expenses support an internal lobbyist staff of 40. The company's advocacy focuses on taxes, defense, federal budget/appropriation, transportation, energy, finance and railroads. Many of these issue areas align directly with the company's business focus. While the majority of the lobbying takes place at the Senate and House, GE also lobbies at the Department of Defense, Department of Transportation, and other administrative agencies. In 2012, GE lobbied on approximately 100 pieces of legislation. The dominant focus was on bills to amend the Internal Revenue Code, the implementation of the Dodd–Frank Act and the Department of Transportation appropriations. Beyond these broad legislative efforts, GE lobbying focused on some "rifle shot" legislation such as Preservation of Access to Osteoporosis Testing for Medicare Beneficiaries Act of 2011.

A more recent addition to the top spenders list is Google. The company's lobbying expenditures went from $1 million in 2006 to $17 million in 2012. The rapid growth is a function of Google's interest in influencing the government's antitrust policy, privacy legislation and cyber security. They have also lobbied on immigration reform to enable more skilled workers to enter the country. In 2012, they focused on legislation such as Protect IP Act 2011, Stop Online Piracy Act, Secure IT, and Cyber Security Act of 2012. Two thirds of the expenditures support internal lobbying resources, including 14 registered lobbyists; the remainder is spent on about 25 independent lobbying firms including Podesta Group, Gephardt Group, Crossroads Strategies, and First Group.

The three profiles above represent direct business interests; in contrast, the AARP agenda is in support of the issues facing their members: Americans who are older than 50. The organization's lobbying spending increased dramatically after 2002, peaking in 2005 when spending reached $30 million. Since that time, AARP's spending level has hovered around $20 million a year. AARP has a large lobbying staff of 74. Only a small portion of their lobbying is contracted to third parties.

The dominant issues addressed by AARP lobbying efforts are related to health and retirement, as would be expected based on the demographics of their membership. In contrast to some of the major spenders described above, the majority of the lobbying by AARP takes place in the executive branch, including the White House.

Another active membership-based lobbying group is the American Medical Association. The AMA consistently spends $15-$20 million annually on lobbying. In the organization's own words, "The AMA is aggressively involved in efforts related to the most vital issues in medicine today, including medical liability reform, Medicare physician payment reform, expanding coverage for uninsured and increasing access to care, improving of public health, managed care reform, and others."[31] In support of these objectives, the AMA hosts of variety of advocacy events including a state legislative strategy conference, national advocacy conference, as well as a medical students "Day on the Hill" where students have an opportunity to meet with policymakers. The vast majority of the AMA's lobbying spending supports a team of 20 in-house lobbyists. The backgrounds of these individuals, legislative directors, legislative assistance, legislative counsel, enable the team to have access to decision-makers. Medicare/Medicaid and health issues are the primary areas of focus for the lobbying team. While two thirds of their contacts are with House and Senate members, they are also active at the centers for Medicare and Medicaid services, DHHS, the White House, the Department of Justice, and the FDA.

The business and membership/trade group orientation of the top lobbying spenders is a microcosm of overall lobbying activity. Baumgartner and Leech analyzed the lobbying reports required under the Lobbying Disclosure Act. Businesses accounted for 44 percent of lobbying reports (a measure of lobbying activity). Trade associations account for an additional 14 percent. At 16 percent of reports, state and local governments lobbying the federal government is an important segment of the industry.[32] The dominance of business and trade associations is even larger when spending is considered. These two groups account for 78 percent of lobbying expenditures.[33] (Exhibit 2-6)

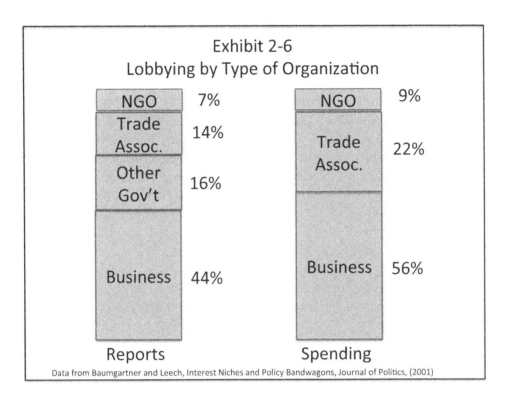

Data from Baumgartner and Leech, Interest Niches and Policy Bandwagons, Journal of Politics, (2001)

Within the business segment, lobbying is undertaken by a relatively small subset of firms. Kerr, Lincoln, and Mishra examined a sample of 3,260 firms in the United States and found that only ten percent engaged in lobbying. [34] The researchers looked for characteristics that define those that lobby from companies that do not. Size was a determining factor; firms that lobby had sales four times that of non-lobbying organizations. The lobbying firms also have two to three times the number of employees and assets of the non-lobbying firms. Spending on research and development was also positively correlated with lobbying, but the statistical strength of the relationship was not as strong as firm size. The researchers found that the small set of lobbying firms was very stable over time. The number of companies becoming active lobbyists or ceasing their lobbying activities was about 10 percent annually.[35] Why do so few firms engage in lobbying and why do those that lobby continue to do so?

> **Notable Quote**
> The probability that a firm lobbies in the current year given that it lobbied in the previous year is 92%.
> (Kerr et al 2011)

The authors proffer that the startup costs of lobbying are a substantial barrier to entry. The group's theoretical model, applied to lobbying associated with increasing the number of H-B1 visas, which enables domestic employers to temporarily hire foreign workers in specialty fields (especially information technology), supports their hypothesis.

The logical follow-on question is: What are these barriers? A potential answer is the energy, resources and expertise needed to create an internal organizational capability to lobby and/or fear of lacking the skills to effectively manage external lobbyists. Another is non-lobbying firms relying on the advocacy of others – trade associations or other corporations in their industry limiting the need for their own lobbyists. Yet another possible explanation is that firms do not think lobbying offers a good return on investment. Finally, some firms might equate lobbying with unethical behavior and simply want to avoid any tie to impropriety. While there is anecdotal evidence to support each of these explanations, a robust analytical assessment is yet to be conducted.

The top spender profiles all highlight the dominance of internal lobbying resources. Third-party lobbyists are hired but account for a small portion of the lobbying effort of these organizations. The decision to lobby with internal versus external resources is often a function of control. Lobbying is a high stakes corporate activity. The potential for gains from lobbying is high as detailed later in the chapter, but there are also risks. At the top of the list is avoiding impropriety and scandal. Second, because messaging is often nuanced, understanding a client's needs from the inside is necessary to communicate effectively. A third concern is cost: Internal resources are often less expensive if the organization plans a sustained lobbying effort. Taken together, these considerations often tip the scales to keeping the majority of lobbying in-house.

The Principle Actors – Third Party Lobbying Firms
While the lion's share of the more than $3 billion spent on lobbying annually is for internal resources; the third-party, for-hire, lobbying firms still generate more than $300 million in billings per year. Third-party firms have their advantages. They often offer specialized expertise on topics that a corporation's in-house lobbyist does not have or it would be expensive to obtain. Second, the lobbying firms add value by keeping abreast of pending legislation and administrative actions. A third benefit is access; dedicated lobbying firms often have staff, including former members of Congress and the executive branch, who have access to key decision-makers. Fourth, for-hire firms can often respond quickly to unanticipated events. Finally, external lobbyists are a variable cost – retain them when you need to, eliminate them when you do not.

There are hundreds of lobbying firms ranging in size from dozens of lobbyists, generating millions of dollars in billings, to sole practitioners whose revenues are in the thousands. The large firms can be roughly divided into three groups – law firms, public relations firms, lobbying firms. The two largest lobbying firms in 2012 -- Patton Boggs and Akin, Gump -- had revenues of $45 and $30 million respectively and are both large multiservice law firms. Ogilvy Government Relations and Podesta Group are examples of public relations firms that also provide lobbying services. Cassidy, Alston & Bird, Holland & Knight are firms whose dominant focus is lobbying and advocacy. All of the organizations mentioned had lobbying revenues in excess of $13 million in 2012.

Patton Boggs (now Squire Patton Boggs), the largest lobbying firm, represented more than 250 clients in 2012 and reported $45 million in revenues. The client list is a Who's Who in business: AT&T, Citigroup, City of San Diego, Exxon Mobil, Microsoft, Northrop Grumman, Tyson Foods, and Wholesale Markets Brokers' Association. Annual billings to their clients range from $5,000 to almost

> **Fun Fact**
> Patton Boggs Lobbying Revenue
> (millions of dollars)
> 2000 - $20
> 2004 - $31
> 2008 - $39
> 2012 - $45
> (OpenSecrets)

$1 million. Exhibit 2-7 shows the distribution of billings for 2012. The majority are in the $100,000-$200,000 range. The firm has a registered lobbying staff of more than 100 including Trent Lott, former Senate Majority Leader; Rodney Slater former Secretary of Transportation; and John Deschauer, former Director of Senate Affairs for the Department of Defense. The range of issues that the firm lobbies on is as broad as their client base but is focused on federal budget/ appropriations, transportation, health issues, urban development, taxes,

> **Food For Thought**
> What might account for such rapid and sustained growth?

Medicare/Medicaid, homeland security, and energy. The vast majority of their lobbying contacts are with members of the Senate and House. They also actively lobby the Department of Transportation, the Department of Housing and Urban Development, the Environmental Protection Agency, and the White House.

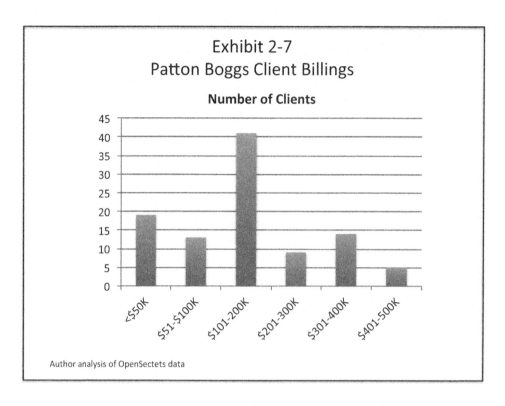

Exhibit 2-7
Patton Boggs Client Billings

Number of Clients

Author analysis of OpenSectets data

The Podesta group has seen its lobbying revenues double from $12 million to more than $25 million since 2009. The firm has more than 100 clients in industries ranging from pharmaceuticals to banking to automobiles to defense to food. Annual billings to these clients ranged from $20,000 to almost $700,000 in 2012. The firm has approximately 50 registered lobbyists on staff. Similar to Patton Boggs, the majority of their lobbying contacts are at the House and Senate.

At the other end of the spectrum sits Capitol Hill Strategy Advocates. This firm, established in 2011, had revenues of $55,000 in 2012. The firm has one lobbyist and three clients and advocates on healthcare, small business, and transportation issues. Sixteen contacts were made with members of the House and Senate in 2012. While the top firms account for the vast majority of lobbying contacts and spending, the preponderance of firms are small operations.

Principle Actors - The Lobbyists
More than 12,000 individuals are registered to lobby at the federal level. A subset of this group meets directly with policymakers. Many others conduct the research and package the materials that are used to support lobbying efforts. In larger, for-hire firms, the lobbying team exhibits a pyramid organization – a few very senior lobbyists supported by a larger group of lobbyists, supported by a larger team of specialist consultants, research and administrative staff. (Exhibit

2-8) shows a stylized typical lobbying firm's organizational structure.) The same structure is often used by organizations that do their lobbying in-house. Smaller firms might have one or two principals supported by one or two support staff. There are also a large number of sole practitioners who perform all the lobbying functions themselves.

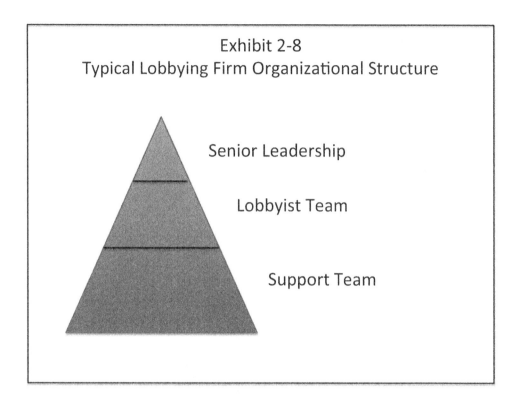

Exhibit 2-8
Typical Lobbying Firm Organizational Structure

Senior Leadership

Lobbyist Team

Support Team

Who are the senior lobbyists? What are their backgrounds? What are the paths used to become an effective advocate? Senior lobbyists are predominantly people who have been members of Congress (or senior executive branch officials) or served on their staffs. These individual have two of the most important attributes required for success in the lobbying industry. First, they have access. Lobbying requires the ability to meet with members and their staffs to share insights and information. To do so you need to get in the door. As a member or senior staff, you get to know everyone who is anyone in Washington. When your public service is completed and you become a lobbyist, your phone calls and emails to current members and staff will be answered. Second, they understand the legislative (or executive branch) processes. Cassidy succeeded in procuring funds for the Tufts School of Nutrition Science and Policy because he understood the appropriations process. Beyond process, having worked in Congress or an Executive Branch department enables the lobbyist to understand the norms of those bodies. Understanding the dos and don'ts can prevent costly mistakes.

There are several other attributes that are required to be a successful lobbyist. While access and process knowledge are important, essential attributes for lobbyists are credibility, integrity, and trust. As Bertram Levine explains in The Art of Lobbying; "Lobbyists are measured by their reliability."[36] Reliability includes (1) accurate, timely and complete information; (2) confidences strictly maintained; and (3) consistent support.

Time is a most precious commodity for members of Congress, senior executives and their staffs. Consequently, the lobbyist must provide the lobbyee with a strong value proposition. Lobbyists create value by providing substantive expertise, process guidance and political insight. Lobbyists are also a source of "arms and legs" who provide what Hall and Deardorff call a subsidy to legislators and executives. Finally, lobbyists also offer value through supporting lobbyees' campaigns with direct contributions and facilitating fundraising.

There is not a single "ideal resume" for senior lobbyists but there are common elements in their career paths. Lobbyists typically complete stints in government as staff to members of Congress or senior executive branch officials. These experiences familiarize aspiring lobbyists with the legislative/administrative process and enable the individual to build his or her network. Lobbyists also have experience working in the private sector/civil society. This provides the substantive expertise and associated credibility to lobby. Often an individual will move from government to industry, back to government and then back to industry. This phenomenon, known as the "revolving door," offers a full understanding of the decision-making process, and its impacts, from all sides. However, it can also spark conflicts of interest. Regulations requiring a cooling off period between public and private sector work seek to balance these interests. (These regulations are detailed in Chapter 3.)

While not a prerequisite, serving in public office is a great asset for a lobbyist. Having walked in the shoes of an elected official gives the lobbyist great credibility and a true understanding of how he or she can add value as a lobbyist. Understanding the campaign process from the inside, provides the lobbyist with special insight into the pressures of the election cycle -- from addressing constituent concerns to raising campaign funds.

Attending certain educational institutions and working with non-profits are other avenues that help round-out the lobbyist's resume. Certain high schools or colleges provide a network of contacts that offer access to policymakers. For example, in Boston, a large number of politicians and lobbyists attended Boston Latin School including House Speaker Robert DeLeo and former House Speaker Thomas Finneran. The connections and credibility associated with those institutions provides a fast path to Massachusetts politics. Many politicians are members of charitable organizations or work for non-profit institutions as a way to build contacts, provide public service, and understand local/constituent issues. Exhibit 2-9 illustrates how these experiences can be combined into a strong lobbying resume, in this case illustrative rather than actual.

Exhibit 2-9
Illustrative "Ideal" Lobbyist Resume

Experience 2010-2012	**Office of Governor Deval Patrick** **Chief of Staff** • Assisted the Governor in the formulation and implementation of his policies • Served as Governor's liaison with cabinet and other agency directors • Administered the management of the Office of the Governor and its staff	Boston, MA
2006 – 2010	**Massachusetts State Senator, 2nd Suffolk and Middlesex District** • Elected to two terms as State Senator • Committees: Ways and Means, Vice-Chair of Joint Committee on Education	Boston, MA
2004 – 2006	**Massachusetts Joint Committee on Education** **Policy Director** • Provided research and policy analysis on all areas of education legislation to House and Senate Committee members • Managed other committee staff • Interfaced with community, advocacy, and lobbying groups	Boston, MA
2000-2002	**Massachusetts Department of Elementary and Secondary Education** **Director of School and District Turnaround** • Oversaw Department activities for intervention of low-performing schools and districts • Coordinated with schools, districts, and external partners	Boston, MA
1998-2000	**Teach for America** **5th Grade Teacher** • Taught 5th graders in low-performing school in Lawrence, MA • Acted as school union representative	Pittsfield, MA
Volunteer Experience	**The Boston Harbor Association** **Board Member (2008-2012)**	Boston, MA
Education	**HARVARD UNIVERSITY, John F. Kennedy School of Government** **Master in Public Administration, 2004**	Cambridge, MA
	HARVARD COLLEGE **Bachelor of Arts, cum laude, May 1998**	Cambridge, MA

The Principle Actors – The "Lobbyees"

In the United States, thousands of internal and external lobbyists advocate to a comparatively small group of key policymakers. The most common targets of lobbying efforts are members of Congress. While there are times when lobbyists directly communicate with members, more commonly, those receiving lobbyists are the members' staff. Who are the most lobbied? The answer is -- the most powerful. In Congress, the House and Senate majority and minority leaders, whips as well as committee chairs wield great power because of control over the legislative agenda and thus are targets of lobbyists. Members who are considered issue experts are extensively lobbied. Executive branch lobbying targets include the White House, department secretaries and their deputies as well as the agencies and their staffs.

The purpose of lobbying meetings can be generally classified into:

- Relationship Building: Establish and reinforce confidence and trust in your work as a lobbyist.
- Information Push: Sharing important insights with a member/executive.
- Information Pull: Learning from the lobbyee about issues and perspectives that are important for your client.

Often, lobbyists seek to accomplish all three objectives during a meeting.

Challenge: Would You Hire Berman and Company?

60 Minutes refers to Richard Berman as "Dr. Evil." The Chicago Tribune writes: Razor-sharp wit and unconventional tactics. Rachel Maddow says: "The people paying Rick Berman are getting way more than their money's worth." Berman and Company's website is titled 'The Power to Change the Debate'. In the words of founder Rick Berman, "My goal is to make people say, I've never thought of it that way before." Berman's company provides research, communications, advertising and government affairs support to clients in a wide array of industries, especially food and beverage, and employment policy and compensation. Trained as a lawyer, Rick Berman worked on labor issues for the United States Chamber of Commerce, Dana Corporation and Bethlehem Steel. He was also Executive Vice President for Public Affairs at Pillsbury Restaurant Group. He created his advocacy group to "blend aggressive, creative thinking with functional expertise to achieve extraordinary results for our clients." From 2002 to 2006, the company was a registered lobbying firm earning annual revenues between $60,000 and $120,000. The American beverage Institute and American Beverage Licensees accounted for the majority of these revenues. Since 2007, Berman and Company has taken a different approach to influencing public policy -- educating policymakers and the public through the media.

> **Notable Quote**
> The people paying Rick Berman are getting way more than their money's worth.
> - Rachel Maddow

> **Notable Quote**
> My goal is to make people say, "I've never thought of it that way before."
> - Rick Berman

"We take special pride in our track record of developing powerful messages on public policy issues that might otherwise seem dry." Doing so has enabled Berman to attract the attention of major news organizations. His firm has also received numerous media awards including four Bulldog Awards and 12 Pollie Awards. Berman's notoriety is driven in large part by the nonprofit organizations he has created to support for-profit interests. Notable examples are The Center for Consumer Freedom and The Center for Union Facts. The Center for Consumer Freedom, which Berman created in 1996, is "a nonprofit organization devoted to promoting personal responsibility and protecting consumer choices." The focus of the organization is to reduce government involvement in health, animal rights, personal finance, and food.

To make its point, the organization created a number of advertisements attacking the "food police." These ads live up to the aggressive, sharp wit attributes ascribed to Berman. The Center for Union Facts created an advertisement with the following dialogue spoken by what appears to be a union employee: "You know what I love? Paying union dues just so I can keep my job... I really like how the union discriminates against minorities! ... Nothing makes me feel better than knowing that I'm supporting their fat-cat lifestyles."

The "in your face" content is only part of the Berman story. The rest of the story is that the organizations that are delivering this material are nonprofits. This structure provides two benefits for Berman's clients. First, the donors are allowed to claim a tax deduction for the funds used to support these "charitable organizations." While it may not seem right that taxpayers are subsidizing these efforts, the IRS has investigated Berman and generally given him a clean bill of health. The second advantage is that donations to a nonprofit, charitable organization are not disclosed. His critics argue that the funding is provided, in large part, by private corporations who use Berman's nonprofits to achieve private gain.

A Cargill executive states: "They are aggressive, innovative, and they played to win." On 60 minutes, Morley Safer said: "Let me just take you through some of the things your critics have said about you. Sleazy, greedy, outrageous, deceptive..." In response to an accusation that he is no more than a hired gun, Berman said: "I do get paid for educating people. If that's my biggest crime, I stand accused."

If you were interested in influencing public policy on an issue that Berman had expertise in, would you hire him? [Watch the 60 Minutes and/or Rachel Maddow interviews and look at some of his websites to bring his strategy to life.]

Lobbying Data

Where does the information come from to provide such detailed profiles of lobbying firms, issues and spenders? Under the Lobbying Disclosure Act of 1995 and the Honest Leadership and Open Government Act of 2007, lobbyists report their activities to the Senate Office of Public Records. While the information is available via the Office's website, it is not that user friendly. OpenSecrets.org, a part of the Center for Responsive Politics, has created an easy to use, searchable database of lobbying activity based on the federal disclosure forms. Data are available on an annual basis back to 1998. The search feature allows the researcher to find individual lobbying clients, lobbying firms and lobbyists. By issue area, any individual can drill down to spenders, lobbying firms, individual lobbyist, contacts (lobbyees) and even bills that were the subject of the lobbying contact. The Center is funded by 18 foundations including The Ford Foundation and the MacArthur Foundation as well as more than 50 individual donors.

Foreign organizations lobbying in the United States may be required to register and disclose under the Foreign Agents Registration Act of 1938. Foreign governments and non-business entities are generally regulated by this Act, which requires that they disclose their advocacy activities to the Justice Department. Images of these reports are then posted on a public access website. However, the site is far from user friendly. The Sunlight Foundation (in collaboration with ProPublica), a non-profit and non-partisan organization, whose mission is to "[use] the power of the Internet to catalyze greater government openness and transparency, and provides new tools and resources for media and citizens, alike" gathers these filings into a searchable database and makes the information available to the public free of charge. [37] The Foreign Lobbying Influence Tracker is searchable by legislator, country, client, lobbyist, and issue.

Individual states have a range of intra-state lobbying information available to the public. The Commonwealth of Massachusetts maintains a database of lobbying activity through the Secretary of State's office. This database allows users to search by lobbyist and/or client as well as by industry. Industry searches can be drilled down to company, to lobbyist and then provides details on the lobbyist's compensation and positions on legislation. While not as user-friendly as the OpenSecrets website, the Massachusetts site does provide a meaningful level of transparency about lobbying in the State. Mississippi, which is new to reporting lobbying activity, has a public view website, but it can only be searched by client or lobbyist name. The Texas Tribune offers a searchable lobbying database, which details actors and spending in the state. Owing to the growing transparency movement at the state level, public access to lobbying information will likely improve in the coming years.

Industry Economics

There is a great deal of transparency about the lobbying industry (e.g. who gets paid what by whom) but the economics of the business are more opaque. Lobbying firms are largely private and therefore do not report their financials. Based on information that is required as part of disclosure filings, the cost structure of the industry appears dominated by expenses for lobbyists and support staff. Operating expenses (e.g. rent, computer equipment, printing, travel) account for 20–30 percent of total costs. Ironically, entertainment expense that were historically sizable (think Sam Ward and Samuel Colt), have been largely eliminated through restrictions on meals, gifts, and travel post the Abramoff scandal.

An additional expense, which is incurred largely by lobbyists directly and not by the firm, is campaign contributions. Supporting candidates' election efforts is an important "ante" to being in the lobbying profession. Washington lobbyists can get dozens or even hundreds of requests for contributions. Federal campaign finance laws limit the donations from a person to an individual candidate to $2,600 per election. Until a recent Supreme Court Ruling, individual contributions to national party committees were capped at $74,600 every two years. Up to an additional $48,600 could be contributed to individual candidates. Once that limit was reached the lobbyist could not contribute more. Saying they have reached the cap was one way a lobbyist could respectfully decline a contribution request.

The Supreme Court eliminated that "excuse" in April 2014 with its ruling in *McCutcheon v. Federal Election Commission*. The effect of the Court's 5-4 decision was the elimination of the limits on party contributions and the aggregate limit for candidates; the $2,600 contribution limit to individual candidates remains. As one Washington lobbyist commented after the ruling: Now you have to say, 'I'm sorry. I just can't...'"[38] The contribution costs can add up. One prominent lobbyist is purported to have contributed more than $1 million since founding his firm.

Lobbying firms most commonly charge for their services on a retainer basis. Two factors lead to the dominance of this approach. First, lobbying activity for an individual client ebbs and flows; the retainer model smooths out revenue streams and makes client payments more predictable. The second reason is the avoidance of contingent contracts, payment only for successful outcomes. In the mid-19th century, when lobbying was less structured, professional payment for lobbying services was often contingent on a successful outcome. The courts, however, voided a number of these contacts because of their potentially corrupting influence. The courts' antipathy toward these contracts was part and parcel with their overall skepticism about the propriety of lobbying. As lobbying became more professional, concerns about contingent contracts diminished.

Today, no federal legislation bars contingent contracts for lobbying Congress and policy makers; although, there are such bans on lobbying for federal procurement contracts and for lobbyist representing foreign principals under the Foreign Agents Registration Act. (This act is detailed in the next chapter.) Many states do ban contingent contracts.

Challenge: Contingent Contracts

The answer to the question -- Should contingent contracts be allowed for lobbying? -- is not obvious. On one hand are concerns that contingent contracts provide an incentive to "win at any cost" even if it involves fraud and corruption because you only are paid if you succeed. On the other hand, contingent contracts allow those who have limited resources to lobby when they otherwise could not. Viewed this way, contingent contracts are a means of leveling the lobbying playing field which is dominated by the better-resourced advocates. Decide how you would answer the question about the use of contingent contracts and write a short, but persuasive memo supporting your view.

Industry profitability is hard to assess from the outside. Comments from successful lobbyists imply that the business is quite lucrative. There is reason to believe this is so. First, the costs structure is largely people: If business is good, you hire; when it is bad, you can layoff. Also, with the expected median salary for a lobbyist in the United States at $100,000, compensation is good, but not outrageous.[39] Second, capital costs are *de minimis*. Third, repeat business is very high. Most lobbying efforts are sustained campaigns rather than one-off events. Thus, lobbying services are likely to be required year-in and year-out, thereby reducing sales expenses.

Moreover, from the client's perspective, lobbying expenses in comparison to the potential return on investment is small. An analytical assessment of the return on lobbying spending conducted by Richter, Samphantharak, and Timmons showed that increasing lobbying expenditures by one percent "appears to lower effective tax rates by somewhere in the range of 0.5 to 1.6 percentage points for the average firm that lobbies."[40] They estimate the return for each incremental lobbying dollar is $6 to $20. Another analysis of the impact of lobbying on tax rates was completed by Lee Drutman of the Sunlight Foundation, who found that Fortune 100 companies that lobbied had lower effective tax rates than those that do not. He also found that the companies that spent more on lobbying exhibited lower tax rates. Strategas, an investment research firm, conducted a

> ### Notable Quote
> Lobbying…might well be the most profitable thing a company spends money on.
> - The Economist
> (Forbes.com 2011)

41

broader based look at the impact of lobbying. They examined the degree of lobbying (measured as a percent of assets) with share prices. Over the 2002 to 2011 period, the lobbying-intensive firms outperformed the S&P 500 by 11 percent per year. With that level of returns, lobbyers are likely to keep right on lobbying. Exhibit 2-10 summarizes the findings of a recent study examining the impact of lobbying on the financial returns of publicly-traded companies. Does lobbying matter? Yes!

Exhibit 2-10
Return on Lobbying Investments

Paper: Corporate Lobbying and Financial Performance

Authors: Chen, Parsley, Yang

Question 1: Is corporate lobbying positively related to financial performance?

Answer: Yes

Question 2: Are the findings robust across empirical specifications and samples?

Answer: Yes

Question 3: Do the findings hold for portfolios of companies?

Answer: Yes, those that lobby intensely earned 5.5% more over 3 years compared to peers.

Source: Corporate Lobbying and Financial Performance, Chen, Parsley, and Yang, (2010)

Challenge: Making the Case for Lobbying
Write a letter to a corporation that does not lobby today to encourage them to explore lobbying as a means to impact public policy that effects their profits. Select a real company so you will have context for the letter.

Association of Government Relations Professionals

Every industry needs a trade group to support and lobby on their members' behalf. Lobbyists are no different. The American League of Lobbyists (ALL) was incorporated as a non-profit in 1980 with a mission to increase public understanding of lobbying and support the professionalization of those who lobby. The organization offers seminars for practitioners, maintains a code of ethics for lobbyists and offers a certification program. The latter combines knowledge of the legislative and rulemaking processes as well as the laws, regulations and ethics for conducting lobbying. Programs range from ethics training to online advocacy to meeting with Congressional members.

The group renamed themselves in 2013 to the Association of Government Relations Professionals (AGRP). While the name change was nominally made to reflect the broader activities of its members, it is likely that the term "lobbyist" carried baggage that the new name seeks to leave in the past.

Exhibit 2-11
The Rebranding

"Even lobbyists think they need rebranding"

AGRP is also a lobbying client. In 2011 and 2012, the fees did not reach the level at which reporting is required. However, the issues that AGRP has lobbied on are constitutional and governmental in nature. Specifically, they have addressed proposed legislation known as the Stock Act, which prohibits "commodities and securities trading based on nonpublic information relating to Congress, to require additional reporting by Members and employees of Congress of securities transactions, and for other purposes."[41] The Sunlight Foundation, an organization committed to transparency in the pubic arena, is supportive of the legislation but raises a concern that -- as drafted -- it would prohibit legislators from offering their perspectives on the outcome of pending legislation.[42] In support of AGRP's position, it retained lobbyists who made contact with the House, Senate, Vice President's office and the White House.

State and Local Level Lobbying

At the state and local level, industry players – clients, lobbying firms, lobbyists, and lobbyees - mirror those at the federal level; however, on a smaller scale. Consider the lobbying industry in Texas. Texas defines lobbying as "direct communications with members of the legislature or executive branch of state government to influence legislation and administrative action."[43] Individuals who lobby for compensation and meet a threshold of activity (more than $1,000 per quarter) are required to register and disclose employers and clients, compensation and reimbursement, and subject matter for which they advocated.

More than 1,500 lobbyists are registered in Texas; although, only about 850 met the reporting thresholds and therefore filed disclosure forms. Annual lobbying spending in Texas varies widely from a few million dollars to more than $20 million, a function of the issues and interests being debated in a given year. On average, lobbying firms represent four to five clients and generate lobbying fees of $100,000-$200,000. Top spenders include telecom companies, healthcare organizations and electric utilities. A portion of the lobbying is undertaken with internal staff but there are also third-party lobbying firms.

The "Top Hired Gun" lobbying firm in 2013 according to Capital Inside, is the Texas Lobbying Group. The firm was started in 2002 to provide advocacy services ranging from legislative lobbying to strategy formation to grassroots mobilization. The organization's clients include: AT&T, Liberty Mutual, UnitedHealth Group, and Texas Instruments.[44] The firms' three partners are all high-profile, well-respected lobbyists. Mike Toomey, one of the founders, has the ideal background to make him a successful lobbyist. A graduate of Baylor and South Texas College of Law, he was chief of staff for two governors, served as a

> **Notable Quote**
> Toomey does his homework, argues his points and caries a voluminous knowledge of a wide range of issues.
> - Dallas Morning News
> (Texas Lobby Group)

state representative, and was chair of the Judiciary Committee. He is known for his "encyclopedic knowledge of state government," "intensity and hard work," and as a "tough, tough negotiator." Toomey was chair of the West Houston Chamber of Commerce and president of the Optimists Club.

The "Texas" example is played out in state capitals throughout the country, though the issues lobbied for, the companies lobbying and the regulations in place may vary slightly from state to state. Like the federal government, there's no shortage of special interest groups at the state and local level, each hoping to affect the outcomes of policymaking.

Industry Insights
- Lobbying is a steadily growing multi-billion industry.
- Lobbying is highly concentrated on a handful of issues – the federal budget, taxation, defense, health, environment, trade and transportation.
- Ten percent of lobbying issues account for 50 percent of lobbying reports.
- Business interests and trade groups dominate lobbying spending.
- Major corporations are large lobbyists and primarily depend on an internal staff.
- While only 10 percent of lobbying expenditures are with third-party lobbying firms, this segment still has billings of more than $300 million.
- The large lobbying firms with dozens of lobbyists account for the majority of spending but there are also thousands of small firms.
- Successful lobbyists have generally held legislative or administrative roles providing them with process insight and access to policymakers; they are also credible and trustworthy.
- Lobbying is likely a lucrative business for those with the attributes listed above; a strong "return on investment" for clients justifies the lobbyist's fees.
- The Association of Government Relations Professionals "lobbies" on behalf of the industry.
- The Center for Responsible Politics (OpenSecrets) and the Sunlight Foundation maintain searchable websites of lobbying activity available free of charge to the public.
- A robust lobbying industry also exists at the state and local level.

Learning by Doing

The lobbying industry thrives on new areas that are subject to public policymaking. Fracking fits the bill. The extraction industry and gas/oil users (e.g. electric utilities, energy intensive manufacturers, homeowners) are keenly interested in the development of this new energy source. Some environmentalists see fracking as a better alternative to coal. Competing energy sources such as coal producers see fracking as a threat. Also opposed to the extensive fracking are environmental groups that are concerned about water pollution. There are strong arguments on both sides of this issue. Your task is to develop a business plan for a new lobbying firm that will advocate about fracking. Decision No. 1: What position will your firm take in the fracking debate? Will you work in support of, against, or potentially on both sides of the issue? Decision No. 2: What is the name of your firm?

Establishing a new firm requires a business plan which details the company's mission, services, differentiation, marketing, staff and financials. A business plan template is provided in Exhibit 2-12. Complete the business plan using insights drawn from this chapter. Some external research on the fracking industry and current lobbying about this topic will make your plan more robust. Expect that there will be unanswered questions. As you learn more about lobbying in subsequent chapters, revise and refine the business plan. A way to test the robustness of your plan is to present it to a colleague, friend, or family member and ask: Would you be willing to provide the seed money to launch my lobbying firm? If the answer is "yes," you are ready to move on to the next chapter. A "no" means you need to rethink and refine the plan.

Exhibit 2-12
Business Plan Contents

Company Description – What is our value added?
Market Analysis – Who needs our services?
Service Offering – What do we provide?
Marketing and Differentiation – How do we sell and why are we selected?
Organization – Who comprises our team?
Funding – Where do we get our seed and working capital?
Financial Projections – Can we make money?

Drawn from Small Business Administration,
http://www.sba.gov/category/navigation-structure/starting-managing-business/starting-business/how-write-business-plan

---

Bibliography for Chapter 2

"American Medical Association Advocacy Topics." Accessed July 22, 2013.
   https://www.ama-assn.org/ama/pub/advocacy/topics.page?

Baumgartner, Frank R., and Beth L. Leech. "Interest Niches and Policy
   Bandwagons: Patterns of Interest Group Involvement in National Politics."
   Journal of Politics 63, no. 4 (2001): 1191–1213. doi:10.1111/0022-3816.00106.

"Be Very Wary of the STOCK Act." *Sunlight Foundation*. Accessed July 22, 2013.
   http://sunlightfoundation.com/blog/2011/11/17/be-very-wary-of-the-stock-act/.

"Federal Election Commission." *Contribution Limits 2013-14*. Accessed July 22,
   2013. http://www.fec.gov/pages/brochures/contriblimits.shtml.

Kerr, William R., William F. Lincoln, and Prachi Mishra. *The Dynamics of Firm
   Lobbying*. Working Paper. National Bureau of Economic Research, November
   2011. http://www.nber.org/papers/w17577.

Levine, Bertram J. *The Art of Lobbying: Building Trust and Selling Policy*.
   Washington, D.C.: CQ Press, 2009.

"Lobbyist Salary | Salary.com." *Salary.com*. Accessed July 22, 2013.
   http://www1.salary.com/Lobbyist-Salary.html.

"OpenCongress." *H.R.1148 STOCK Bill (STOCK Act)*. Accessed July 22, 2013.
   https://www.opencongress.org/bill/112-h1148/show.

Richter, Brian Kelleher, Krislert Samphantharak, and Jeffrey F. Timmons. *Lobbying
   and Taxes*. SSRN Scholarly Paper. Rochester, NY: Social Science Research
   Network, October 22, 2008. http://papers.ssrn.com/abstract=1082146.

Stolberg, Sheryl Gay. "How Tom Donohue Transformed the U.S. Chamber of
   Commerce." *The New York Times*, June 1, 2013, sec. Business Day.
   http://www.nytimes.com/2013/06/02/business/how-tom-donohue-transformed-
   the-us-chamber-of-commerce.html.

"Sunlight Foundation." *Sunlight Foundation*. Accessed July 22, 2013.
   http://sunlightfoundation.com/.

"Texas Ethics Commission." *Lobbying in Texas: A Guide to the Texas Law*.
   Accessed July 22, 2013. http://www.ethics.state.tx.us/guides/LOBBY_guide.htm.

"Texas Lobby Group." *A Full Service Lobbying and Government Relations Firm*.
   Accessed July 22, 2013. http://txlobby.com/.

Chapter 3: Lobbying Regulations and Enforcement

In recent years, lobbying has become a highly-regulated function. At the Federal level, lobbyists must register and report their detailed lobbying activities to the House and Senate and/or the Department of Justice. This information ultimately finds its way onto OpenSecrets.com and the Foreign Influence Tracker, where anyone can view the lobbyist's activities. Lobbyists are prohibited from providing members/senior officials or their staffs with gifts, meals, or travel. There are also restrictions on moving from industry to government and back. And if that weren't enough, to prevent bribery and conflicts of interest, an ethics pledge is required for many jobs in state and federal government. This chapter explores how we arrived at these regulations and if they are sufficient to prevent corruption.

Exhibit 3-1 shows the 200+ year timeline of regulatory actions governing lobbying at the federal level. Legislation was passed in spurts and was generally triggered by scandals and external events. However, the episodic nature of the timeline does not imply there was no activity during the intervening years. Legislation to regulate lobbying was introduced frequently in both chambers of Congress. Rather the gaps illustrate how difficult it is to pass laws even when there are pressures to do so.

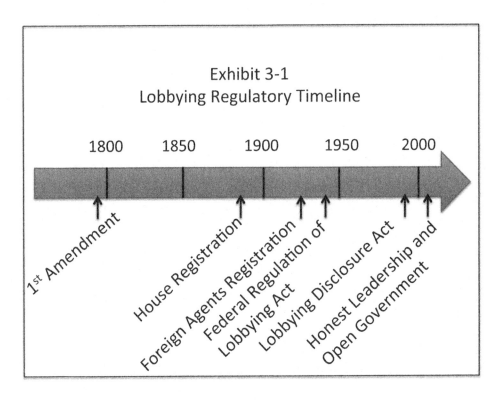

Foundational Concepts

The path to the current regulatory environment and its associated transparency begins in 1791 when the Bill of Rights was ratified. The First Amendment protects the rights of United States citizens to petition, or lobby, the government. These rights have been consistently reinforced by the courts using the concept of "strict scrutiny" – the government must meet a high standard of state interest to permit any infringement on First Amendment rights.

The Supreme Court has not, however, affirmed that the rights to petition and assembly specifically apply to lobbying (i.e. establishing a constitutional right to lobby). The only reference to such a constitutional right was a statement by Justice Harry Blackmun in *Regan v. Taxation with Representation* in which he wrote of his concurrence with the majority, "Lobbying is protected by the First Amendment." [45] The support for this conclusion stemmed from the 1961 Supreme Court decision in *Eastern Railroad Conference v. Noerr Motors* where Justice Hugo Black wrote for the majority: "The right to petition is one the freedoms protected by the Bill of Rights, and we cannot, of course, lightly impute to Congress an intent to invade these freedoms." [46]

There are several lower court decisions which support the constitutional protection of lobbying. The California Supreme Court supported the First Amendment rights of lobbyists in *Fair Political Practices Commission v. Superior Court*. The issue in this case was whether the state could require lobbyists to register and report their activities. The Court wrote "among the fundamental rights guaranteed by the First Amendment to the United States Constitution is the right to 'petition the government for redress of grievances.' The lobbyist's function obviously is to exercise such right on behalf of his employer." [47] The federal district court ruling in *ACLU v. New Jersey Election Law Enforcement Commission* crisply articulates the degree of constitutional protection afforded to lobbyists, "Freedom of speech and the right to petition for the redress of grievances are among the most precious of the liberties safeguarded by the Bill of Rights." [48] Therefore the court required that any regulation be the least restrictive in order to achieve the state's compelling interest.

There is, however, a counter-balance to unfettered petitioning of the government – the prohibition on buying legislation or using a corrupting influence. *Tool Company v. Norris* was detailed in Chapter 1. Another key decision limiting the unfettered right to petitioning the government was *Marshall v. Baltimore & Ohio Railroad Company*. In 1853, the Supreme Court passionately articulated the limitations. The railroad had contracted with Marshall to secure a grant from the Virginia legislature for a right-of-way through Virginia to the Ohio River. Marshall proposed to secure this legislation through his lobbying efforts. In a letter to the company, he described his lobbying approach; a key feature of his strategy was to conduct his lobbying in secrecy. In the letter, he describes several subterfuges to explain his time in Richmond. Doing so would enable him to influence legislators without facing opposition from those who did not want to see the grant issued. He writes: "In considering the details of the plan, I would suggest that all practical secrecy is desirable. I contemplate the use of no improper use... I require secrecy from motives of policy only, because an open agency would furnish ground of suspicion and unmerited invective, and might weaken the impression we seek to make." Compensation for his successful efforts was set at $50,000. Marshall's attempt to obtain this legislation failed initially; however, the desired access was subsequently obtained. He then sought compensation from the railroad. When the railroad refused to pay him Marshall went to court to enforce his contract and ensure he was paid.

Mr. Justice Grier, writing for the majority, unambiguously articulated the unenforceability of such a contract. One line of argument was the issue of secrecy. "Influences secretly urged under false and covert pretenses must necessarily operate deleteriously on legislative action," Grier wrote. Had Marshall acted legally and ethically, there would have been no reason to conceal his activities. The court was also concerned that Marshall would only be paid in the event of a successful outcome. A contract that is paid only when efforts are victorious often drives lobbyists to engage in wrongful acts as they are willing to employ all tactics necessary to guarantee some sort of payment. Moreover, the court feared that the contract would have a corrupting influence on the political system. Grier wrote, that such contracts "tend to corrupt or contaminate, by improper influences, the integrity of our social or political institutions."[49]

The right to petition and the prohibition on buying legislation have been combined into a single regulatory framework for lobbying – registration and disclosure. Registration has long been accepted as a means of knowing who is petitioning the government. (Exhibit 3-2) The House introduced the concept in 1876 as lobbying became perceived as a "dangerous and corrupting influence."[50] The rationale for disclosure stems from the compelling interest in (1) policy makers' understanding the positions of their constituents; and (2) "promoting openness in the system by which its laws are created."[51] Disclosure is viewed as one of the least onerous means of achieving the state's interests. "Lobbying disclosure laws are traditionally subject to less scrutiny than laws that sanction 'pure speech.'"[52] There are, however, limitations on the burdensomeness of the reporting. A California law requiring lobbyists to report their activities only tangentially related to lobbying was deemed so broad and burdensome that it was nullified.[53]

```
┌─────────────────────────────────────────────────────────┐
│                                                         │
│                    Exhibit 3-2                          │
│          The Balancing Act of Regulating Lobbying       │
│                                                         │
│                                                         │
│   Right to Petition        v.        Prohibition on     │
│                                      "buying" legislation│
│                                                         │
│                                                         │
│                       Solution:                         │
│          Registration: Does not impinge rights          │
│                                                         │
│          Disclosure: Narrowly focused, least onerous    │
│                                                         │
│                                                         │
└─────────────────────────────────────────────────────────┘
```

Regulation Via the Pocketbook

The increasing influence of lobbying in the late 19th and early 20th century, and the many scandals that accompanied it, gave rise to numerous calls for regulation. However, attempts at regulating lobbying legislatively were unsuccessful. Presidents Theodore Roosevelt and Woodrow Wilson railed against lobbying but could not muster support to pass legislation. In 1915, during the Wilson Administration, the Internal Revenue Service (IRS) did the next best thing to passing legislation: To curb lobbying, it denied the tax deductibility of expenses "...expended for lobbying purposes, the promotion or defeat of legislation, the exploitation of propaganda..."[54] The impact of this change in the tax code made lobbying more expensive. Prior to the change, businesses were able to deduct lobbying expenses for tax proposes which provided an indirect subsidy to those who lobbied. The business community was not pleased with the loss of deductibility of lobbying expenses and challenged the IRS in court. The Supreme Court in *Cammarano v. United States* ruled that denying the tax deduction put all taxpayers on the same footing: The Court stated that the regulation simply requires all taxpayers to fund their lobbying "entirely out of their pockets, as everyone else engaging in similar activities is required to do..."

> **Key Decision**
> Lobbying expenses are NOT tax deductible.
> *- Cammarano v. United States*

Lobbying costs remained a non-deductible expense until 1962 when Congress changed course and permitted a tax deduction for business expenses associated with the "direct connection with appearances before, submission of statements to, or sending communication to, the committee, or individual members, of Congress or any legislative body of a state..." The rationale for the change was

(1) the difficulty in accounting for lobbying versus other advocacy expenditures; (2) a concern that the regulation only covered Congressional lobbying; and (3) the desire to encourage taxpayers to present their views to Congress. By the 1990s, the anti-lobbying sentiment was high enough to reverse direction – Congress passed legislation that not only eliminated the tax deductibility of lobbying expenses for Congress, but also for lobbying of senior members of the executive branch.

Restricting Lobbying as a Tool of Propaganda
The first lobbying regulation was enacted into law in 1938. Ironically, it was concerns about foreign influence on American public policy, which led to the legislation, not worries about domestic lobbying. Specifically, in the 1930s, there was growing concern that Hitler was encouraging the spread of Nazism in the United States. The McCormack Committee investigating "un-American activities" recommended legislation that would regulate propaganda. The approach adopted by Congress was registration and disclosure. Under the Foreign Agents Registration Act of 1938 (FARA), agents of foreign principals (foreign governments, political parties, corporations and individuals) were required to register with the Secretary of State and disclose their client and foreign interests. Moreover, materials distributed by such agents needed to be clearly marked as propaganda. (Exhibit 3-3)

FARA is still in effect although it has been amended several times. A major change was enacted in 1966 when the Act was revised to focus on lobbying and grassroots activism by foreign principals rather than its initial emphasis on propaganda. By this time, Congress was most concerned about foreigners impacting tax, trade and other business policies.[55] In conjunction with the Lobbying Disclosure Act of 1995 (LDA), described below, foreign corporations lobbying in the United States were permitted to register and disclose their activities under that act rather than FARA. The less restrictive rules of the LDA make this an attractive option for foreign corporations.

Whether one needs to register under FARA is determined by whether an agent of a foreign principal "intends to, in any way, influence any agency or official of the Government of the United States or any section of the public within the United States with reference to formulating, adopting, or changing the domestic or foreign policies of the United States or with reference to the political or pubic interests, policies, or relations of a government of a foreign country or foreign political party."[56] Information required for registration includes details on the foreign principal as well as the agent and the nature of their relationship. Foreign agents are also required to file a disclosure statement outlining specific activities conducted every six months. A searchable database of these filings is maintained by the Sunlight Foundation.

Regulating Lobbying – A First Try (1946)

Decades of frustration over the degree of domestic lobbying and the periodic scandals resulted in the passage of the Federal Regulation of Lobbying Act of 1946. The driving force behind the Act was the need for legislators to know who was petitioning – constituents or lobbyists -- and who lobbyists represented. The Act was an adjunct to a broader legislative reorganization bill which may account for its passage.

The 1946 Act Content. The intent of the Act was to provide the public with information about who was lobbying their elected officials. The legislation required those who lobby to register and disclose their activities. The key sections are:

- Section 305 requires individuals to report lobbying expenditures used to influence legislation.
- Section 307 defines what individuals/organizations are required to fulfill these obligations. Specifically, the act states "the provision of this title shall arrive at any person, who by himself, or through an agent or employee or other persons in any manner whatsoever, directly or indirectly, solicits, collects, or receives money or any other thing of value to be used principally to aid, or the principal purpose of which person is to aid, in the accomplishment of any of the following purposes: (a) the passage or defeat of any legislation by the Congress of the United States.

(b) to influence, directly or indirectly, the passage or defeat of any legislation by the Congress of the United States."

- Section 308 requires registration. The section reads: "Any person who shall engage himself for pay or for any consideration for the purpose of attempting to influence the passage or defeat of any legislation by the Congress of the United States shall, before doing anything in furtherance of such object, register with the Clerk of the House of Representatives and the Secretary of the Senate and shall give to those officers in writing and under oath, his name and business address, the name and address of the person by whom he is employed, and in whose interest he appears or works, the duration of such employment, how much he is paid and is to receive, by whom he is paid or is to be paid, how much he is to be paid for expenses, and what expenses are to be included . . . " [57]

The legislation provides sanctions for those who violate its provisions. Those convicted of a violation are subject to a fine of up to $5,000 or imprisonment for not more than 12 months or both. A violator is also prohibited from lobbying for three years. [58] (Exhibit 3-4)

Exhibit 3-4
Lobbying Legislation Profile:
Federal Regulation of Lobbying Act of 1946

Rationale: Frustration about unscrupulous lobbying practices

Requirements: Registration and disclosure of activities

Improvements: First comprehensive attempt to regulate domestic lobbying

Lasting Impact: Established constitutionality of registration and disclosure; forced clearer definitions

---

Concerns about the effectiveness of the law surfaced quickly. President Harry Truman sought to revise the law only two years after he signed it. This effort was unsuccessful. As William Eskridge observed, the law failed to empower the

Clerk of the House and Secretary of the Senate to penalize those who did not register and disclose. Moreover, the sanctions for violating the law were criminal in nature "rather harsh for most violations of the statue."[59] Finally, there was ambiguity about the role of the Department of Justice in enforcing the law.

Legal Challenges to the 1946 Act. Congress was also concerned about the effectiveness of the law. In 1949, Congress established a select committee to assess lobbying activities. The committee was tasked with conducting a "study and investigation of all lobbying activities intended to influence, encourage, promote, or retard legislation" and lobbying of federal government agencies.[60] An organization called the Committee for Constitutional Government, refused to disclose to the committee who purchased their books and was convicted for failing to provide materials requested by a congressional committee. The conviction was challenged on First Amendment grounds. In *United States v. Rumely,* the court decision foreshadowed the problems stemming from the lack of definitions of "lobbying" and "lobbying activities" in the 1946 Act. In the absence of a statutory definition, the court determined that its duty was to define the terms in a way that would prevent constitutional challenges. The implication of the ruling was a narrow definition of lobbying and lobbying activities. In the words of the court: "Certainly it does [no] violence to the phrase 'lobbying activities' to give it a more restricted scope. To give such meaning is not barred by intellectual honesty. So to interpret is in the candid service of avoiding a serious constitutional doubt."[61]

> **Notable Quote**
> If 'lobbying' was to cover all activities of anyone intending to influence, encourage, promote or retard legislation, why did Congress differentiate between 'lobbying activities' and other 'activities'?
> - Mr. Justice Frankfurter
> (*U.S. v. Rumely*)

The Lobbying Act was directly challenged in *United States v. Harriss.* In deciding this case, the Supreme Court paved the way for registration and disclosure by lobbyists; however, their decision so narrowly defined those who were subject to the 1946 Act that it became largely irrelevant. The case arose because the National Farm Committee, a Texas corporation, failed to report the fact it had received contributions to influence policymaking relating to commodities and commodity futures.[62] Two of the organizations principals also failed to register with the House and Senate.

The Court focused on three concerns. First was whether the lobbying act was invalid because sections 305, 307, and 308 were so vague and indefinite as to not meet the requirements of due process. A second challenge centered on Sections 305 and 308, which were argued to violate of First Amendment guarantees to freedom of speech, press and the right to petition the government. A final challenge was that the penalties themselves violated the right of people to petition their government, a right protected by the First Amendment.

The Court determined that the statute did not violate the Due Process Clause. The rationale for this conclusion came from the Court's determination that Section 307, which limits who must comply with the act, is controlling. Thus, the statute did not apply to any person making contributions to influence legislation; it only applied to a subset of individuals. Specifically, in order to be covered by the statue, a person must (1) solicit, collect or receive contributions; (2) the main purpose must be to influence legislation; and (3) the method of influence must be direct communications with Members of Congress. Regarding the main purpose, the Court determined that those "contributions and persons having only an incidental purpose of influencing legislation" were to be excluded from coverage by the Act. Lobbying was interpreted to mean direct communication with members of Congress on pending or proposed federal legislation. Based on the narrow definition of who must comply with the Act, the requirements for direct contact with members of Congress to influence the passage or defeat of legislation, and not being *de minimus* in nature, "the lobbying act meets the constitutional requirement of definiteness."

Addressing the question of First Amendment protections, the court recognized the variety of pressures exerted on legislators as well as the importance of direct advocacy to our ideal of representative government. But Justice Earl Warren also acknowledged the importance of the public to know and evaluate these pressures. "Otherwise the voice of the people may all too easily be drowned out by the voice of special-interest groups seeking favored treatment while masquerading as proponents of the public weal. This is the evil which the lobbying act was designed to help prevent," he wrote. Moreover, "Congress has not sought to prohibit these pressures [lobbying]. It has merely provided for a modicum of information from those who hire, attempt to influence legislation, or who collect or spend funds for that purpose. Under these circumstances, we believe that Congress, at least within the bounds of the act as we have construed it, is not constitutionally forbidden to require the disclosure of lobbying activities. To do so would be to deny Congress, in large measure, the power of self–protection." Justices William O. Douglas and Hugo Black did not agree with this logic. For them the Act "can easily ensnare people who have done no more than exercise their constitutional rights of speech, assembly, and process."

> ### Key Decisions
> Lobbyist registration and disclosure are permitted but to a very limited set of advocates.
> - United States v. Harriss

Finally, the court avoided addressing the question of whether the penalties in the act were a violation of First Amendment rights. Since the sanctions were not applied to the litigants, there was no need to address this question.

Notwithstanding the limited constitutionality of requiring registration and disclosure resulting from the *Harriss* decision, the Act was a failure. First, it failed to cover important lobbying targets including Congressional staff and senior members of the administration. Second, the Act did not cover grassroots lobbying. Third, the itemization of expenditures "failed to require what the public needs to know most about lobbying: how much was spent overall and for what policy objective."[63] House and Senate recipients of the data viewed their responsibility as merely a repository of the information. Thus, there was no effective way for the public to access the information and there were no audits of compliance. Finally, the legislation was poorly drafted as key terms were not defined. The legislation was largely eviscerated by the courts.

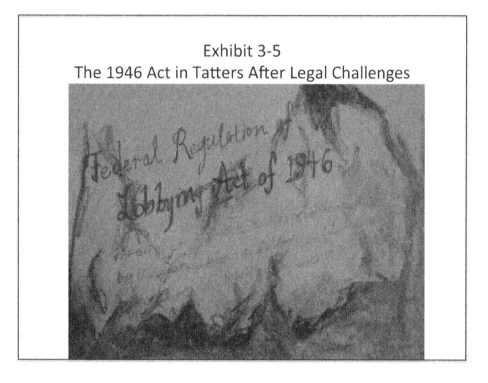

Exhibit 3-5
The 1946 Act in Tatters After Legal Challenges

The Impact of the 1946 Act. The result of the legal decisions and the limitations of the Act itself was that it became irrelevant. It remained on the books with its limited scope but it was not effective. Evidence of its irrelevance was highlighted in a General Accounting Office (GAO) study in 1991. The specific failings of the legislation were (1) its narrow focus following Harriss

> **Fun Fact**
> Only 6,000 of the 13,000 Washington "influencers" were registered lobbyists.
> (GAO 1991)

and thus excluding "other significant activity clearly recognized as lobbying...;" (2) a lack of enforcement authority; and (3) "arcane" and "confusing" forms and instructions. The results were that many lobbyists neglected to register and those that did submitted incomplete forms. Quantitative proof supported the GAO's conclusions. The GAO compared a list of lobbyists registered under the 1946 Act with those identified in the *Directory of Washington Representatives*, a listing of those who engage in government affairs, public relations and related activities. Less than half of individuals in the directory were registered lobbyists. The GAO interviewed a small sample of those who were not registered and learned that three-quarters said they did seek to influence legislation with Members of Congress or their staffs, and officials in the executive branch.[64] The GAO also found that 90 percent of the disclosure reports were incomplete. Sixty-two percent of reports were filed late. Only 10 percent of reports contained expenditures for salaries and wages (this is, after all, a people-centric business) and 40 percent of lobbyists showed financial activity.[65]

Challenge: The Right Regulation

Draft legislation that would not only achieve effective registration and disclosure (the goals of the 1946 Act) but also withstand a Constitutional challenge on First Amendment grounds.

The Byrd Amendment. One new regulation on lobbying was enacted in 1989/1990 with the passage of the Byrd Amendment. Senator Robert Byrd introduced the amendment to the 1990 Department of the Interior Appropriations Act. The Senator's motivation was his observation that: "In recent months, there has been a constant stream of news articles relating to lobbyists who exert undue influence to steer the executive branch decision-making process away from merit selection and toward political favoritism..."[66] The legislation bars private parties from using government funds to influence the award of federal contracts. The US code reads: "None of the funds appropriated by any Act may be expended by the recipient of a federal contract, grant, loan, or cooperative agreement to pay any person for influencing or attempting to influence an officer or employee of any agency, a Member of Congress, an officer or employee of Congress or employee of a Member of Congress in connection with any federal action..."[67] The agency issuing the contact was responsible for collecting disclosure reports and providing them to the Clerk of the House and Secretary of the Senate. The issuing agency was also responsible for monitoring compliance. The Department of Justice was the enforcement authority against violations. Federal employees are also prohibited from using federal funds to lobby on federal legislative or administrative actions. Civil penalties of up to $100,000 can be levied against violators.[68]

The philosophy of the Act remains in force. However, the Amendment was substantially altered with the passage of the Lobbying Disclosure Act of 1995. The disclosure process was significantly streamlined and the issuing agencies are no longer required to file compliance reports.

Regulating Lobbying – A Second Try (1995)

A combination of factors came together for Congress to pass the first comprehensive lobbying regulation in 50 years and, in terms of impact, the first ever. Scandal was one driver. Wedtech Corporation was founded by John Mariotta, a Puerto Rican, in New York City. The company grew from a manufacturer of baby carriages to a major defense contractor. The success of the company, in large part, was due to its status as a minority–owned business which allowed it to obtain no-bid contracts from the Department of Defense. The problem was, however, the company was not minority owned. Mariotta had brought in a partner who owned a majority of the company who was not a minority. The company engaged in fraud and bribery to maintain this facade. Wedtech retained a variety of lobbyists, including former members of Congress, to help secure its contracts.[69] The firm's lobbying activities were not reported. A congressional investigation into the scandal focused attention on the limited effectiveness of lobbying regulations. Following this investigation, legislation to revise lobbying law was introduced.

A second driver was the anti-lobbying rhetoric that was prevalent in the 1992 presidential election campaign. Third-party candidate Ross Perot, in a televised national debate, stated: "I think the principle that separates me is that five and a half million people came together on their own and put me on the ballot...I was not put on the ballot by any PAC money, by any foreign lobbyist money, [or] by any special interest money." Candidate Bill Clinton offered the following perspective: "It's long past time to clean up Washington. The last twelve years were nothing less than an extended hunting season for high-priced lobbyists and Washington influence peddlers. On the streets where statesmen once strolled, a never ending, stream of money now changes hands -- tying the hands of those elected to lead."[70]

> Fun Fact
> Lobbying legislation was introduced in the following Congresses: 91st-92nd , 94th , 95th ,96th , 98th , 102nd , 103rd , 104th
> (Luneburg, Susman, Gordon)

A third factor was the GAO study, noted above, which found that lobbyists were not registering and disclosing their activities. According to the House Judiciary Committee, the Act would streamline disclosure requirements and ensure that lobbyists filed semiannual reports on their clients, the issues on which they lobby and their compensation. The Committee wrote: "The Act is designed to strengthen public confidence in government by replacing the existing patchwork of lobbying disclosure laws with a single, uniform statute."[71]

Objectives of the Legislation. The goals of the Act were similar to those of the legislation 50 years earlier. Specifically, Congress sought to foster "responsible representative government" by making the public aware of the "efforts of paid lobbyists to influence the public decision making process in both the legislative and executive branches of the Federal government." President Bill Clinton offered the following perspective when he signed the Lobbying Disclosure Act of 1995 (LDA) into law: "I am very proud to sign this legislation to bring lobbying in Washington into the sunlight of public scrutiny."[72] There is, however, a subtle but important shift in focus from the 1946 Act. The motivation for the LDA was disclosure to enable the public (rather than legislators) to know who was influencing legislation and policy making.[73]

LDA Profile. LDA avoided the ambiguity issues that plagued the 1946 Act. The following key terms were clearly defined:

- "The term "lobbyist" means any individual who is employed or retained by a client for financial or other compensation for services that include more than one lobbying contact, other than an individual whose lobbying activities constitute less than 20 percent of the time engaged in the services provided by such individual to that client over a six-month period."
- "The term "lobbying activities" means lobbying contacts and efforts in support of such contacts, including preparation and planning activities, research and other background work that is intended, at the time it is performed, for use in contacts, and coordination with the lobbying activities of others."
- "The term "lobbying contact" means any oral or written communications (including any electronic communication) to a covered executive branch official or a covered legislative branch official that is made on behalf of a client with regard to – the formulation, modification, or adoption of "federal legislation, federal rules/regulations, or administration of programs /policies." Lobbying contacts exclude communications made by a public official in the execution of their responsibilities, representatives of media organization, testimony before a committee, and in response to a specific information request of Congress/executive official and/or in response to a subpoena.

The Act provides a detailed list of covered officials in executive and legislative branches. Covered executives include the President, Vice President, employees in the Executive Office of the President as well as employees in position levels I-

V. Those covered in the legislative branch include Members of Congress and their staff.

Lobbyists must register with the Clerk of the House and Secretary of the Senate within 45 days of making their first lobbying contact or being retained to make a contact. (See Exhibit 3-6) A *de minimus* exemption eliminates the need for registration if the total income from a particular client is not expected to exceed $5,000 or total expenses in connection with lobbying activities are not projected to reach $20,000 in a six month period. (These threshold amounts change with the Consumer Price Index.) The registration form is streamlined in comparison to that required under the 1946 Act. Required information includes name and address of the lobbyist, name and address of the registrant's clients, and the issues to be discussed.

Exhibit 3-6
Lobbying Disclosure Act – Registration Requirement

Individual Lobbyist
If: Retained by client for compensation, **and**
If: You will make more than 1 contact**, and**
If: You will write or speak with a covered official about legislation or policy making**, and**
If: you will spend 20+ percent of your time lobbying in the next 6 months, **then** you must register
Lobbying Firm
If: in a 6 month perod income from lobbying exceeds $5,000, **and/or** lobbying expenses exceed $20,000,
then you must register

Registered lobbyists are required to file a semiannual report with the Clerk of the House and Secretary of the Senate. The report details the name of the registrant and name of the client, the issue area being addressed, a good faith estimate of the income from the client (or payments for internal lobbyists), and a good faith estimate of total expenses incurred. (See Exhibit 3-7.)

```
Exhibit 3-7
Lobbying Disclosure Act – Disclosure Highlights


        Registrant
        Address and principle place of business
        Contact
        Senate and House ID numbers
        Client name
        Income or expenses
        Lobbying activity and issues
        Interests of any foreign entities
        Signature
```

The Clerk and Secretary are in turn required to:

- Review and verify that the forms are complete, accurate and timely.
- Notify lobbyists of non-compliance.
- Contact the United States Attorney in cases of no response to notification.
- Provide public accessibility to the information.

LDA includes sanctions to ensure compliance. Failure to remedy a violation is subject to a civil fine of not more than $50,000.

Strengths of the LDA. The Act was well designed and crafted. The LDA addresses many of the limitations of prior efforts to regulate lobbying. First, the Act clearly defines the key terms such as lobbyist and lobbying activities as detailed above. Second, the *de minimus* exemption cures the Court's concerns about an overly broad statute and incidental violation. Third, covered officials are defined to include not just Members of Congress but also their staffs and senior officials in the administrative branch. Fourth, lobbying activities include not just meeting with covered officials but also the planning, research and preparation for lobbying meetings.

LDA has not been met with legal challenge since its passage. The Act is well within the bounds established in *Harriss*. It maintains the concept of <u>direct</u> communication with policy makers, rather than <u>any</u> contact, which avoids the issue of being overly broad and therefore introducing First Amendment concerns. LDA does not impact grassroots lobbying which is more likely to raise Constitutional questions about infringing on core political speech. The 1995 law also avoids a prohibition on future lobbying for violations of the statute, another area of Constitutional concern. In sum, "[it] does not directly prohibit any political activity but only requires that such activity be disclosed."[74] The disclosure provisions were upheld in *Harriss* and are also akin to disclosure associated with campaign finance laws which have been supported by the courts.

Concerns About the LDA. The LDA does have its critics. Some suggest that disclosure alone is not enough to achieve the objective of keeping lobbyists from undue influence in policy making and enforcement. Three issues that the legislation does not address are gifts/entertainment, the revolving door, and campaign contributions. The accessibility of the information is also problematic; although, OpenSecrets.com does make the information more useful to the concerned citizen. There is also the issue of the missing link. The information disclosed under LDA does not directly tie lobbying activity with individual Members or senior executive branch officials. The concern about effective administration and enforcement which was prominent post the 1946 Act remains somewhat problematic as evidenced by the United States Attorney's Office assigning only five of its 700 personnel to enforcing LDA.[75] William Luneburg, a law professor at the University of Pittsburgh, offers the following solution: Vest the power to administer and enforce LDA with an independent agency "outside of the Congress and not under the thumb of the President."[76] In this way, the industry could be regulated by an entity other than those directly affected by it. A final issue – which is perhaps the most disconcerting – is that the Act does not address grassroots lobbying, mobilizing a group of people to influence public policy by contacting their representatives. This form of lobbying is not regulated, enabling individuals, groups and/or organizations to impact public policy without disclosure. (Exhibit 3-8)

> <u>Food For Thought</u>
> What are the implications of not tying lobbyist contacts directly with Members?

```
┌─────────────────────────────────────────────────────────────┐
│                      Exhibit 3-8                             │
│              Lobbying Legislation Profile:                   │
│              Lobbying Disclosure Act of 1995                 │
│                                                             │
│                                                             │
│   Rationale: Scandals and concerns about the power of       │
│   lobbyists                                                  │
│                                                             │
│   Requirements: Registration and disclosure of activities   │
│   with Congress and the executive branch                    │
│                                                             │
│   Improvements: Well-conceived and drafted – clear          │
│   definitions and Constitutional                            │
│                                                             │
│   Lasting Impact: Still how lobbying is regulated           │
│                                                             │
└─────────────────────────────────────────────────────────────┘
```

Notwithstanding the adoption of the most comprehensive lobbying reform legislation ever, ten years later the country faced one of the largest lobbying scandals in history – the Abramoff affair.

Regulating Lobbying Post-Abramoff
Great optimism surrounded the passage of the LDA in 1995. At last the public would be able to see who was lobbying whom, on what issues, and with what resources. There was an expectation that the lobbying scandals that plagued lobbying would come to an end. Such hopes were dashed a decade later with the Abramoff affair. His illegal lobbying activities not only led to his own incarceration, but also the conviction of many others who were on the receiving end of his largess. Congressional action to correct the flaws in the lobbying regulations illustrated by Abramoff was swift, reflecting the anger in Congress, the media and the general public. The legislative efforts culminated in 2007 with the passage of the Honest Leadership and Open Government Act (HLOGA). An example of real bipartisanship, the bill passed the House 411 to 8 and in the Senate the vote was 83 to 14. Then-Senator Barack Obama said the legislation was "the most sweeping ethics reform since Watergate."[77]

The Act addressed a variety of ethics and lobbying issues including accepting gifts, travel, disclosure and the revolving door. Regarding gifts, the act prohibits Members of Congress from accepting gifts from lobbyists or their clients. HLOGA also addresses travel funded by outside groups, a key strategy used by Abramoff to influence Members. The Act requires members to disclose travel which is financed by outside groups on a public website. Members of Congress and senior executive branch officials are allowed to travel on non-commercial aircraft; however, they must pay fair market value for the use of the aircraft. Candidates for the House of Representatives are prohibited from using noncommercial aircraft. Lobbyists are required to certify that they have not provided gifts or travel in violation of House and Senate rules.

HLOGA also enhanced disclosure of lobbying activities. The Act requires more frequent and timely disclosure. Reports are required on a quarterly rather than semiannual basis. They must be filed within 20 days rather than the 45 days in the LDA. The *de minimus* exception is also lowered from $5,000 to $2,500 for total income from lobbying and from $20,000 to $10,000 for total expenses in conjunction with lobbying.[78] The new legislation also requires lobbyists to report campaign and presidential library contributions on a semiannual basis. The civil penalty for "knowing and willful violations" of the disclosure requirements was increased from $50,000 to $200,000. A criminal penalty with the potential for a prison term was added: "Whoever knowingly and corruptly fails to comply with any provision of this act shall be imprisoned for not more than five years or fined under title 18, United States code, or both."[79] The act also sought to enhance the efficiency and effectiveness of disclosure. Electronic reporting was enhanced and the Government Accountability Office was tasked with an annual audit of disclosure compliance.

Government officials leaving their posts to become lobbyists, leveraging their contacts and influence over remaining policy makers, has been a long-standing concern. Equally troublesome is the move from private sector to public sector where individuals have decision-making authority that directly impacts their prior employer. Specifically, the worry is that the individuals would have a conflict of interest or have undue influence on policy makers or decision making as they change roles. The combination of these issues is known as the "revolving door." Prior legislation established a limited "cooling off" period for some senior government officials. The 2007 Act enhanced and broaden the cooling-off period.

- The period for senators increased from 1 to 2 years.
- The two-year cooling-off period also applies to cabinet secretaries and other senior executive personnel.
- House members face a one-year cooling-off period.
- Senate staff and officers have a one-year prohibition from lobbying-related contacts with the entire Senate.
- House staff members are restricted from lobbying their former office for a period of one year.

The actual language of the restriction is instructive: "Any person... after that person leaves office, knowingly makes, with the intent to influence, any communication to or appearance before any Member, officer, or employee or either house of Congress or any employee of any other legislative office of Congress, on behalf of any other person in connection with any matter

Food For Thought
How effective are the revolving door restrictions likely to be in preventing conflicts of interest?

on which such former [covered official] seeks action by a Member, officer, or employee of either house of Congress, in his or her official capacity, shall be punished as provided in section 216 of this title."[80] In essence, a covered official may not influence any member of government during the cooling-off period. (Exhibit 3-9)

Exhibit 3-9
Lobbying Legislation Profile:
Honest Leadership and Open Government Act
Of 2007

Rationale: Abramoff scandal - gifts/travel regulation gap and concerns about revolving door

Requirements: Restriction/prohibition on gifts and travel; extended cooling-off periods

Improvements: Covers missing elements

Lasting Impact: Still law of the land

President Obama on Lobbying

HLOGA addresses both Congress and the executive branch; however, its focus is on Congress. President Barack Obama, a long-standing critic of lobbying excesses, has enhanced the regulation of lobbying for the executive branch. He issued Executive Order 13490 on January 21, 2009, his first day in office. The order is titled Ethics Commitments by Executive Branch Personnel. The centerpiece of the order is an ethics pledge required of employees in every executive agency that contractually commits the appointee to the following: "As a condition, and in consideration, of my employment in the United States government in a position vested with the public trust, I commit myself to the following obligations, which I understand are binding on me and are enforceable under law..." The specific obligations include a ban on accepting gifts from registered lobbyists or their clients and a two-year cooling-off period. The cooling-off period extends in both directions – appointees from industry are prevented from participating in matters relevant to their prior employer and restricted from lobbying the government on policy matters they were responsible for while in office once they return to the private sector.

Challenge: The Ethics Pledge

Would you sign the Ethics Pledge to work in a presidential administration? If not, what caveats would you require to sign the pledge?

President Obama also addressed lobbying head-on in his 2010 State of the Union address. He remarked that he came to Washington to give the people and the government what they deserve and reduce the distrust that exists between the citizens and federal government: "To close the credibility gap, we have to take action on both ends of Pennsylvania Avenue – to end the outsized influence of lobbyists; to work openly; to give our people the government they deserve... But we can't stop there. It's time to require lobbyists to disclose each contact they make on behalf of a client with my administration or with Congress."

One action he took to fulfill this vision was limiting the impact of lobbying associated with Recovery Act funds. In a memorandum to executive branch department heads, the President wrote: "In implementing the Recovery Act, we have undertaken unprecedented efforts to ensure the responsible distribution of funds for the Act's purposes and to provide public transparency and accountability of expenditures. We must not allow recovery act funds to be distributed on the basis of factors other than the merits of the proposed projects or in response to improper influence or pressure." The "influence" and "pressure" referred to in the memorandum are from lobbyists. To address these concerns, the president established the following guidelines for interactions with lobbyists:

- "Executive departments and agencies cannot consider the views of lobbyists concerning projects, applications, or applicants for funding."[81]
- Officials are prohibited from communicating orally with registered lobbyists about recovery act projects.
- Written communications must be posted on the agency's website.

Yet another restriction placed on lobbyists by the Obama Administration limits the number of federally-registered lobbyists serving on advisory boards and commissions. The goal of this action is to "reduce the influence of special interests in Washington." This action has been quite controversial. Representatives of the Industry Trade Advisory Committees wrote a letter to the administration highlighting concerns, including the quality of information and decision making available to advisory committees, an incentive for lobbyists to deregister so they can be appointed, and letting the illegal actions of a few to dictate restrictions on the majority.

> **Food For Thought**
> Should lobbyists be prohibited from serving on government advisory committees?

The regulations outlined above are constantly being reviewed, interpreted, and revised. The most up-to-date information is contained in the Lobbying Disclosure Act Guidance which is updated semiannually. This is the best source for federally lobbying "dos and don'ts."

The *Citizens United* Angle

Prior to state level discussion on lobbying regulations, a last federal issue warrants mention – the Supreme Court's *Citizens United* decision. The Supreme Court, in their *Citizens United* decision, addressed whether the McCain-Feingold campaign finance reform bill could limit the spending of corporations in federal elections. In a 5-4 and highly-controversial ruling, the Court determined that corporations have the unfettered right to speak in political campaigns. Justice Anthony Kennedy, writing for the majority, stated the First Amendment "must be given the benefit of any doubt to protecting rather than stifling speech." He went on to write that restricting speech based on the identity of the speaker is more often than not a means to control content. He added that voters should be free to obtain information from diverse sources to better inform their vote. [82] Justice Paul Stevens wrote spirited dissent arguing that McCain-Feingold is not a categorical ban on corporate speech as companies can speak through political action committees. Moreover, the decision should be narrow (not broad) and the majority abandons *stare decisis* "blaz[ing] through our precedents, overruling or disavowing a body of case law…" Nevertheless, the decision stands and corporations may use an unlimited amount of general treasury funds to support their candidates in elections.

What does this decision have to do with lobbying? A *Washington Examiner* columnist offers this perspective: Businesses have two options to influence lawmakers – (1) lobbying and (2) encouraging voters to support their candidates in elections. He argues that since the passage of McCain-Feingold, corporations have favored lobbying. [83] With the *Citizens United* ruling, corporations have an alternative to lobbying for influencing public policy outcomes. Lobbying expenditures since the ruling have been flat lending some credibility to the *Washington Examiner* columnist's contention. It is likely too early to tell whether the ruling will have a long-term impact on lobbying or if corporations will continue to use both avenues for influence.

Assessment of the Current Regulatory Regime

Lobbying registration and disclosure is now well ensconced. Congress has adopted a set of regulations that balance the desire to "control" lobbying through disclosure with the First Amendment right to petition. The recent limits and prohibitions on gifts and travel have helped to reduce concerns about unfair, if not undue, influence on lobbyists. The GAO's 2012 Lobbying Disclosure assessment paints a picture of success. The GAO report begins:

> Fun Fact
> 97% of lobbyists could substantiate their income and expenses.
> (GAO 2012)

"Most lobbyists were able to provide documentation to demonstrate compliance with the disclosure requirements" of LDA and HLOGA.[84] More important than simply reporting, almost all lobbyists could provide documentation to support reported income and expenses.[85] This is a substantial improvement from the findings in the 1990s. The GAO also concluded that resource constraints were not limiting the enforcement of lobbying regulations.

Nevertheless politicians and the media continue to rail against lobbying. The American Bar Association sponsored a task force to consider ways to improve the system of lobbying regulation "to restore the honor and enhance the efficacy of those in our profession who advocate for clients in the forum of public policy."[86] Charles Fried, a Harvard Law School professor who served on the task force and wrote the preface to the

> Food for Thought
> Would you advocate for eliminating the 20% rule? Why? What are the implications of segregating advocacy from fundraising?

report, highlights the criticality of this function: "Lobbying, and therefore lobbyists, are indispensable to the functioning of government, and they embody a constitutional right of the highest order, enshrined in the First Amendment..." The task force recommendations center on increasing transparency and segregating advocacy from fundraising. The group proposes two actions to improve the efficacy of disclosure. First, the government should broaden those required to register and disclose by eliminating the exemption for advocates who spend less than 20 percent of their time lobbying. Their recommendation does suggest retaining the dollar threshold. Second, the task force would add the requirement that lobbyists disclose the specific individuals with whom they have advocated. Turning to fundraising, Fried writes: "Nothing so contributes to the perception of lobbyists as agents of corruption, rather than public policy advocates, as confounding of these two [lobbying and fundraising] functions." The group therefore proposes that "so far as practicable, those who advocate to elected officials do not raise funds for them, and those who raise funds for them do not advocate for them."

State Level Regulations

States also regulate lobbying. State level regulations are typically based on the federal model and involve registration, disclosure and transparency. The definitions of "lobbying" and "lobbyist" are quite similar across the states, as are the requirements for registration. Where state regulations vary is in the information that must be disclosed. Most require an enumeration of lobbying expenditures especially for gifts, entertainment and travel. Some states also require the lobbyist to identify the issues they lobby on and in which body of government. The National Conference of State Legislatures maintains a database of all state-by-state requirements. One important contrast from federal lobbying concerns contingent contracts. These are contracts in which the lobbyist is paid only if he or she is successful such as securing earmarks in appropriations bills or passing legislation. While there is no federal prohibition on contingent contracts, 43 states ban the practice.[87]

One of the most stringent state lobbying laws is in Massachusetts. The Act to Improve the Laws Relating Campaign Finance, Ethics and Lobbying was passed in 2009 in response to yet another scandal. In this case, the recently reelected speaker of the Massachusetts House had been indicted, and subsequently convicted, in a bribery scandal. Speaker Salvatori DiMasi and a lobbyist were found guilty of corruption in which DiMasi was paid $65,000 to secure a multi-million dollar software contract for a company that the lobbyist represented. DiMasi lobbied Governor Deval Patrick to get the software contract approved. DiMasi was not the first speaker to run afoul of the law; two prior speakers resigned amid allegations of ethics violations. The result was the passage of a new Massachusetts Lobbying Law, which became effective in January 2010.

The new law expanded the definition of lobbying to include interactions with legislative, executive, and municipal levels of government. Lobbying at the legislative and executive levels included not only direct contacts with covered officials but also "strategizing, planning, and research if performed in connection with, or for use in, an actual communication with a government employee..." This broader construction increases the likelihood of meeting the financial thresholds which require registration. The definition also has the potential to increase the number of individuals required to register through their participation in development of advocacy materials. One law firm, writing to their clients about the new Massachusetts law, distributed a white paper entitled "You, Too, Could be a Lobbyist (Even if You Don't Want to Be)."

The specific criteria to determine if an individual is considered an executive or legislative agent are fourfold, all of which must be met to be an agent. The individual must (1) engage in lobbying as defined in the statute; (2) receive compensation for lobbying in excess of $2,500 per six-month period; (3) conduct more than 25 hours of lobbying activities in a six month period; and (4) have at least one direct contact with a covered official.

The Massachusetts lobbying law has several other interesting attributes:

- Contingent contracts are prohibited.
- Disclosure of lobbying expenses is itemized at a detailed level (meals, gifts, transportation, entertainment, advertising, public relations, printing, mailing and telephone expenses are each separately identified).
- Late filing fees ($50 per day for 20 days, increasing to $100 per day thereafter) encourage timely filing.
- Fines ($100-$10,000) and the potential for prison sentences (not more than 5 years) are used to enforce the statute.

A final notable aspect of the Massachusetts lobbying law is the requirement for lobbyists to complete a State-designed and implemented lobbyist training program each year prior to registration. The training can be completed online or in a classroom. The topics covered include: an overview of lobbying requirements and explanations of registration and disclosure processes.

Challenge: Massachusetts Lobbying Law FAQs

Lobbying laws can be challenging to interpret; yet, accurate understanding is essential to avoid violations. The Massachusetts law is no exception.

Read the actual text of the law available at: https://malegislature.gov/Laws/SessionLaws/Acts/2009/Chapter28 and answer the following questions:

- *Are employees of organizations who testify before legislative committees required to register as agents?*
- *Is an individual who is retained to advocate on behalf of a client before a municipal government subject to registration?*
- *Is an individual who provides pro bono testimony in a regulatory hearing advocating on behalf of their client's position required to register as a lobbyist?*
- *Can a registered lobbyist participate on boards and commissions at the municipal and state level of government?*

Regulation Redux

- Lobbying has generally been viewed as a constitutionally-protected right; however, there is a prohibition on "buying" legislation.
- Regulation of lobbying through registration and disclosure has been the balance between the protection and the prohibition.
- The first legislated limitation of lobbying focused on lobbying on behalf of foreign principals; the Foreign Agents Registration Act of 1938 is still in force.
- The first attempt at regulating domestic lobbying in 1946 was eviscerated in the courts, but it did establish the constitutionality of some restrictions.
- The Lobbying Disclosure Act of 1995 is the dominant lobbying regulation statute; it centers on registration and disclosure.
- Clear definitions and restricted application of the 1995 Act minimized legal challenges.
- Gift and travel prohibitions were adopted in 2007 to complement the 1995 Act.
- *Citizens United* opens an alternative means of influencing public policy.
- The current regulatory structure has its critics; one proposal is to broaden disclosure requirements and separate lobbying from fundraising.
- States also regulate lobbying; most laws are based on the federal registration and disclosure model.

Learning by Doing

One of the first official acts of your new lobbying firm is registration. If you will be lobbying at the federal level you must register with the Secretary of the Senate and Clerk on the House under LDA and HLOGA. Obtain the registration Form L-1 from the Secretary of the Senate website and compete the form. Also, draw up an internal policy for tracking lobbying activities and an associated spreadsheet so you will be able to easily complete your disclosure requirements under LDA (Form L-2) and HLOGA (Form 203). If your plans are to lobby at the state level, determine the lobbying requirements in the relevant state(s) and complete the necessary actions.

Bibliography Chapter 3

"2012 Lobbying Disclosure: Observations on Lobbyists' Compliance with Disclosure Requirements." Accessed July 28, 2013. http://www.gao.gov/products/GAO-13-437?source=ra.

ACLU of New Jersey v. New Jersey Election Law Enforcement Commission (United States District Court, District of New Jersey 1981).

An Act to Provide Greater Transparency in the Legislative Process, 2007.

Babington, Charles. "Bush Signs Lobby-Ethics Bill." *The Washington Post*, September 15, 2007, sec. Nation. http://www.washingtonpost.com/wp-dyn/content/article/2007/09/15/AR2007091500589.html.

Browne, Steven. "The Constitutionality of Lobby Reform: Implicating Associational Privacy and the Right to Petition the Government." *William & Mary Bill of Rights Journal* 4, no. 2 (February 1, 1995): 717.

———. "The Constitutionality of Lobby Reform: Implicating Associational Privacy and the Right to Petition the Government." *William & Mary Bill of Rights Journal* 4, no. 2 (February 1, 1995): 717.

Byrd, Robert. "United States Senate." Government. *Lobbyists*, September 28, 1987. http://www.senate.gov/legislative/common/briefing/Byrd_History_Lobbying.htm.

Canady, Charles. *Lobbying Disclosure Act of 1995*. 104th Congress, 1st Session, House of Representatives, Committee of the Whole House on the State of the Union, November 14, 1994.

Carney, Timothy. "Why Lobbyists Dislike Citizens United | WashingtonExaminer.com." *Washington Examiner*. Accessed July 28, 2013. http://washingtonexaminer.com/article/2515086.

Citizens United v. Federal Election Commission (United States Supreme Court 2010).

Clinton, William J. "Remarks on Signing the Lobbying Disclosure Act of 1995 and an Exchange with Reporters." Roosevelt Room of the White House, December 19, 1995.

"Eastern R. Conference V. Noerr Motors - 365 U.S. 127 (1961)." *Justia US Supreme Court Center*. Accessed July 28, 2013. http://supreme.justia.com/cases/federal/us/365/127/case.html.

"Ethics: Contingency Fees for Lobbyists." *National Conference of State Legislatures*, March 2013. http://www.ncsl.org/legislatures-elections/ethicshome/50-state-chart-contingency-fees.aspx.

Fair Political Practices Com. v. Superior Court, Supreme Court of California (1979).

"History of the Lobbying Disclosure Act." *Public Citizen: LobbyingInfo.org*, July 26, 2005. http://www.lobbyinginfo.org/laws/page.cfm?pageid=15#_edn11.

Holman, Craig. "Origins, Evolution and Structure of the Lobbying Disclosure Act." *Public Citizen*, May 11, 2006. http://www.citizen.org/documents/LDAorigins.pdf.

Limitation on Use of Appropriated Funds to Influence Certain Federal Contracting and Financial Transactions. 31USC1352.

Levin, Robert M. *Lobbying Law in the Spotlight: Challenges and Proposed Improvements*. Report of the Task Forc e on Federal Lobbying Laws Section of Administrative La w and Regulatory Practice American Bar Association, January 3, 2011.

Luneburg, William V. "The Evolution of Federal Lobbying Regulation: Where We Are Now and Where We Should Be Going." *McGeorge Law Review* 41 (2009).

Luneburg, William V., Thomas M. Susman, and Rebecca H. Gordon. *The Lobbying Manual: A Complete Guide to Federal Lobbying Law and Practice*. American Bar Association, 2009.

"Marshall V. Baltimore & Ohio Railroad Company - 57 U.S. 314 (1853)." *Justia US Supreme Court Center*. Accessed July 28, 2013. http://supreme.justia.com/cases/federal/us/57/314/case.html.

"Regan V. Taxation With Representation - 461 U.S. 540 (1983)." *Justia US Supreme Court Center*. Accessed July 28, 2013. http://supreme.justia.com/cases/federal/us/461/540/.

Socolar, Milton J. "Federal Regulation of Lobbying Act of 1946 Is Ineffective." United States General Accounting Office Testimony, July 16, 1991. http://www.gao.gov/assets/110/104007.pdf.

Straus, Jacob R. *Lobbying Registration and Disclosure: Before and After the Enactment of the Honest Leadership and Open Government Act Of 2007*. DIANE Publishing, 2011.

———. *Lobbying Registration and Disclosure: The Role of the Clerk of the House and the Secretary of the Senate*. Congressional Research Service, June 20, 2013. http://www.fas.org/sgp/crs/misc/RL34377.pdf.

———. *Lobbying the Executive Branch: Current Practices and Options for Change*. DIANE Publishing, 2010.

"The Lobbying Game: Influence-brokers In D.c. How Representatives Of Foreign Interests Push Their Agendas Among Washington's Decision-makers." *Philly.com*. Accessed July 28, 2013. http://articles.philly.com/1996-09-17/news/25631817_1_trade-deficit-mfn-trading-status.

"United States V. Harriss - 347 U.S. 612 (1954)." *Justia US Supreme Court Center*. Accessed July 28, 2013. http://supreme.justia.com/cases/federal/us/347/612/case.html.

"United States V. Rumely - 345 U.S. 41 (1953)." *Justia US Supreme Court Center*. Accessed July 28, 2013. http://supreme.justia.com/cases/federal/us/345/41/.

Chapter 4: Ethics and Endless Scandals

Even a casual reading of the first three chapters reveals a recurring theme – the fact that lobbying is perpetually intertwined with scandals. Whether detailing the history of lobbying, the industry, or regulation, a key feature has been periodic but ever-present scandals. The prior chapter explored regulating lobbying to minimize the corruption associated with lobbying. Regrettably that has not proven enough to avoid illegal behavior. There is, however, another avenue to avoid scandal – the promotion of ethical behavior by lobbyists and lobbyees.

Ever-Present Scandals

Notwithstanding The Lobbying Disclosure Act and The Honest Leadership and Open Government Act of 2007, the scandals continue. At the federal level, the successful lobbying firm PMA abruptly closed after federal prosecutors reportedly raided the firm and the home of its principal. The *New York Times* reported that prosecutors were focused on inappropriate campaign contributions and potentially Congressional ethics rules violations associated with gifts.[88] PMA was founded by Paul Magliocchetti, a former senior staffer to the House Appropriations Committee, and grew rapidly from revenues of $3 million in 1998 to $15 million in 2007 at its peak.[89] The growth was spurred by the firm's success in obtaining hundreds of millions of dollars in earmarks for its clients.[90] The firm's clients, ITT Industries, General Dynamics, and Finmeccania SpA to name a few, were dominantly in the defense, technology and healthcare industries. More than 30 lobbyists provided services to PMA's clients, including the founder's son, Mark.

Father and son were charged with "funneling hundreds of thousands of dollars to lawmakers to enhance [the] firm's stature and business prospects.[91] Campaign contributions served as the vehicle used to "funnel" the funds. Magliocchetti requested that PMA employees, including his son, provide campaign contributions to officials and then reimbursed the donors from personal or firm funds – a clear violation of campaign finance laws. Mark Magilocchetti admitted to wrongdoing, indicating he did not know this was a violation of law initially, but came to realize it sometime later. With his son cooperating with authorities, Paul admitted to campaign law violations. In the words of the U.S. Attorney: "Mr. Magliocchetti is answering for his brazen disregard for the law to achieve political influence and enrich himself...Campaign finance laws give transparency to political contributions, and protect the public's ability to see who's really funding a campaign."[92] Magliocchettti served a 27-month prison sentence for his illegal activity. His lobbying career was over and his personal life fell into disarray.

Impropriety has also been prevalent in state government. In New York, State Senator Carl Kruger pled guilty to corruption charges and is serving a multiyear prison sentence. He admitted that he directed clients to a lobbyist, Richard Lipsky, in exchange for a 50 percent kickback on Lipsky's fees. The lobbyist received only a few months in jail as he cooperated with authorities in the case. Notwithstanding his cooperation with the government, Judge Jed S. Rakoff insisted on some prison time. "I think it still has to be the case that to engage in a form of public corruption you must understand that you go to jail."[93]

Understanding Dishonesty. What drives this behavior? The psychology of lobbying fraud is similar to other forms of violating trust. In the book 'Trust and Honesty', Tamar Frankel explores the erosion of trust in the United States. She highlights "everyone does it" as a key justification for dishonesty.[94] Lipsky, the New York lobbyist who paid kickbacks to a state senator, explained his behavior this way: "I simply forgot everything I had learned and lived by and failed to apply the same accountability and high standards to my own behavior. Instead of remaining skeptical and righteous, I went along."[95] Abramoff offers this excuse in his autobiography: "The worst part for me was the hypocrisy of the whole thing. Most of these senators had taken boatloads of cash and prizes from my team and our clients."[96]

Frankel also writes about "intellectualizing" deceitful behavior. The following quote from Abramoff illustrates this point: "In my weakness of character, and my desire to get the client to do quickly what I thought would be necessary to save them, I didn't reveal that I was the one who set up this company and subsequently profited from it."[97] He rationalizes his actions based on serving the client; the fact the he personally benefited from the arrangement above and beyond his fees was merely an

> **Notable Quote**
> Human beings have limits, but I refused to recognize mine and, instead I used my creativity, intellect, work ethic and the power of manipulation to get what I wanted. It didn't matter that I believed my actions were of the good of my clients; they were wrong – I was wrong.
>
> Jack Abramoff
> (Abramoff 2011)

afterthought. He himself recognizes this justification: "In doing each of these things and more, I had intellectualized and rationalized my actions. I found— and sometimes created—loopholes and shortcuts. In my rush to do a million things simultaneously, I did some of them incorrectly and illegally. As I reviewed actions taken years before, I cringe in horror. Had I really done that? What was I thinking?"[98]

A third explanation that Frankel identifies is what she calls the slippery slope – the gradual shift from appropriate, to questionable, to wrong/illegal behavior.

Again, Abramoff uses this explanation to shed light on his behavior. "Over the next few weeks, I reflected on my stupidity, my mistakes (my crimes). How could I have allowed things to get so far out of hand?"[99] Ironically, those who take the slippery slope do not realize they are going down it until it is too late. "...I continued to pour over my emails. Eventually, it became clear that I was not as blameless as I first thought. I had broken the law. I might not have intended to do so, but as I came to understand, under federal criminal law, intentions didn't matter."[100]

Another explanation for illegal behavior is to consider the idea that power corrupts. Simply stated: When people are in positions of power, they come to believe they are above the law and ethical restraints. The concept of power corrupting has a long history. Lord Acton, a historian and moralist, wrote in 1887: "Power tends to corrupt, and absolute power corrupts absolutely. Great men are almost always bad men."[101] The idea is intuitively attractive and matches anecdotal evidence. For evidence, look no further than Napoleon Bonaparte, Adolf Hitler, Francisco Franco, and Richard Nixon. Recent academic research also confirms the power corruption hypothesis. For example, in one experiment students were put in high-power and low-power positions. Those in the high-power positions held a higher sense of morality (i.e. cheating on expense reports is bad) than those in the low-power position, yet the high-power participants were significantly more likely to cheat when playing a game in isolation than their low-power counterparts.[102]

Concerns about the role of lobby in policymaking are not new. Just after the millennium, a Gallup poll found that almost 80 percent of respondents agreed or strongly agreed that "special interests have too much control over what government does." The most frequent responses to the question --'What bothers you most about American politics?' -- were (1) too little involvement with the public; (2) too much bureaucracy; and (3) the need to "get rid of lobbying/interest groups."[103]

> ### Fun Fact
> 71% of respondents think lobbyists have too much power in contrast to 22% who think local government has too much power.
> (Gallup)

The scandals of the past decade have reinforced the public's skepticism of lobbying. A Gallup poll reported that lobbyists were rated the lowest of more than a dozen professions when it comes to honesty and ethical standards. Even car sales people and Congress members were rated higher than lobbyists.[104] Moreover, the public believes lobbyists have too much power – they top the list of those with too much 'say and sway' as reported in *Gallup Politics*. Interestingly, this assessment is largely the same for Republicans, Democrats and Independents.[105]

Implications of Distrust

The negative attitude of the public toward lobbying is problematic for lobbyists on several fronts. First, the skepticism threatens the continued growth of the industry. The tarnished image of lobbying makes selling the role of public affairs officer (as it is often called since most don't want the title of lobbyist) inside an organization more difficult. The public affairs role competes for resources with other functions of the organization. The rationale for supporting these activities is the return on investment discussed in Chapter 2. However, if lobbying represents reputational risk, the function is likely to receive fewer resources. Numerous stakeholders – shareholders, customers, employees, communities - could pressure the organization to reduce or cease lobbying. The risk of employing a lobbyist might be amplified if an organization is hiring an outside lobbying firm as the organization has less direct control over the process. Compounding the problem is the *Citizens United* decision that creates an alternative path to influence public policy. If that path is deemed less risky, organizations are likely to divert funds from lobbying to campaign financing.

It is true that lobbying expenditures exceed $3 billion and have grown in the past despite the scandals; however, something new has been taking place. For the first time (with the exception of the 2007/8 financial crisis), lobbying expenditures decreased in 2012 by $250 million. At the firm level, some of the declines were sizable.[106] This could be an anomaly or it could be the beginning of a trend – only time will tell.

A second negative impact for lobbyists is the potential for more regulation. Each major scandal results in calls for more restraints. While the First Amendment limits the restrictions, more detailed, frequent and generally more onerous disclosure is a real possibility. The thresholds for registration could also be lowered increasing those who must comply with the LDA and HLAOG. This was the approach used in Massachusetts in response to a lobbying scandal involving the Speaker of the House. Among the changes, it became necessary to register if lobbying activities amounted toward more than 25 hours (the ceiling was 50 hours previously.)

Policymakers are also negatively impacted by the perpetual scandals and associated public anger about lobbying. Some face the direct fallout of being associated with a scandal. Abramoff tainted literally dozens of policymakers and staff members, destroying many careers. Even those who are not directly involved in corrupt activities are guilty by association. The approval rating of Congress has dropped to less than 20 percent in the past few years compared to above 40 percent in 2000.[107]

Less lobbying also reduces the legislative subsidy described by Hall and Deardorff. Policymakers do not have the resources to be knowledgeable about all relevant issues. Lobbyists provide valuable insights.

Corruption tied to lobbying also takes a toll on democracy itself. Lobbying, the right to petition the government for redress, is a core tenet of democracy, but when legislation is for sale or only a subset of the public has access to decision makers, the foundation of the democracy can be eroded. *'The Ethics of Lobbying'* published by the Woodstock Theological Center captures this thinking: "The pervasive belief that government serves the interests of the powerful has demoralized American democracy. It has weakened support for government, generated distrust of public officials, and significantly reduced the civic engagement of ordinary citizens."[108] The judge, in sentencing Abramoff, reached a similar conclusion: "You've impacted seriously the public confidence in the integrity of the government. These activities corrupted the political process and deprived the public of the honest services of their own public officials, both in the legislature and executive branch."[109]

The regulations enacted are part of the solution and there are opportunities to increase their effectiveness within the boundaries of the First Amendment such as broadening those who must register and disclose and increasing penalties. One non-legal or regulatory solution that might help tip the scales toward "good" lobbying is a focus on lobbying ethics – creating a culture where ethical behavior is not only the norm but also bad behavior is self-policed and minimized.

Association of Government Relations Professionals
The Association of Government Relations Professionals (AGRP), formerly the American League of Lobbyists, understands the need for the lobbying industry to enhance its trustworthiness. A primary focus of the organization is on the ethical behavior of its members. AGRP has its Code of Ethics for its members. The Code is "utilized as a model by various organizations and serves to strengthen our image and enhance our role as a vital and respected link in the democratic process."[110] The premise for the code is that lobbyists have a proactive obligation to "preserve and advance public trust and confidence in our democratic institutions and the public policy process..."[111] AGRP "strongly" urges that its members comply with its Ethics Code. As to sanctions, "[a]ny AGRP member found guilty by a court of a crime of moral turpitude or of violating a law directly related to any professional lobbying or political campaign activity shall forfeit AGRP membership."[112]

The Ethics Code consists of nine articles outlined in Exhibit 4-1. The Code begins with a call for conducting lobbying with honesty and integrity (Article I). Truthful and accurate information should be provided. Inaccuracies or changes should be relayed to the policymaker as soon as they are known. Article II calls for compliance with all laws, regulations and rules. This rather evident requirement has two noteworthy aspects. First, lobbyists should know the law and regulations that apply to the profession. While this would seem obvious, the law is nuanced and a clear understanding takes work. Mark Magliocchetti of the PMA Group, who helped his father funnel thousands of dollars in campaign contributions to members of Congress, argued for leniency based on his lack of understanding that his actions were illegal. The second noteworthy aspect is that a "lobbyist should not cause a public official to violate any law, regulation, or rule..."[113]

Exhibit 4-1
Association of Government Relations Professionals
Code of Ethics

Article I – Honesty and Integrity

Article II – Compliance with Applicable Laws,

Regulations & Rules

Article III – Professionalism

Article IV – Conflicts of Interest

Article V – Diligence & Best Efforts

Article VI – Compensation and Engagement Terms

Article VII – Confidentiality

Article VIII – Public Education

Article IX – Duty to Governmental Institutions

Article III is devoted to professionalism. Lobbyists should understand legislative and governmental process, treat allies and adversaries with respect and civility, and participate in continuing education. Article IV addresses conflicts of interest. The article reads: "A lobbyist should not continue or undertake representations that may create conflicts of interest without the informed consent of the client or potential client involved."[114] AGRP highlights the need to avoid advocating for a client's position that would adversely impact another client. Indeed, it was just such a conflict that brought the spotlight onto Jack Abramoff, ultimately revealing his violations of the law as well as ethical standards.

Article V covers due diligence and best efforts. Section 5.2 is particularly noteworthy as it states "lobbyists should exercise loyalty to the client's or employer's interests." Articles VI and VII address compensation and confidentiality. The details are typical of any professional service business.

The last two articles are outward facing and highlight the role of the lobbyist in supporting the industry and protecting the government institutions that it supports. Article VIII is titled Public Education and encourages lobbyists to teach the public about the legitimacy and necessity of lobbying. The article also encourages lobbyists to provide pro bono services to those who do not have the resources to advocate for their cause. The final article details the duty of the lobbyist to governmental institutions (Article IX). Lobbyists are enjoined to respect government institutions and "not act in any manner that will undermine public confidence and trust in the democratic governmental process."

The Woodstock Principles
The AGRP is not the only group thinking about lobbying ethics. The Woodstock Theological Center at Georgetown University has devoted significant energy to this area. The Center focuses on issues of social or political importance that involve theology or ethics. They organized a project on lobbying titled 'The Ethics of Lobbying: Organized Interests, Political Power and the Common Good' for three reasons – lobbying's rapid growth, increasing suspicion about the function and the call for standards and principles by members of the lobbying community. The Center's staff began their research with a robust set of interviews and discussions with lobbyists, legislators, lawyers, ethicists, philosophers and political scientists.

The resulting information was used to identify the ethical challenges associated with lobbying. The first challenge is that "money talks." Those with access to extensive resources hire lobbyists and their positions are heard by policymakers. The researchers do not question the right of people with funds to spend them lobbying. They do question how the voices of those without money can be heard. A second challenge is campaign finance. In the words of an interviewee: "... members will do a lot more for you if you have both given and raised money for them than if you haven't."[115] Third, under the heading of 'Truth Telling', respondents emphasize the importance of telling the truth -- "You can't lie; what you've basically got is your word and reputation." The challenge lies in the difference between the letter and spirit of truth – "Lobbyists think about just how much you can shade the picture without losing your own soul, short of that, losing your credibility with the person you're talking to."

A fourth challenge is commonly referred to as the revolving door. The cycle of people moving from government to lobbying and back to government provides great value but also raises significant risks. On the value front, experience in government makes lobbyists more effective. They understand governmental process in great detail. They also have a network which enables them to know who to call to get things done. Lobbyists who move to the government have deep perspective on issues that face policymakers. Lobbyists are also skilled researchers and communicators; capabilities that improve government operations. The revolving door, however, carries the risk of conflicts of interest. Lobbyists for defense contractors who move to the Pentagon might have a bias toward their former employer's positions, especially if they are likely to return to the company after government service. There is a similar concern that policymakers will provide more access and attention to the advocacy of lobbyists if they are likely to join that person's firm in the future. In the words of Jack Abramoff: "In almost every congressional office, the Chief of Staff is the center of power. Nothing gets done without the direct or indirect action on his or her part. After a number of meetings, with some possibly including meals or rounds of golf, I would say a few magic words: 'When you are done working for the Congressman, you should come work for me at my firm.' With that, assuming the staffer had any interest in leaving Capitol Hill for K St. (and almost 90% of them do), I would own him and consequently, that entire office.... This paycheck may have been signed by the Congress, but he was already working for me, influencing his office for my clients' best interests."[116]

A final challenge is the role of the lobbyist in supporting the common good. What obligation does the lobbyist have to support the common good? What is the common good?

The Woodstock researchers provide a set of ethical guidelines in response to these challenges. They begin with an overarching normative charge: "The universal norms that cover all human action also apply to the conduct of lobbyists. These include prescriptive norms like telling the truth, promoting justice, treating other persons with integrity and respect. They also include the prospective norms that forbid bribery, distortion, flattery, and fraud." Moreover, lobbyists have responsibilities not only to their clients and to those who they lobby but they also have "civic obligations to their country, for the hired lobbyist is also an engaged citizen with a citizen's duty to promote the public good."[117]

> ### Food For Thought
> Do lobbyists have an obligation to serve the common good as well as their client? How would you operationalize this concept?

From these lofty pronouncements, the Woodstock team enumerates seven principles for the ethical conduct of lobbying. (Exhibit 4-2) The first principle, and potentially the most controversial, is that lobbyists should take account of the "common good" as well as their client's needs. Common good is defined as "the comprehensive and enduring well-being of the political community as a whole." The rationale for this position is that lobbyists seek to influence public policy outcomes and therefore have an obligation to ensure their advocacy reflects the needs of the country as a whole. They are especially concerned that the lobbyists' actions do not unfairly burden the most vulnerable. Lobbyists represent their clients' interests but also "the lobbyist retains a personal responsibility as a citizen for the fairness, integrity, and effectiveness of the policymaking process, as well as for the substantive political outcomes to which it leads."[118]

Exhibit 4-2
Woodstock Principles

1. Take into account the common good
2. Candor and mutual respect
3. Candid disclosure
4. No concealing and misrepresentation
5. Avoid conflicts
6. Avoid inappropriate tactics
7. Promote integrity of lobbying

The second Woodstock principal is that the relationship between lobbyist and client be based on candor and mutual respect. They see this as an obligation for both lobbyist and client. The lobbyist should consider the ethical behavior of the potential client. The implication is obvious – lobbyists should not work for unethical parties. Moreover, the lobbyist should only accept assignments with clients whose senior management is committed to acceptable ethical standards including support for the common good. The client should evaluate the ethics of the lobbyist based on the lobbyist's prior record. The client should also understand the lobbyist's strategies and tactics before hiring the lobbyist.

The third Woodstock principle addresses the relationship between lobbyists and policymakers. The themes are candid disclosure as well as accurate and reliable information. The lobbyist should clearly disclose the issues being addressed and the client being supported. Reliable and comprehensive information must be provided including the opposition's perspective. The lobbyist has a proactive obligation to update the policymaker if information provided in the past changes materially. The lobbyist-policymaker relationship also requires that the lobbyists never compromise the independence of the government official.

The relationship between lobbyists and the media is the focus of the fourth Woodstock principle. The core obligation is that the lobbyist presents full and accurate information to the media. The Woodstock team recognizes the importance of communicating through the media, but cautions the lobbyist against misrepresentation. A specific concern is the use of phantom grassroots campaigns intended to either imply public support when it may not be factual or conceal the identity of a client. This principle seeks to address "the growing public relations and advertising mentality in lobbying [which] threatens greater reliance on half-truths, distortion, scare tactics, and misinformation in pursuing political goals."[119]

Woodstock Principle 5 requires that lobbyists avoid conflicts of interest. The lobbyist has "professional obligations to clients and personal obligations to his or her conscience." Lobbyists should avoid taking assignments where a conflict might arise. Potential conflicts should be reviewed with clients before the advocacy begins or as soon as it arises. The tone of the text implies that lobbyists err on the side of avoiding potential conflicts.

Principle 6 elaborates on the normative prohibition of inappropriate strategies and tactics. The lobbyist must not share false or misleading information or intentionally divert attention from important information. Personal attacks on individuals are also prohibited.

The final principle seeks to "promote the integrity of the lobbying profession in public understanding of the lobbying process."[120] The Woodstock team highlights the critical and legitimate need for lobbying. Adopting the prior six principles helps achieve this last objective. Moreover, the lobbyist has a role in educating policymakers and citizens about the role and value creation of lobbying.

Challenge: Your List of Ethical Principles
The Association of Government Relations Professionals and the Woodstock Theological Center address the need for ethical behavior by lobbyists. However, they come at this issue from different perspectives. AGRP approaches ethics as a means of sustaining the viability of the lobbying industry. Woodstock seeks to maximize the positive aspects of lobbying through ethical behavior. Compare the ethical principles adopted by AGRP and Woodstock. What are the

similarities and differences? From your own perspective, what should be the set of ethical principles for lobbyists?

Complements to Ethics

This chapter began with examples of how lobbying scandals persist despite federal and state regulations. Ethical behavior has been proffered as a means of filling the gaps in regulation. Having considered the AGRP and Woodstock codes, we are left with a core question: Is this enough to end scandals? The answer for many is: The codes help keep the honest from becoming dishonest, but do not address those on the fence or those willing to "stray into the gray." If you reach the same conclusion, what else can be done? Four complements to regulation and ethics codes warrant consideration – (1) adopting American Bar Association (ABA)–style sanctions; (2) regulating lobbying based on a national economic welfare argument; (3) establishing a fiduciary duty for lobbyists; and (4) industry self-regulation/certification.

The ABA Approach. The ABA Model Rules of Professional Conduct offers a complementary approach to enhancing the ethical behavior of lobbyists. The idea is to include "lawyer-lobbyists" under the Model Rules that govern the behavior of lawyers practicing law.[121] "Many lawyers lobby, and by explicitly incorporating lawyer-lobbyists' activity into the Model Rule of Professional Conduct, ethics scandals should decrease as lawyer-lobbyists receive increased ethical guidance and face the prospect of discipline for breaking the Model Rules."[122] The Model Rules address many of the AGRP Code of Ethics and the Woodstock Principles including: competency, conflicts, confidentiality, truthfulness, candor and fairness, and public service.

The ABA Model Code, however, involves an enforcement mechanism and sanctions for violations. Each state bar association adopts specific rules relating to enforcement and sanctions. Those adopted by the Florida Bar are emblematic. The purpose of the disciplinary process "is to protect the public

> ### Food for Thought
> Why would a state bar association include lawyer-lobbying in its Model Rules?

and the administration of justice from lawyers who have not discharged, will not discharge, or unlikely to discharge their professional duties to clients, the public, the legal system, in the legal profession properly."[123] In this excerpt, notice the obligation to clients, the public, and the profession. A variety of sanctions can be imposed if there is "clear and convincing evidence that a member of the legal profession has violated a provision of the rules..." including disbarment, suspension, public reprimand, probation and restitution.[124] The sanctions associated with failing to avoid conflicts of interest, a topic which is relevant for lobbyists, include disbarment if the lawyer has interests that are adverse to the client's, if the lawyer fails to get the informed consent of the client, and if the lawyer causes serious or potentially serious harm to the client.

This approach offers several advantages over the mere "encouragement" that AGRP and Woodstock provides. First and foremost, it offers direct incentives for professional and ethical behavior backed by serious sanctions. Second, it utilizes an existing structure and does not seek to reinvent the wheel. Third, such formal conduct rules enhance the professionalization of lobbying.

> ### Food For Thought
> Should AGRP include sanctions in its Code? How could this be implemented? Why would lobbyists agree?

However, there are several challenges associated with the ABA Model Code. First, only lawyer-lobbyists are covered, which excludes lobbyists who are not lawyers. This could put lawyer-lobbyists at a disadvantage to other lobbyists not covered by such stringent rules. (Of course the reverse could also be true – lobbyists covered by the rules would be more desirable as the risks of using them would be lower.) Another concern is the First Amendment. Would such rules be an unconstitutional restriction on the right to petition? Finally, would the ABA be willing to take on this issue?

Challenge: Legislators and Judges– Money and Power

The right to petition dates back to King Solomon in biblical times. The right to petition the government was really an opportunity to appeal to the king himself. Solomon was both law-maker and judge. In the United States, we have multiple elected legislators rather than a king. In this model the opportunity for corruption abounds as money enables the electoral process, and personal gains for the legislators are often very tempting. Lobbyists too often lubricate this machine. The result is the endless scandals described in this chapter. But, what about the judges? While many are appointed, many others are elected. Yet, we rarely see the same level of corruption in the courts as in legislatures. What accounts for the difference? Are there lessons that are transferable from the judiciary to legislative branch?

The State Interest Argument. In Chapter 3, the role of regulation in preventing lobbying scandals was explored. The fundamental constraint on this approach is the First Amendment right to petition, which limits the extent of legal restrictions on lobbying. Richard Hasen of the University of California, Irvine, School of Law offers an alternative legal argument that would permit greater regulation of lobbying. Specifically, he proposes regulating lobbying based on "the state's interest in promoting national economic welfare."[125] His logic for the proposal is the following: Lobbyists expend resources in order to capture government spending. These transfers, from taxpayers to lobbyists' clients, are not a productive economic activity; rather they are merely rent-seeking. Moreover "lobbyists tend to lobby for legislation that is itself an inefficient use of government resources..." These two activities threaten national economic welfare and therefore create a compelling state interest in regulating lobbyists, one that he argues would at least compete with if not trump First Amendment concerns.

Hasen acknowledges that there is no court precedent for the national economic welfare argument. However, he offers some evidence to support his argument that a court could balance the First Amendment right petition with the national economic welfare threat. He quotes Hugo Black (when he was a Senator) who declared, "our government has lost hundreds of millions of dollars which it should not have lost and which it would not have lost if there had been proper publicity given to the activities of lobbyists."[126] He also highlights public concerns about the inefficiency of earmarks, an approach often used by lobbyists to secure government funding for their clients. Because of the lack of legal precedents for his national economic welfare argument, Hasen limits the restrictions on lobbyists that he seeks to attain. Rather than propose a ban on lobbying, which he acknowledges his novel argument could not support, he focuses on restricting lobbyists' ability to conduct fundraising for candidates. He hypothesizes that this lower scrutiny activity could be limited based on the economic threat and that limiting campaign contributions would significantly reduce the adverse effects of lobbying.

While Hasen's national economic welfare argument is innovative and intriguing, it is unlikely to have any near-term impact. Perhaps, longer-term and after another major scandal, elements of the concept will be considered by both policymakers and the courts.

Fiduciary Obligation. Another approach to increasing lobbyists' accountability is for lobbyists to carry fiduciary obligations. There is not a single codified definition of a fiduciary. Rather, the obligation is associated with characteristics of the relationship between parties. Four attributes can be linked to the creation of a fiduciary relationship based on the work of legal scholar Tamar Frankel.[127] The first is that the empowered party provides a socially desirable outcome through expertise. Second, the party providing the service is entrusted with property, power or a "critical resource" in order to provide the desired benefit. Third, by entrusting the service provider, the entrusting party faces risk. "The services cannot be performed unless the property or power is entrusted first. The services can be evaluated only afterwards. In addition, the services involve various degrees of discretion that must be vested in the fiduciaries."[128] Finally, it is expensive to monitor the performance of the entrusted party again increasing the risk of the entrustor.

Examples of functions that are often associated with a fiduciary relationship include financial advisors, accountants, doctors and lawyers. It is important to note that the creation of the fiduciary duty is dictated by the specific facts of the relationship, not the nature of the function. Thus, some accounting relationships are those of a fiduciary (e.g. providing personally financial and/or tax advice to a client or directly managing the assets of the client) while others are not (e.g. auditing the financial statements of a corporation[129]). A clear example of a fiduciary is a financial advisor. An individual entrusts funds to an advisor because of his/her expertise. The advisor has direct control of the funds and how they are invested. Clearly that individual faces the risk of loss of funds, satisfying the third criterion above.

The appeal of applying such a concept to lobbying is that failure to fulfill the fiduciary obligations leads to sanctions that carry some weight. Courts have imposed a variety of remedies. Compensatory damages seek to make the entrustor whole from the breach. A less severe remedy is denying the fiduciary of their fees. The court can also impose punitive damages "to punish a party for outrageous conduct and to deter that party and other parties from similar future conduct."[130]

There are two paths to lobbyists becoming fiduciaries. Court decisions is one avenue. The likelihood of this is very low. There is little court precedent to rely upon. Also, there is the potential challenge to such an obligation on First Amendment grounds. (However, fiduciary obligations are not a ban on the right to petition.) The second path is legislation. This would provide clear guidance to lobbyists and empower the government and the courts to enforce fiduciary obligations on their activities. The probability of legislative action is also very low as other efforts to expand fiduciary relationships such as to broker/dealers, have faced an uphill battle. In the case of broker/dealers, the need for the protections offered through fiduciary duty is high as entrustors risk their financial assets. Yet, even in this case, legislators are unwilling to mandate fiduciary obligations. Of course, another major lobbying scandal could provide the impetus for Congress to adopt fiduciary requirements for lobbyists.

> Food For Thought
> Is there a role for Angie's List and/or Yelp in rating lobbyists?

Industry Self-Regulation. The group that benefits most directly from improved reputation is the lobbyists themselves. Therefore, lobbyists could establish a voluntary certification program that provides training and commitment to a set of ethic behaviors. Participants would receive a certification akin to the Good Housekeeping Seal of Approval. A directory of certified lobbyists would differentiate participants from those who have not committed to the code. A process to identify violators and an adjudication mechanism would provide necessary enforcement. Going one step further, lobbyists could voluntarily agree to fiduciary responsibilities.

Challenge: Voluntary Self-Regulation and Certification System

The First Amendment limits the ability to regulate lobbyist behavior yet there is likely value for lobbyists to voluntarily self-regulate as a means of lobbyist differentiation. Moreover a certification program would reduce the legal and reputational risk for clients.

Self-regulation is used in the brokerage business to maintain the integrity of the investing process. The Financial Industry Regulatory Authority, Inc. (FINRA) is a private sector corporation that is responsible for "investor protection and market integrity through effective and efficient regulation of the securities industry."[131] The group achieves this mission by (1) registering and educating all brokers; (2) examining securities firms; (3) writing the rules they must follow; and (4) enforcing the rules. The scale of this activity is very large; 4,250 brokerage firms and more than 600,000 registered securities representatives.

Prospective brokers must pass examinations administered by FINRA and demonstrate competence in a wide array of relevant topics, including securities laws, FINRA regulations, operation of financial markets, economic theory, risk management, portfolio theory, and fair sales practices.

Not only does FINRA license individuals and firms, but also they are empowered to enforce the rules that govern brokerage. Sanctions include ordering restitution. The organization also seeks to educate the customers of brokers through interactive educational content and alerts.

Based on the brokerage analog, create a lobbyist self-regulation program. Consider:

- *What constitutes certification?*
- *How are violators identified and adjudicated?*
- *What sanctions would be used for violations?*
- *What remedies, if any, are available to clients?*
- *Who would administer the program and how would it be funded?*

While any or even all of the above would provide clients with a greater sense of comfort in using lobbyists, and the general public might have more confidence in the system, they will not eliminate those lobbyists who willfully intend to violate the law and/or ethical standards. For them, we can only hope that the damage they do is minimal and they only do it once.

Ethics Endgame
- Despite regulations, lobbying scandals persist.
- The scandals in turn lead to skepticism about lobbying and lobbyists.
- The negative public attitude directly threatens the continued growth of the lobbying industry.
- It also leads to more regulation making lobbying more costly.
- Beliefs that legislation is for sale and only certain parties have access to policy makers, erodes the foundation of participatory democracy.
- Regulations are only a partial solution given the limitations on impacting the First Amendment rights of lobbyists.
- Ethics codes, adopted and enforced, by the lobbying industry is one means of bolstering regulations.
- The professional lobbying community represented by the Association of Government Relations Professionals has a code of ethics but it lacks meaningful enforcement and sanctions.
- The Woodstock Theological Center of Georgetown University adds an additional complexity to lobbying ethics – should the lobbyist take into account the common good?
- Complements to ethics include an ABA-style Model Code of Conduct, which has sharp teeth and/or limits lobbyists' ability to raise campaign funds for legislators.
- Industry self-regulation is the best, albeit, difficult path to avoiding more scandals.

Learning by Doing
Define an ethics policy for your lobbying firm. Provide guidelines and supporting rationale. Do not forget to consider sanctions for violations.

Bibliography Chapter 4

"About the Financial Industry Regulatory Authority." Accessed August 4, 2013. http://www.finra.org/AboutFINRA/.

Abramoff, Jack. *Capitol Punishment: The Hard Truth About Washington Corruption from America's Most Notorious Lobbyist*. Washington, D.C.; New York: WND Books ; distributed to the trade by Midpoint Trade Books, 2011.

"Annual Lobbying by PMA Group." *Open Secrets: Center for Responsive Politics*. Accessed August 4, 2013. http://www.opensecrets.org/lobby/firmsum.php?id=D000000501&year=2009.

Baumgartner, Frank R. "Converting Expectations: New Empirical Evidence on Congressional Lobbying and Public Policy." *University of North Carolina at Chapel Hill* (2013).

"Code of Ethics." American League of Lobbyists. Accessed July 6, 2013. http://www.alldc.org/ethicscode.cfm.

"Congress and the Public." Accessed August 4, 2013. http://www.gallup.com/poll/1600/Congress-Public.aspx#1.

Eggen, Dan, and Maria Glod. "Ex-lobbyist Paul Magliocchetti Charged with Campaign-finance Fraud." *The Washington Post*, August 6, 2010, sec. Metro. http://www.washingtonpost.com/wp-dyn/content/article/2010/08/05/AR2010080504416.html.

Frankel, Tamar. *Fiduciary Law*. Oxford; New York: Oxford University Press, 2011. http://site.ebrary.com/id/10476943.

Frankel, Tamar. *Trust and Honesty: America's Business Culture at a Crossroad*. New York: Oxford University Press, 2008.

Gardiner, Sean. "Lobbyist Gets Prison In Bribery Scandal." *Wall Street Journal*, September 29, 2012, sec. Ny Politics. http://online.wsj.com/article/SB2000087239639044338960457802484251428403 4.html.

Hasen, Richard L. "Lobbying, Rent-Seeking, and the Constitution." *Stanford Law Review* 64, no. 1 (January 1, 2012): 191.

"John Emerich Edward Dalberg Acton, 1st Baron Acton (English Historian and Moralist) : Supplemental Information." *Encyclopaedia Britannica*. Accessed August 4, 2013. http://www.britannica.com/EBchecked/topic/4647/John-Emerich-Edward-Dalberg-Acton-1st-Baron-Acton/4647suppinfo/Supplemental-Information.

Jones, Jeffrey M. "Lobbyists Debut at Bottom of Honesty and Ethics List." *Gallup*, December 10, 2007. http://www.gallup.com/poll/103123/lobbyists-debut-bottom-honesty-ethics-list.aspx.

Kirkpatrick, David D., and Charlie Savage. "Star Lobbyist Closes Shop Amid F.B.I. Inquiry." *The New York Times*, March 30, 2009, sec. U.S. / Politics. http://www.nytimes.com/2009/03/30/us/politics/30pma.html.

"Paul Magliocchetti Pleads Guilty - John Bresnahan." *POLITICO*. Accessed August 4, 2013. http://www.politico.com/news/stories/0910/42690.html.

Saad, Lydia. "Americans Decry Power of Lobbyists, Corporations, Banks, Feds." *Gallup Politics*, April 11, 2011.

"Standards for Lawyer Sanctions." *The Florida Bar*. Accessed August 4, 2013. http://www.floridabar.org/tfb/TFBLawReg.nsf/9dad7bbda218afe8852570020048 33c5/ca758a1382421b60852574ba00649949.

The Psychology of Power Absolutely, The Economist, Jan 21, 2010.

"The Shadow Lobbyist." *Opinionator*. Accessed August 4, 2013. http://opinionator.blogs.nytimes.com/2013/04/25/the-shadow-lobbyist/.

Woodstock Theological Center. *The Ethics of Lobbying: Organized Interests, Political Power, and the Common Good.* Washington, D.C.: Georgetown University Press, 2002.

Chapter 5: Persuasion and Lobbying

Successful lobbying requires a solid understanding of the psychology of persuasion; a well-designed strategy that reflects the context, substance and politics of the issue; and a set of tactics that efficiently and effectively implement the plan. This chapter addresses persuasion and the next chapter tackles strategy and tactics.

The power of persuasion is the starting point for effective lobbying. Why should a policymaker support your position? What will sway the thinking of the government official? While the psychology of persuasion is a course unto itself, this chapter provides an overview of key concepts as they apply to lobbying.

A set of foundational principles underlies the study of persuasion. These principles are implemented through a variety of enabling tactics meant to bring the principles to life. Additionally, persuasion is not one dimensional. Yes, you want to persuade the lobbyee of your position, but the lobbyee will likely hear from multiple sources on most policy issues. Assuming your opposition is also skilled in persuasion, how do you achieve your end result? Moreover, the lobbyee is aware that you are seeking to persuade and therefore may erect "anti-persuasion" barriers that you must overcome. Thus, persuasion can be viewed as a multiparty interaction or game; "game" in the sense of game theory. The foundational principles, tactics and multiparty game aspects of persuasion are detailed below, and are supplemented with lobbying-specific applications.

Foundational Principles

The literature on persuasion is extensive. However, there are two sources that are especially powerful. The first is Robert Cialdini who has been studying persuasion for decades. Do an Internet search for "persuasion principles" and Cialdini dominates Page One of the results. Why? His six principles are well-structured, easy to digest, intuitive and well supported. The second source of foundational materials is drawn from Harvard professor Howard Gardner. His book, Changing Minds, gives us another complementary set of principles. While several of the principles offered by Cialdini and Gardner are similar and reinforce each other, others expand the foundation. The combined principles provide a solid basis for understanding persuasion.

At its root, lobbying is the art of persuading a policymaker to support or not oppose your position. In his book Influence: The Psychology of Persuasion, Cialdini outlines six core principles of persuasion:

- Reciprocity: If you do something for me, I feel obligated to do something for you, often of even greater value.

- Consistency and Commitment: Once a decision is made, subsequent decisions support the original position. Committing to the position and documenting a plan to take action greatly increase the likelihood that it will be done.
- Social proof: Relying on the decisions of others, especially those like us or who we respect or admire, provides a shortcut for decision-making.
- Liking: Persuasion is enhanced when we like the person who seeks to influence us. We like those who are similar to ourselves and those who share our attributes and interests including age, race, religion, politics, geography, sports teams and extra-curricular activities.
- Authority: Duty to authority is a powerful motivating force. Obedience to authority is learned from an early age and persists. Authority is signaled through title, institutional affiliations and trappings such as clothes, office location, etc.
- Scarcity: People are persuaded by the thought of scarcity – the lack of …fill in the blank… increase its desirability and the urgency of having it.

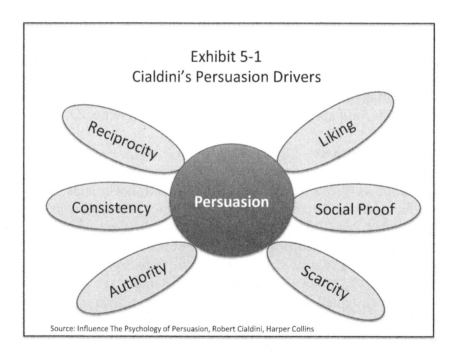

Exhibit 5-1
Cialdini's Persuasion Drivers

Reciprocity · Liking · Consistency · Persuasion · Social Proof · Authority · Scarcity

Source: Influence The Psychology of Persuasion, Robert Cialdini, Harper Collins

The power of these factors is their ability to provide automatic agreement rather than an extended analysis. They provide us with a short cut for decision-making. Details of each of Cialdini's core principles and their applicability to lobbying are provided below.

Reciprocity. Perhaps the most fundamental means of persuasion is reciprocity – you scratch my back and I scratch yours. The principle is a long established social norm. Its development is linked to the evolution of society, as the associated mutual obligation was an early solution to the free rider problem. Obligation is a very strong norm – if you help me, then I must at some time repay the favor. The basis for the norm is multifold. First, individuals are concerned about what others think of them. Society ostracized those who were always takers but not givers. Cialdini illustrates this social stigma with the words "moocher" or "welsher"; words with a strong negative connotation, which describe a person who does not practice reciprocity. Second, people tend to feel good when they return favors for others. Researchers from Santa Clara University use this natural inclination to explain why subjects of their 2009 study were more likely to do a reciprocal favor for another (in this case, respond to a survey) after they were given a gift. [132]

Other studies have documented the power of the reciprocity norm, finding that favors are returned regardless of whether the provider is liked by the receiver. Dennis Regan of Cornell demonstrated this in 1971.[133] Exhibit 5-2 below shows the results of his study. Regan found that an individual is able to sell more raffle tickets if he or she does a favor for the buyer regardless of whether the buyer likes the seller. In other words, in reciprocity, 'liking' the individual is significantly less important.

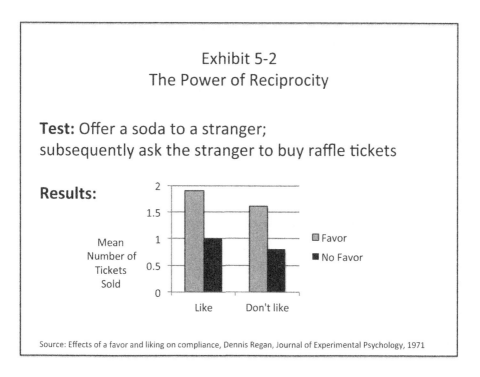

Exhibit 5-2
The Power of Reciprocity

Test: Offer a soda to a stranger;
subsequently ask the stranger to buy raffle tickets

Results:

Source: Effects of a favor and liking on compliance, Dennis Regan, Journal of Experimental Psychology, 1971

The results hold true regardless of whether anyone knows the favor was returned.[134] Moreover, it is common for the returned favor to be of greater value than the original. It is important to note that the reverse is true if reciprocity is in reaction to taking rather than giving. Individuals who are the victim of anti-social acts have more selfish responses.[135]

The concept of reciprocity extends beyond the simple tit-for-tat. It also explains the power of the "rejection and retreat" approach to persuasion. This concept builds on the idea of reciprocity but the value provided is not gifts, funds or information. Rather it is a concession to another party's request, even if the request is unreasonable. Consider the following dialogue:

Political Activist: "Hi, we hope you will support Ms. Jones for Congress. She is a remarkable leader and will help bring jobs to our community. Would you be able to attend a dinner with her next week? The contribution to attend is $1000."
Homeowner: "I do like her policies but I cannot afford such a contribution."
Political Activist: I am delighted that you support her candidacy. I agree that the fundraiser is very pricy. Would you consider putting this campaign sign on your lawn?"
Homeowner: "Certainly."

In this case, the concession was that the activist retreated from the funding request to only posting a sign. The retreat is the "gift" and researchers consistently find it is effective in establishing a reciprocity relationship.

Reciprocity in Lobbying. Reciprocity is a central tenet of persuasion in lobbying. In the 1800s, the direct exchange of favors was the norm. Samuel Colt, the famed manufacturer of the revolver, sought to extend his patent on this firearm through Congressional

> ### Notable Quote
> "The money has been used…in paying the costs and charges in getting up costly and extravagant entertainments, to which ladies and members of congress were invited, with a view of furthering the success of this measure."
> - Samuel Colt
> (Byrd 1987)

legislation. Colt manufactured elaborate custom revolvers and gave them as gifts to family members of Congressmen. He also wined and dined members for their support. Fast-forward 150 years and the power of gifts is front and center in the Jack Abramoff scandal. Abramoff provided members of Congress and senior staff with golf trips, sporting event tickets and expensive meals in exchange for supporting his clients' interests.

Concern with the undue influence that is associated with reciprocity in conjunction with Abramoff's transgressions led Congress to pass the Honest Leadership and Open Government Act of 2007, which places more restrictions on gifts for members of Congress and Congressional staff. Similar fears led

President Barack Obama to require an ethics pledge of all Executive Branch employees that they will not accept gifts while serving in office.

These regulations limit one type of exchange but there are several others that enable lobbyists to potentially gain from reciprocity. Helping members finance their campaigns is the most obvious and widespread source of reciprocity. Candidates need money and lobbyists are excellent funding facilitators. Lobbyists' extensive networks make them especially effective at hosting campaign events. However, the "gift" lobbyists provide is not substantial personal funds: It is access to well-heeled campaign financiers. The reciprocity engendered by hosting campaign events is captured in the exchange below with Charles Keating, then-president of a failing savings and loan company. He was asked if there was a relationship between his $1.5 million donations to senators' election campaigns and his attempt to influence bank regulators. He responded: "I want to say in the most forceful way I can: I certainly hope so."[136] He was subsequently convicted on multiple counts of fraud.

Reciprocity can also be achieved in the absence of campaign funds and gifts. Recall President John F. Kennedy's explanation of lobbyists' value. He said lobbyists help government officials understand the wide array of complex issues that policymakers face. The lobbyist therefore earns some degree of reciprocity by providing information and insight to the policymaker. The same logic applies if you agree with the lobbying as a legislative subsidy argument.

What is the reciprocity that the lobbyist receives? There is broad consensus that the exchange offered by members is an opportunity for the lobbyist to meet with the member or staff to share a perspective and/or make a request. The information flow can also move in the other direction where the member provides important guidance to the lobbyist about policy actions.

In the case of lobbying, there is little incentive for policymakers to avoid reciprocity. Offering access, which may be gained albeit with more work in the absence of reciprocity, is hardly a disincentive to receive the value provided by lobbyists. In contrast, lobbyists can provide substantial value, whether its campaign support or compelling policy analysis.

Consistency and Commitment. While reciprocity addresses an obligation to an external party, consistency is largely internally focused. Simply put: Consistency says my decision today must be consistent with those made yesterday. "In order to attain or preserve such consistency, individuals often comply with requests that are

> **Notable Quote**
> There is no expedient to which man will not resort to avoid the real labor of thinking.
> - Sir Joshua Reynolds
> (Cialdini 2006)

aligned with their beliefs, values and existing commitments — especially when these commitments reflect personal choices. The tendency to feel committed to past personal choices and to behave consistently with these commitments has been shown to have a profound impact in various compliance settings."[137]

Why? First, people are loath to admit they were wrong. Inconsistency is an admission of error; few rush to admit their mistakes. There are clearly times when people admit errors but, for the most part, researchers find people default to support past decisions even if they are costly. Second, society has a bias against inconsistency. Without consistency, our lives would be chaotic, erratic and therefore more difficult. Evidence of this bias can be seen in the negative connotation associated with the word "inconsistent." Perhaps a more powerful and colorful example is referring to those who change their positions as "flip-floppers", a term that was effectively used to undermine the presidential candidacy of John Kerry in 2004. According to a 2008 *New York Times* article, "operatives in both parties agree that John Kerry's apparent equivocation on the Iraq war damaged his 2004 campaign." The article quoted Jonathan Prince, a strategist for John Edwards, who said, "It spoke to a pattern of calculation and indecisiveness that make him look like a weak commander in chief compared to [George W.] Bush."[138] Third, consistency is very efficient. Rather than taking the time and mental energy to evaluate a position anew, adopting a prior stance not only takes less effort. As we face increased time pressure and the amount of information for us to digest explodes, we will continue to default to prior decisions when we face difficult decisions.

Our desire for consistency is amplified with commitment; a verbal or written agreement to a decision greatly increases the likelihood of sticking with the choice. Public statements further increase commitment. The North Carolina Department of Environment and Resources leverages this concept to increase recycling. They find small commitments lead to larger commitments. They also find that written commitments are very powerful; signing a recycling pledge greatly increases the likelihood of action.[139] The combination of consistency and commitment is a very powerful and persuasive force. So powerful is the force that it can lead to, in Cialdini's words, "the absurdity of foolish consistency."[140] How does the absurdity arise? Consider the interactions between consistency and reciprocity: Trivial requests and harmless concessions create commitment and then reciprocity expands the degree of obligation.

Consistency has been observed across cultures but there are differences. Cialdini, along with Petia Petrova and Stephen Sills, examined consistency behavior of United States and Asian individuals in a 2007 paper. They found that U.S. participants were less likely to agree to complete an online survey than their Asian counterparts; however, once they had committed to do so the U.S.

participants were more likely to complete subsequent requests. [141] The conclusion: When it comes to consistency and commitment, culture matters.

Consistency and Commitment in Lobbying. The persuasive power of consistency drives two aspects of lobbying – how the advocate behaves and what the lobbyist can expect of the lobbyee. Lobbyists must be consistent in their positions, strategy, and framing, among other things. Consistency is linked to trust and reliability, which are requirements for successful lobbying. For-hire lobbyists have an even greater need for consistency to overcome their image as "hired guns."

In lobbying, consistency is also important on the part of policymakers. The requirement for politicians to avoid being seen as flip-flopping on issues is very strong. Lobbyists must expect policymakers in general and, politicians in particular, will only adopt positions that are consistent with their core ideology, past voting patterns and past statements. Positions can be changed but the process is long and the rationale for the altered course must be extremely compelling.

The psychology of commitment encourages lobbyists to secure agreement for action before leaving a meeting with a lobbyee. Verbal or written commitment greatly increases the chance of having the request fulfilled, especially if the commitment is shared with the policymaker's senior staff.

Social Proof. Decision-making is hard, especially when information is limited or there is uncertainly. One means of simplifying the process is looking for social proof – what are others, similar to myself, doing? The logical thought process is, "If I follow the crowd, the chances of making a mistake are much lower". Thus, leveraging social proof by showing others support a particular position can be a very powerful means of persuasion. Social proof is extensively used in the marketing arena. Statements such as "fastest growing" and "most popular" are examples. Social proof is more powerful when provided by those we respect, idolize or wish to emulate. The direct evidence of the power of this form of social proof is the use of attractive models to sell everything from cars to cosmetics. It's why Adidas just paid soccer star David Beckham $160 million to promote Adidas products.[142]

Ironically, many view the results of social proof decision-making with contempt. The expression "following like lemmings off a cliff" is often heard. Lemmings, small rodents, do indeed follow the herd even to their detriment. They are not alone. The American bison was noted for a willingness to follow the herd, right off a cliff.

> **Fun Fact**
> 95% people are imitators; only 5% are initiators.
> (Cialdini 2006)

Humans are similarly subject to group-think. Although following the crowd may have a negative connotation, sales consultant Cavett Robert argues that most people are imitators not initiators.[143] The media is a powerful force in leading people to blindly following the crowd. Experts, celebrities, users, friends and crowds also enhance social proof. (Exhibit 5-3) The power of social proof is sufficiently strong that people will often overlook subtle or not so subtle errors in logic leading to what Cialdini calls "pluralistic ignorance."[144]

Exhibit 5-3
Evidence of Social Proof

25% of U.S. TV commercials have used celebrities.

A one-star improvement in Yelp ratings leads to a 5-9% increase in restaurant sales.

The first negative user review on eBay has been shown to reverse a seller's weekly growth rate... It also hurts pricing; a 1% increase in negative feedback has been shown to lead to a 7.5% decrease in sale price realized.

Source: Social Proof Is The New Marketing, Aileen Lee, November 27, 2011.
http://techcrunch.com/2011/11/27/social-proof-why-people-like-to-follow-the-crowd/

Social Proof in Lobbying. The concept of social proof as a persuader has several implications for lobbying. First, demonstrating a broad base of support for a lobbyist's position enables social proof to persuade the lobbyee. The support can come from policymakers' peers, fellow members of Congress, White House staff or regulators. From letters and phone calls of support to coauthoring legislation, peer-based social proof takes a broad spectrum of forms. Constituent support is also powerful social proof. Here, social media can be used to leverage the voice of the voter. The media is also a powerful source of social proof. An op-ed by an influential person, placed in a well-regarded newspaper has real impact.

The effectiveness of these approaches to social proof is increased with (1) highly respected leaders or examples; (2) visible, pubic support; and (3) consistency and commitment. Quantitative proof is also desirable as people find statistics compelling. While detailed studies from well-respected researchers and pollsters such as Gallup, Pew and others are the gold standard; even basic statistics such as the number of supporters of a policy position are helpful. For policymakers, the power of this information is its ability to reduce the risk of adopting a position.

Liking. We are more persuaded by those we like than those we do not. The "liking heuristic" says people agree with people they like or, phrased differently, 'people I like usually have correct opinions'.[145] What makes a person likeable in the context of persuasion? Similarity is one of the most powerful drivers of liking someone. This is logical as we are most familiar with "our own kind" and most of us like who we are. Similarity factors include age, race, religion, politics, geography, and involvement in sports or extracurricular activities.

Psychologists also find we like others who are attractive and/or accomplished. Association with these people seems to provide a halo effect for us. Politicians routinely leverage this form of persuasion by appearing with military heroes, sports icons or movie idols. There is strong evidence that we like to associate with winners. Cialdini reports on research that finds sports fans wear their team's shirts more when they are winning than losing and the frequency of donning the team's apparel increases with the margin of victory.

Research also indicates a positive correlation between frequency of contact and liking. The more time you spend with others, especially those who are different, the more you come to like them. This finding is being used to break down barriers and reduce animosity between combative groups. For example, Seeds of Peace Summer Camp in Maine increases interaction between Israeli and Arab students in a non-threatening environment. The program is credited with breaking down barriers and thinking creatively about this longstanding conflict."[146] Incorporating a common goal into the interaction increases the chances of success. Familiarity in general has been correlated with liking. In a study published in a 1982 edition of the *Bulletin of The British Psychological Society*, Wladyslaw Sluckin, David Hargreaves and Andrew Colman examined familiarity and liking and concluded: "We are not suggesting, of course, that familiarity is the only factor that determines people's likes and dislikes. However, it is probably one of the most important factors, and its theoretical significance is enhanced by the absence of any other consistent conceptual framework in this field."[147]

The forgoing paragraphs focuses on the positive aspect of liking as a persuasive force. There is also a reverse – disliking people can keep us from rationale behavior. Differences and unfamiliarity between us and someone trying to influence our actions can be a strong barrier to change. Finally, we generally do not like people who bring bad news. Phases such as "don't shoot the messenger" and "blaming the bearer of bad tidings" are indicative of how bad news infects the teller.

Liking in Lobbying. Scan the people at a political fundraiser for members of Congress sponsored by a lobbying firm. You will likely conclude that everyone looks like everyone else. This is not a coincidence. First, many lobbyists are former members of Congress or senior staff. Second, since we have a favorable disposition toward people who are similar to us, the lobbyists who mirror the members increase their likability. Lobbyists understand this persuasion factor and leverage it. From tailored suits to Rolex timepieces to even speech patterns, lobbyists emulate their lobbyees.

A second implication of liking for lobbyists is the need to find similarity beyond looks and dress. Connections including schools, sports, arts and charities are used to cement similarities.

A third lesson for lobbyists is to build "liking" through frequent meetings. Access to members is best achieved at public events, where you are seen supporting the members' interests. One-on-one sessions are infrequent and reserved for substantive information exchange. However, more frequent meetings with senior staff can be used to build a liking relationship. Of course, it is the quality of the meeting not the quantity that will build the desired relationship.

A final implication for lobbyists regarding liking deals with bad news. While it is generally true we are not positively disposed to bearers of bad news, the lobbyist must not shy away from doing so when necessary. Policymakers count on trusted lobbyists to share all the news, good and bad. The lobbyist may well feel discomfort in the moment, but sharing the bad news will pay off in the future. Simply put: It is better for you to take the heat than allow the lobbyee to do so.

Authority. Duty to authority is a very powerful means of persuading people to act. Authority and obedience are essential ingredients for a well-functioning society. We are taught (and learn) from a young age about the importance of respecting authority figures be they parents, teachers or police. Perhaps the most famous example of the persuasive power of authority is the Milgram Study. Yale professor Stanley Milgram

> **Fun Fact**
> 65% of Milgram's subjects exhibited complete obedience in applying the maximum electric shocks to another person.
> (McLeod 2007)

explored the strength of our responsiveness to authority when it is in conflict with our values and conscience. His research demonstrates that people will inflict serious pain through electric shocks on others (they think they are doing so but the pain is acted out). Moreover, if they hesitate to administer the shock, they continue simply because an authority prods them with prompts ranging from "please continue" to "the experiment requires you to continue" to "you have no other choice but to continue." Insights stemming from the research include:

- Status locations increase the level of obedience.
- Perceived moral or legal authority increases compliance.
- Less personal responsibility increases compliance.
- Distance from the authority reduces obedience.
- Symbols of legitimate authority (such as a uniform) increase compliance.[148]

Symbols of authority and reputation and stature were used by the two great pyramid schemers of the last 100 years to persuade people to invest in their frauds. In 1920, Charles Ponzi, the namesake for such schemes, named his business Securities Exchange Company, located his business in the heart of the Boston financial district, dressed impeccably, and rode in a chauffeured Locomobile (the same vehicle used by the Asters and Morgans) to create confidence in his venture.[149] These symbols deflected questions about the veracity of his business, which ultimately was nothing more than paying old investors with the cash from new investors. Bernie Madoff used his reputation as a former head of NASDAQ and architect of financial regulation to keep regulators and investigators from identifying his $60 billion, two decade fraud.

Authority in Lobbying. Lobbyists find themselves in a challenging environment when it comes to leveraging authority to persuade lobbyees because the person they are lobbying is an authority figure. In response, lobbyists often mirror the lobbyee to leverage the persuasive power of authority. From office location and adornment to clothing to club memberships; many lobbyists seek to stand on equal footing with their targets. Look at photos of lobbyists on their websites – They are well dressed, pose in fancy offices adorned with American flags, and of course, are photographed alongside lots of senior officials. Yes, you get the benefits of others' authority simply by being shown with them.

Lobbyists who enter the profession after serving as a member of Congress, in a senior staff position or in another leadership position bring their prior authority with them. This prior experience is an asset that makes these lobbyists especially valuable. With half of senior government officials migrating to lobbying after public service, there is a cadre of authority-carrying lobbyists in Washington.

Lobbyists who do not have this source of authority can leverage the authority that arises from association. Authority is gained through participation in civic organizations and nonprofits especially if the lobbyist takes a leadership position with these entities. Lobbyists also build their stature attending political and charitable events. Participating in these events has a side benefit: the creation of a powerful network.

The insight from Milgram's research offers three specific recommendations for lobbyists seeking to use authority for persuasion. First, meeting in person increases the effectiveness of authority. Second, more frequent meetings increase the obligation. Third, the status of meeting location increases the level of compliance.

Scarcity. Cialdini's last persuasion driver is scarcity. Marketers understand this and therefore advertise limited time offers. The online airline reservation systems leverage this concept as well. Have you seen taglines such as "only 1 seat left at this price". You can see this type of advertising on sites such as Expedia and Travelocity. At the trivial end of the spectrum is a going out of business sale which motivates us to buy now and perhaps more than we otherwise would. At the other end of the spectrum are the Continuation War between the Finnish and Soviets which was fought over nickel deposits and the Iraq invasion of Kuwait to control oil reserves.[150]

The scarcity effect is even greater when there is competition. Auction houses use this principle to maximize the value for the items they offer. A well-known example is the bidding for Edvard Munch's painting "The Scream". The art world was stunned as the winning bid rose to $119.9 million in May 2012, substantially greater than other more highly regarded works. Competition and scarcity were likely at work in sending the price of this work of art so high as five bidders competed during the auction that lasted for 12 minutes.[151] Have you ever tried to catch beads during Mardi Gras in New Orleans? The competition to catch beads that are tossed from floats is fierce. This behavior exists despite the minimal value of the beads. In the moment, the combination scarcity and competition makes otherwise calm and rationale people act the opposite.

Scarcity in Lobbying. Lobbyists can leverage several forms of scarcity to effectively deliver their services. First, lobbyists can provide detailed information; strong analysis and effective packaging which are often in short supply. The Hall and Deardorff model of lobbying as a legislative subsidy rests on the value lobbyists provide by adding to the resource base of policymakers. A second different but often powerful form of scarcity is campaign funds for candidates. Office seekers spend a sizable portion of this time raising money to finance their campaigns. To the extent that lobbyists can help facilitate raising these funds, they are likely to gain more access to the officials once they are elected.

Another powerful example of scarcity in lobbying can be seen when there is an upcoming congressional vote or regulatory deadline. In these cases, time becomes the scarce resource. There is a premium for access to key policymakers and a burden to make your case quickly and convincingly. The scarcity often leads to one and only one chance to assert your position. The burden to "get it right" is increased as, at these times, there is often intense competition for policymakers' ears.

Howard Gardner's Changing Minds. Cialdini's framework is only one of many that are helpful in understanding the process of influencing policymakers. Howard Gardner of Harvard University's Graduate School of Education offers a complementary rubric in his book <u>Changing Minds</u>. Gardner offers seven "REs" as detailed Exhibit 5-4.

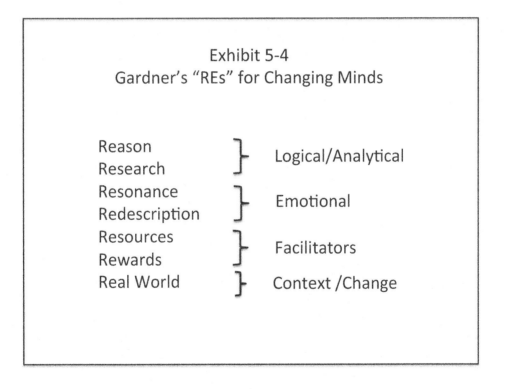

Exhibit 5-4
Gardner's "REs" for Changing Minds

His first two, <u>rea</u>son and <u>res</u>earch, appeal to cognitive-oriented people. This cohort is persuaded by data driven, systematic tests of well-reasoned propositions. Logic, analogs and taxonomies are leveraged to establish and evaluate hypotheses. Lobbyists adopting President John F. Kennedy's experts approach to advocacy seek to persuade through reason and research. Gardener next turns to influencing those who are more responsive to affective considerations. Here he highlights the importance of <u>re</u>sonance; the message and argument just seem right. "Resonance often comes about because one feels a 'relation' to a mind-changer, finds that person 'reliable', or 'respects' that person..."[152] Resonance parallels with Cialdini's pillar about liking.

The cognitive and affective approaches can be combined through representational <u>re</u>-description where the analysis is shown in multiple forms such as text, data and diagrams, each reinforcing the other. As detailed below (Exhibit 5-5), Gardener argues that there are multiple intelligences and therefore we learn in different ways. The effective lobbyist communicates using a variety of methods assuming at least one will resonate for the lobbyee.

Exhibit 5-5
Example of Redescription

Text	The temperature today will be an all time high 40C. Stay by a fan.
Data	6AM 12PM 6PM 12AM 36 40 38 37
Visual	

Regardless of the persuasive approach taken, <u>re</u>sources and <u>re</u>wards are relevant motivating factors. Offering support to the decision-maker, be it material or emotional, can make the target more receptive. These factors tie directly to Cialdini's reciprocity argument. Providing resources and rewards make the recipient beholden to the provider. The lobbyist has an arsenal of resources and rewards to offer the policymaker ranging from information and analysis to campaign contributions and public support for a lobbyee's position.

Real world events are also powerful persuasive forces. An individual's openness to persuasion is in part a function of external events and environment. Following the September 11, 2001 terrorist attack, there was greater receptivity to policies that restrict visitors to the United States. Those limitations would have been hotly contested prior to the terrorist attack. Similarly, coastal building codes in the U.S. Northeast were strengthened in the months following Hurricane Sandy in 2013. Effective lobbyists are abreast of external events and understand their impact on policymaking. In some circumstances, this means holding an issue until the environment is favorable. In others, it is jumping into action because the context favors action. The message for the lobbyist is, 'Be prepared'.

Gardener's final persuasive factor is resistance. People don't like change because it represents risk and uncertainty. This aspect of persuasion will be explored in the last section of the chapter.

Multiple Intelligences. Gardner's work on psychology and education opens another path to understanding persuasion – the multiple intelligences people have. The traditional view of intelligence was that it was singular, largely endowed at birth, hard to enhance, and measurable with an Intelligence Quotient (IQ) test. The intelligence quotient was largely determined by the individual's ability to complete logical operations. Gardener found this difficult to reconcile with luminaries in music, dance and painting who used visual and auditory imagery to create celebrated works of art.

Gardner hypothesized that there is not a single assessment of intelligence; rather there are multiple intelligences. For example, a pianist is able to play an extremely challenging concerto with ease but struggles with modest math problems. This person might have a low IQ but a high "musical" intelligence. A basketball star, who can leap at just the right time to do an alley-oop, has body kinesthetic intelligence that most people with high IQ do not. Another intelligence is interpersonal intelligence – knowing how to discriminate between people, understand their motivations and how best to collaborate with them. The full list of Gardner's intelligences is shown in Exhibit 5-6. Scan the list of intelligences and think of an individual, a teacher, a politician, yourself. Which intelligence does each exhibit? Most people have several intelligences; although their facility in each may vary.

Exhibit 5-6
Gardner's Multiple Intelligences

Logical/Mathematical – Strong reasoning/calculating
Linguistic –Effective use of words
Interpersonal – Interact well with others
Intrapersonal – Understand yourself
Musical – Sensitive to rhythm and sound
Body/Kinesthetic – Skilled in using your body
Visual/Spatial – See the world in terms of physical space

Source: http://www.tecweb.org/styles/gardner.html

There are several implications of this concept for lobbyists. First, the advocate must understand the relevant intelligences of the lobbyee. This enables the lobbyist to deliver messages most effectively. Depending on the individual, the most effective means of

> **Food For Thought**
> What are your intelligence types? What are your strongest intelligences? Weakest?

telling your story may be (1) oral or written; (2) analytic or analog; and (3) using images, data or a personal narrative. Second, assuming the lobbyist's communications are targeted to a larger audience, the messaging should be re-descriptive to reach the widest range of learning styles. Third, the lobbyist should undertake a self-assessment of his or her own intelligence. In other words, it's important to not only understand how your target learns, but how you learn. The lobbyist should understand the most effective means that he or she understands, analyzes and communicates issues.

Additional Implementation Tactics

The Cialdini and Gardener frameworks provide a strong foundation upon which to shape a persuasive program. There are additional, very pragmatic, tools and tactics that build from and/or cut across aspects of their frameworks that can aid in the persuasion process.

Leverage Your Network. Ask a lobbyist to name the three most important assets for effective advocacy; most lists will include network. In this context, the "network" has the breadth of many options for contact as well as the depth of relationship that each contact will respond. The lobbyist's network supports persuasion in two important ways. First, a robust network enables

the lobbyist to gain access to the right policymakers at the right time. The network should also allow for direct access to the target. If not, a broad network of contacts will permit the advocate to gain the desired access via others who do know the target. Stanley Milgram demonstrated in 1967 that we are all linked together by no more than six people – popularized as six degrees of separation. The lobbyist seeks to build a network so policymakers are no more than two degrees of separation. Therefore, if the lobbyist cannot directly access the target, he or she can reach the person with only one other colleague's help. Second, a robust network enables lobbyists to persuade via social proof because they have first-hand knowledge of a wide array of influencers' positions.

Challenge: Map Your Network

Network equals access and access is necessary for influence and persuasion. What does your network look like? Mapping social networks is an easy yet powerful way of understanding your connectivity. A variety of software applications are available to help you create the map and visualize the network. The core methodology is to identify who you know and who they know. Visually, this is portrayed by dots (nodes) to indicate people and lines (links) to connect people. Beyond connectivity, the map can be used to indicate the importance of the relationship, strength of the relationship, frequency of interaction and degree of reciprocity.

Exhibit 5-7 illustrates three simple maps. The Hub and Spoke map shows that a single person is connected to several others but those people are not connected to each other (aside from being connected through the person in the center or hub). The Core and Periphery map indicates that many people are networked with each other, densely at the core and looser at the periphery. The Stove Pipe or Silo map illustrates how multiple core networks exist but the connections between them are limited.

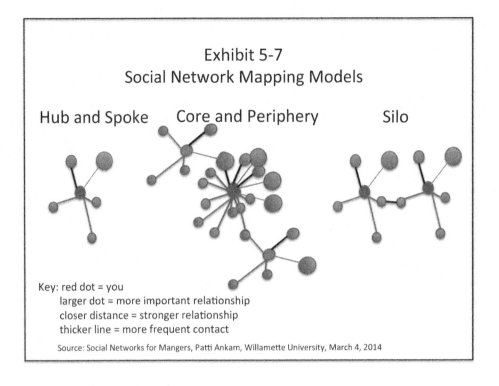

Exhibit 5-7
Social Network Mapping Models

Hub and Spoke   Core and Periphery   Silo

Key: red dot = you
   larger dot = more important relationship
   closer distance = stronger relationship
   thicker line = more frequent contact

Source: Social Networks for Mangers, Patti Ankam, Willamette University, March 4, 2014

Lobbyists desire to have core networks - dense, highly connected relationships. Such relationships facilitate a robust two-way flow of information between the lobbyist and other stakeholders. Networks are built by conscious effort, not happenstance. Using the node and link methodology, map your network and assess its strengths and limitations. What can you do in the next three months and coming year to bolster your network?

Use Body Language with Intention. Your body language says a great deal about what you are thinking and feeling; therefore, it has significant impact on your ability to persuade. Researchers have shown that your body language not only influences how others perceive you, but also how you perceive yourself. Researchers suggest that what you say and how you say it go hand in hand. If there is a mismatch

> **Notable Quote**
> The most important thing to understand about body language is not how to communicate with it, but how to keep from sending the wrong messages.
> - John Stefano
> (Body Language and Persuasion 1977)

between the two, the message is likely to be discounted.[153] Albert Mehrabian, a psychology professor at UCLA, reports that body language accounts for 55 percent of first impressions, tone of voice explains 38 percent, and only 7 percent is drawn from your verbal content.[154] The following dialogue captures the importance of using the right body language to persuade:

"I just do not believe him."
"Why not?"
"It isn't what he says: It's how he says it."[155]

What are techniques to build trust and enhance persuasion through body language? John Stefan, an actor and academic, offers guidance.[156] First, align your words with your feelings. If you do not believe in what you are saying, it will ring hollow to others. Logic and emotion must be consistent. Second, use a natural, voice, facial expressions, gestures, etc. Overacting is transparent and a credibility buster. Third, be confident. A certain amount of nervousness can be expected in a high-stakes environment, but being too edgy raises doubts about your content. The best solution to nerves is preparation: Develop great content and be familiar with it.

The body language you adopt should also reflect that of the person you are communicating with. While strictly mirroring another person can be off-putting, matching styles can be very effective. Recall Cialdini's liking principle: We like people like us. The more someone acts as we do, the greater the likelihood of us liking them.

Effective body language is especially important for lobbyists as many of their interactions with lobbyees are face to face. For the lobbyist this means becoming facile at reading the body language of others, relying on great content to avoid nervousness, and matching body language with oral content. Conducting a trial run of a meeting with a friendly audience is an effective means of learning these skills.

Persuade the Persuadable.[157] Understanding the principles of persuasion is necessary but not sufficient for ensuring a successful outcome. Sufficiency requires that the policymaker be in a persuadable mindset. There are situations when the lobbyee cannot or will not be persuaded due to ideology, consistency or simply poor timing. Making an 'ask' of a legislator just after the member has had a bad day is unlikely to be successful. The lobbyist must determine if the "no" is a function of timing and therefore the request may succeed at another time, or is foundational and will never change. This understanding will allow the lobbyist to avoid spending time and resources trying to convert the unconvertible or, worse yet, offend the member and damage the lobbyist's relationship. Exhibit 5-8 portrays a conversation with the unpersuadable.

```
┌─────────────────────────────────────────────────────┐
│                                                     │
│                    Exhibit 5-8                      │
│           Persuade Those Who Can Be Persuaded       │
│                                                     │
│                                                     │
│        No.                                          │
│        No.                                          │
│        No.                                          │
│        No.                                          │
│        No!!!!                                       │
│        Which part of NO                             │
│        do you not get!                              │
│                                                     │
│                                                     │
└─────────────────────────────────────────────────────┘
```

Persuasion – A Multiparty Interaction

This chapter lays out a set of principles and tactics that can persuade the lobbyee to adopt your position. But it is not that easy! There are two forces that combine to make the process of persuasion more complex: (1) others, perhaps those representing a different side of the issue, will also be using persuasion to get their view adopted and (2) the lobbyee is aware of being persuaded and therefore may use counter strategies to blunt your efforts. Thus, your persuasion strategy must reflect that there are other forces at play and the effort is much more of a "game." The use of the word "game" puts persuasion in the context of game theory where multiple parties influence the outcome of a persuasive attempt. The lobbyist's job is to define a lobbying persuasion approach that maximizes the likelihood of his or her position being adopted.

The lobbyee expects you to identify the opposition's arguments and provide a realistic assessment of their merits. Nevertheless, several actions can enhance the probability of success while maintaining your obligation for robust disclosure. First, with the knowledge that the opposition will lobby for their desired outcome, build a "reciprocity bank". Reciprocity should be viewed over a period of time, not as a single, immediate event. Several lobbyists have said: The time to build reciprocity is when you do not need it; so that when you do, it will be available. The bank enables you to gain access, share your perspective and, if necessary, gain a second hearing. Second, leverage opportunities to demonstrate consistency. Showing that your position is consistent with the lobbyee's prior votes and public statements is a very powerful persuasive force. Third, use social proofs not only to support your position but also to demonstrate the limitations of the opposing view. A list of powerful, respected or charismatic supporters taps Cialdini's authority and liking tenants along with social proof.

Be cognizant that the lobbyee may well adopt persuasion tactics to blunt your efforts or co-opt you to support his or her position. How does the lobbyist prevail? There is clearly not a guaranteed approach; however, the lobbyist increases his or her chances of success by:

- Providing outstanding substantive information and insight.
- Strategically applying persuasion tactics.
- Knowing the lobbyee.

Regarding the latter, knowing how the lobbyee best receives, processes and understands information based on Gardner's intelligences, enables the advocate to maximize the impact of her message.

Persuasion Postulates
- Understanding the power of persuasion is foundational to developing effective lobbying strategies.
- Reciprocity is integrally linked to persuasion: The lobbyist providing policymakers with information/insight and facilitating campaign financing can yield access and a full hearing.
- Policymakers' decisions can be expected to be consistent with past commitments.
- Social proof provided by constituents, fellow policymakers, academics and celebrities increases persuasion.
- Being likeable and having authority significantly enhance the lobbyist's ability to influence policy.
- Minds are changed by a combination of logical/analytical and emotional arguments.
- We all have multiple intelligences – understanding the intelligences of the lobbyee increases the receptivity of the lobbyist's message.
- Build your social network to increase your access to information and policymakers; the Core and Periphery model is the gold standard.
- Using body language to support your substantive message is beneficial, but make sure it does not undercut your efforts.
- Persuade the persuadable.
- Persuasion is a multi-party game: The lobbyee may seek to neutralize your efforts.

Learning by Doing

Shale gas extraction is very controversial. The passion around this issue is evident in New York ,where a moratorium on fracking has been in place since 2008. The pro-fracking forces view point is captured in the following quote from the Executive Director of the New York Petroleum Council at the 2013 extension of the moratorium: "Today's vote by the State Assembly to further delay natural gas development is tantamount to telling the people of the Southern Tier to 'Drop Dead.' Once again, Albany politicians are putting politics before science, and the special interests before the people. The people of New York deserve better, to say the least."[158]

The rationale of those who oppose fracking is reflected in this quote from Alex Beauchamp of *Food and Water Watch:* "Hundreds of New York health professionals agree with the State Assembly that we should not move forward without a full, comprehensive examination of the health impacts of fracking ... Moving forward would simply enrich oil and gas companies that want to ship their gas overseas and their profits to Texas at the expense of New York's public health and environment."[159]

The arguments on both sides largely rest on assertions. Scientists are still collecting fact-based research. While waiting for greater insight, public officials are making policy. In this environment (complex issues, research uncertainty, passionate opposing positions) persuasion is an especially powerful tool of the advocate. In the absence of a compelling fact base, the "softer" aspects of decision-making come into play. Cialdini's reciprocity, liking, consistency, and even social proof are powerful tools for influencing policy. Understanding the lobbyee's intelligences for learning can make your pitch have maximum impact.

Using the concepts in this chapter, develop a persuasion game plan for meeting with the Governor of New York to argue for or against the fracking moratorium.

Bibliography Chapter 5

Badkar, Mamta. "9 Wars That Were Really About Commodities." *Business Insider*. Aug 15, 2012. Accessed August 2, 2014. http://www.businessinsider.com/nine-wars-that-were-fought-over-commodities-2012-8.

Burger, Jerry M., Jackeline Sanchez, Jenny E. Imberi, and Lucia R. Grande. "The Norm of Reciprocity as an Internalized Social Norm: Returning Favors Even When No One Finds out." *Social Influence* 4, no. 1 (2009): 11–17. doi:10.1080/15534510802131004.

Cialdini, Robert B. *Influence: The Psychology of Persuasion, Revised Edition*. Revised edition. New York: Harper Business, 2006.

"Commitment." *Environmental Assistance and Customer Service - N.C. Department of Environment and Natural Resources*. Accessed August 2, 2014. http://portal.ncdenr.org/web/deao/outreach/recycling-education-campaigns/social-marketing/strategies/commitment.

Converse, Benjamin A., Boaz Keysar, Jiunwen Wang, and Nicholas Epley. "Reciprocity Is Not Give and Take, Asymmetric Reciprocity to Positive and Negative Acts." *Psychological Science* 19, no. 12 (2008).

Fagan, Mark, and Tamar Frankel. *Trust and Honesty in the Real World*. 2 edition. Anchorage, AK: Fathom Publishing Company, 2009.

Gardner, Howard. *Changing Minds: The Art And Science of Changing Our Own And Other People's Minds*. First Trade Paper Edition edition. Boston, Mass.: Harvard Business Review Press, 2006.

Harwood, John. "Flip-Flops Are Looking Like a Hot Summer Trend." *The New York Times*, June 23, 2008, sec. U.S. / Politics. http://www.nytimes.com/2008/06/23/us/politics/23caucus.html.

Horn, Steve. "NY Assembly Passes Two-Year Fracking Moratorium, Senate Expected to Follow." *Huffington Post*, March 7, 2013. http://www.huffingtonpost.com/steve-horn/ny-assembly-fracking-moratorium_b_2831272.html.

McLeod, Saul. "The Milgram Experiment." Http://www.simplypsychology.org/milgram.html. *SimplyPsychology*, 2007.

Nazar, Jason. "The 21 Principles of Persuasion." *Forbes*, March 26, 2013. http://www.forbes.com/sites/jasonnazar/2013/03/26/the-21-principles-of-persuasion/.

O'Keefe, Daniel. "Persuasion Theory and Research." *Sage*, 1990.

Petia K. Petrova, Robert B. Cialdini, and Stephen J. Sills. "Consistency-Based Compliance across Cultures." *Journal of Experimental Social Psychology* 43 (2007): 104–11.

Regan, Dennis. "Effects of a Favor and Liking on Compliance." *Journal of Experimental Psychology* 7 (1971): 627–39.

Said, Sammy. "The Top Five Biggest Athlete Endorsement Deals." *TheRichest*. Accessed August 2, 2014. http://www.therichest.com/expensive-lifestyle/money/the-top-five-biggest-athlete-endorsement-deals/.

"Seeds of Peace: Building Peace at Summer Camp Transcript." United States Institute of Peace. Accessed August 2, 2014. http://www.buildingpeace.org/teach-visit-us-and-learn/exhibits/witnesses-transcripts/seeds-peace.

Sluckin, W., D.J. Hargreaves, and A.M. Colman. "Some Experimental Studies of Familiarity and Liking." *Bulletin of the British Psychological Society*, 1982.

Stefano, John. "Body Language and Persuasion." *Litigation* 3 (1977 1976): 31.

Vogel, Carol. "'The Scream' Sells for Nearly $120 Million at Sotheby's Auction." *The New York Times*, May 2, 2012, sec. Arts / Art & Design. http://www.nytimes.com/2012/05/03/arts/design/the-scream-sells-for-nearly-120-million-at-sothebys-auction.html.

Chapter 6: Lobbying Strategies and Implementation

Successful lobbying depends on the ability to design a strategy that responds to the context, substance and politics of an issue. It also depends on the ability to implement that strategy in an efficient and effective manner. The strategy should answer questions including: What objectives are desired? Who are the stakeholders and what are their positions? How should the issue be framed? Who should be lobbied? What resources should be brought to bear? The answers to these and associated questions provide the plans for the lobbying effort. Finally, the lobbyist must determine what tactics can be used to execute the strategy. The chapter elaborates on lobbying strategies and concludes with two case examples.

Strategy Formulation

The term "campaign" is used to describe the overall lobbying effort. The definition of campaign is: "a connected series of operations designed to produce a particular result."[160] While the term originated to describe a sequence of military battles, it is now applied to all types of industries and professions, including lobbying. The operative words in the definition are (1) "series" – lobbying is an ongoing process not a one-time event; (2) "connected" – lobbying efforts are tied together by design; and (3) "result" – lobbying is about achieving a desired outcome.

Strategy is the plan by which the campaign is executed. The term strategy is derived from the ancient Greek word "strategia" which literally translates as generalship. Today, strategy is commonly defined as a careful plan or approach to achieving an objective. There is not, however, a single definition of strategy. Henry Mintzberg identifies five ways to define strategy.[161] (Exhibit 6-1) His first way is the most common, a plan. It is purposeful, deliberate and made in advance to achieve a specific outcome. Strategy can also be defined as pattern, a routine of events that becomes practice. The results of the strategy may or may not match the plan. The strategy should be consistent with past and emergent contexts. Thus, position refers to how the strategy defines where the organization fits into the environment. Perspective is internally focused, centering on how the organization perceives itself in regard to executing objectives. Mintzberg's final "P" is ploy; what schemes or tactics will be used to outmaneuver the competition.

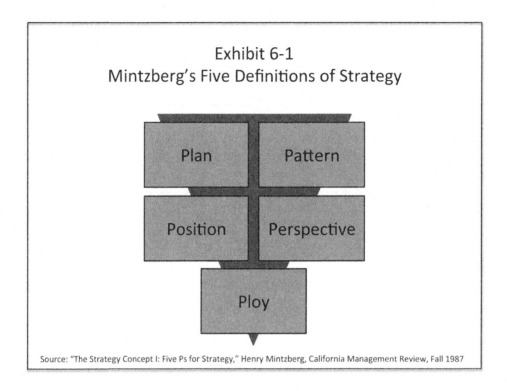

Exhibit 6-1
Mintzberg's Five Definitions of Strategy

Plan

Pattern

Position

Perspective

Ploy

Source: "The Strategy Concept I: Five Ps for Strategy," Henry Mintzberg, California Management Review, Fall 1987

At its most basic level, strategy answers three questions[162]:

- Who are the targets?
- What is being "sold"?
- What enables the sale?

Consider Apple Computer's iPhone strategy. Their target customers are those who value a phone that offers a unique "experience" and are willing to pay more for that opportunity. The product combines leading-edge capabilities with a differentiated design – from look to touch to image. The sales are enabled by focusing on a small number of offerings, innovative marketing and hype. Apple also put profits ahead of market share. This strategy has been successful in "creating a halo effect that makes people starve for new Apple products."[163]

Business has been the primary focus of academic and practitioner work regarding strategy. In the business context (which can be directly applied to lobbying and is elaborated in the next section of this chapter) Michael Porter's "How Competitive Forces Shape Strategy" and "What is Strategy" are seminal. For Porter, "competitive strategy is about being different."[164] Successful strategies customize the delivery of products and services that

> **Notable Quote**
> The essence of strategy is choosing to perform activities differently than rivals do.
> - Michael Porter
> (Porter 1996)

meet customer needs as no one else does. Consider Apple's iPhone, which sells for more than twice the price of a Google Android smartphone with comparable functionality.[165] Why? The strategy described above – great phone, great experience, high-end customers – has been very successful. Another example of strategy through differentiation is Southwest Airlines, which became an aviation powerhouse by offering low fares, reliable service and fun for its passengers. Their strategy was to attract less affluent travelers with low fares, increasing the market size. Outstanding operational efficiency and reliability kept their costs low so they could generate profits despite the low fares. Over time Southwest's image as a reliable, low-cost carrier has remained; although, they are no longer consistently the lowest fare carrier.[166]

One of Porter's most significant contributions is his exploration into the impact of competition on strategy. His Five Forces Model highlights the following competitive factors:

- <u>Rivalry Among Existing Competitors</u> – Swirling at the center of the Five Forces is the rivalry of existing competitors. Limited barriers to entry and lack of customer stickiness intensify the rivalry.
- <u>Bargaining Power of Buyers</u> – Dominant buyers are able to restrict your profits, choking off funds for R&D and innovation, thus weakening your future position.
- <u>Bargaining Power of Suppliers</u> – Strong suppliers who face little competition or have leverage over their customers enabling them to capture your rents and potentially vertically integrate into your space.
- <u>Threat of New Entrants</u> – New entrants bring added capacity and therefore put downward pressure on margins; they also introduce new products/services, which can threaten incumbents.
- <u>Threat of New Products/Services</u> – Innovation is always afoot. New offerings can reduce the desirability of your products or substitute for your products/services.

Economic and technical characteristics of the market dictate the importance of each force. The strongest force(s) is where your strategy is focused.

Harvard Business School's Francis Frei extends the work on strategy by highlighting some very pragmatic requirements for a successful strategy. Her first observation is the need for an integrated, holistic strategy. "When we look at service businesses that have grown and prospered, it is their effective integration of the elements that stands out more than the cleverness of any element in isolation."[167] A second observation is eye opening: "Strategy is often defined as what a business chooses not to do well ... To create a successful service offering, managers need to determine which attributes to target for excellence and which to target for inferior performance."[168] Her argument is that while most organizations strive to be the best at everything, realistically, this is not possible. Therefore, an important part of the strategy process is agreeing on what will not be addressed or what will be done with reduced rigor.

An undercurrent to the forgoing strategy discussion is that context matters. Several Boston Consulting Group consultants make a compelling case that predictability and malleability of the environment significantly impact strategy definition. Predictability addresses the question: "How far into

> **Fun Fact**
> 75% of firms that developed strategies assume "predictability" even when that is not the case.
> (Reeves et al 2012)

the future and how accurately you can confidently forecast demand, corporate performance, competitive dynamics and market forces."[169] Malleability refers the ability of you and your competitors to impact those factors. Based on the combination of predictability and malleability, four types of strategy emerge.

- Classical – When the world is predictable and non-malleable, well-defined expectations and Porter-style Five Forces analysis leads to long-term strategic plans. These detailed blueprints are developed over weeks or months and communicated throughout the organization over a similar timeframe. The performance of these plans is reviewed against targets and refined on an annual basis. Longstanding markets such as food, transport and utilities effectively use the classical planning model.
- Adaptive – In some arenas, the external environment changes frequently, rapidly and with little forewarning. In these cases, a classical strategy becomes outdated in short order. The adaptive approach shrinks the planning time horizon and formality of the plan. Rather than a blueprint, the strategic plan becomes "rough hypotheses based on the best available data."[170] The adaptive strategic plan is more of a decision tree that is constantly updated than a step-by-step program. Moreover, changes are immediately communicated to the organization, which easily adjusts to new directions and requirements. Biotechnology and computer hardware are examples of adaptive industries.
- Shaping – Where the world around you is changing rapidly and you, as well as your competitors, can influence the operating environment, even the adaptive model might not be responsive enough. A shaping strategy enables the organization to not only be agile and responsive but also test approaches to reshape the environment and to leverage its comparative advantage. The shaping strategy can be thought of as a series of "experiments." Smartphone apps and social media fall into this category.
- Visionary – On rare occasions, a new market that is highly likely to develop is identified and an organization has the opportunity to help shape it. Here a vision strategy is developed. There is time for careful

planning and execution, but a focus of the plan is how to influence the market environment to suit the strengths of the organization. Examples include healthcare delivery and big box retailing.

Challenge: Predictability and Malleability in Lobbying
BCG's Predictability and Malleability approach can also be used for strategy development in lobbying. Consider the movement for legislation that allows for medicinal use of marijuana. If you were developing a strategy for supporting such legislation in Florida, would you adopt a Classical, Adaptive, Shaping or Visionary approach and why?

A final observation is that strategy development is a continuous process. Whether the strategy is classical and updated annually, or shaping and therefore in a constant state of flux, strategies must be reviewed and refined.

Lobbying Strategy Development
In the context of lobbying, strategy development is a multi-step process (Exhibit 6-2). The first step is to define the near and long term objectives of the lobbying campaign. The second step is to understand the needs and wants of the stakeholders and determine "targets." The third step is framing the issue to maximize the probability of success. The fourth step is determining the resources that will be brought to bear, what venue(s) will be used, and who will be lobbied. The fifth step is developing the substantive content to support the effort. Finally, the strategy is implemented, progress is monitored and the approach is refined as necessary.

Exhibit 6-2
Strategy Development Roadmap

- Establish near-term and long-term objectives
- Map stakeholder needs and wants
- Frame the issue to maximize success
- Determine resources and venues
- Develop the substantive content
- Execute the strategy
- Monitor progress and refine strategy

Considerations for developing each strategy element and the associated implementation tactics are detailed in the subsequent sections.

Strategic Objectives. The starting point for developing a lobbying strategy is defining objectives. Lobbying is a campaign; there are often near-term and long-term objectives. Strategists often begin with the outcome that is desired and work backward to establish the near-term objectives that support the long-term goal. For example, a lobbying campaign to protect coastal fisheries might have as its long-term objective federal legislation that establishes specific catch limits as a function of overall fish population. Such legislation is a multi-year campaign; therefore, the advocates might establish 12-month objectives of mapping stakeholders, identifying potential supporters and building general public awareness. Goals for 24 months might include securing sponsorship for the legislation from at least five members and building a coalition of supporters.

Dartmouth College Office of Human Resources has coined the concept of "MASTERful" in goal-setting exercises.[171] The goals should be **m**easureable so progress can be tracked. Quantitative metrics are preferable. For lobbyists, measures could include the number of legislators supporting desired legislation, the number of op-eds in support of the position or the number of meetings with senior staff. The goals should also be **a**chievable and **s**pecific. "T" is for time-based; each goal should have a target date for achievement. Lobbyists need to reflect election and legislative cycles in setting timetables. The last two aspects are **e**nergizing and **r**elevant. This framework effectively highlights the importance of goals in building and sustaining enthusiasm for the effort. Most lobbying campaigns span multiple years. Maintaining a sense of progress is essential for the lobbyist's morale as well as for client's interest and resources. The relevance of goals is a final check to confirm that the goals really drive to the desired policy outcome.

In defining strategic objectives, the predictability/malleability concept can be applied. If the Classical environment exists, the lobbying strategy can focus on achieving longer-term objectives using a comparatively stable approach. The decades long process of achieving healthcare reform typifies the classical strategy. In a more volatile situation, the lobbying objectives will be shorter term and may be subject to more frequent change. Policymaking about Internet Neutrality requires a more agile set of objectives.

Stakeholder Mapping and Target Identification. People are the key to achieving the lobbyist's objectives. Stakeholders range from policymakers to interest groups to civil society, any of whom may be for or against your position. A simple but effective tool for tracking stakeholders and their positions is the Who/What matrix illustrated in Exhibit 6-3. The vertical axis enumerates all the stakeholders who care about the issue. A comprehensive list increases the probability that the lobbyist will garner all the support that is available and understand those who will oppose the desired policy outcome. A sub-organizing scheme is helpful if there are a large number of interested parties. Stakeholders can be sequenced from most to least supportive or from most to least influential. A complementary segmentation is the strength of relationship between the lobbyist and the stakeholders.

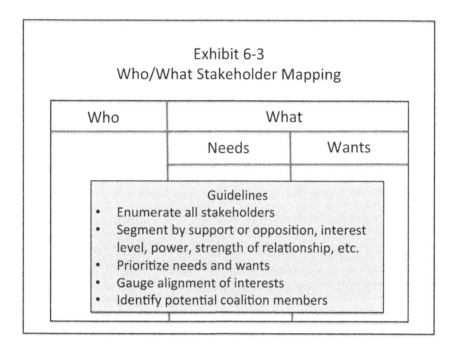

Exhibit 6-3
Who/What Stakeholder Mapping

Who	What	
	Needs	Wants

Guidelines
- Enumerate all stakeholders
- Segment by support or opposition, interest level, power, strength of relationship, etc.
- Prioritize needs and wants
- Gauge alignment of interests
- Identify potential coalition members

The horizontal axis of the matrix is for the "wants" of each group. What is their desired outcome on the issue? Here also, a full enumeration is beneficial. Stakeholders rarely have a single preference on key policy issues. Understanding the nuances of each interest group increases the chances for finding win-win solutions. Differentiating between needs and wants helps to prioritize a stakeholder's requirements versus desires.

The completed matrix enables the lobbyist to see who will be supportive and what positions will bolster their support as well as who can be convinced and what will win them over. Moreover, the Who/What visually illustrates alignment of interests and potential coalition members.

Coalitions are essential for lobbying campaigns. Even interests that are well endowed with access and resources find it beneficial to team with others to strengthen the support for their position. The amount of energy that goes into coalition building (and it does take effort) is generally a function of the amount of competition, be it legislative focus, opposing viewpoints, or media interest. Controversial issues clearly require more coalition building. However, there is a point of diminishing returns; keeping coalition members satisfied becomes more difficult as the number of parities increases. Coalitions only form if they are mutually beneficial. Many come together to achieve a specific objective and then end.

Coalitions often make for strange bedfellows. Typically, an environmental organization and an energy exploration/development group would have little in common. However, at present both seek to restrict coal-fired power plants. The American Natural Gas Alliance advocates for public policies that support natural gas exploration and production. The primary competitor to natural gas for electricity production is coal. Therefore, the Alliance lobbies for polices that make gas more attractive and coal less desirable. The National Wildlife Federation is dedicated to protecting wildlife and its habitat. The mining and movement of coal through the nation's sensitive wildlife areas is a primary concern. While coming at the limitation of coal from two very different perspectives, the two organizations are a natural coalition -- at least regarding the reduction of coal mining. Once coal is reduced or eliminated, it is certainly plausible the environmentalists will turn their sights to reducing natural gas use.

The Who/What matrix also highlights who are in opposition. Porter's 'Rivalry Among Competitors and Bargaining Power' concepts can be applied to assess the strength and impact of the opposing position.

The insights from the Who/What also enable the lobbyist to identify who will be targets during the campaign. The targets are the set of people who – taken together – are necessary to successfully execute the strategy. The targets can be segmented into the primary and secondary decision-makers, their staffs, and those who are in supporting roles.

Issue Framing. How the issue is described/explained to the policymakers, other stakeholders and the general public is key to building support for the lobbyist's positions. "Framing can be thought of as a competition among perspectives describing the same underlying phenomenon," wrote Jeffrey M. Berry et al. in a paper presented

> **Notable Quote**
> The way in which the world is imagined determines at any particular moment what men will do.
> - Walter Lippmann
> (FrameWorks Institute)

before the Annual Meeting of the American Political Science Association in 2007.[172] Frames are powerful because they are an efficient way to understand information. In a 2002 pamphlet published by the FrameWorks Institute, authors wrote, "These mental shortcuts rely on 'frames,' or a small set of internalized concepts and values that allow us to accord mental to unfolding events and new information. These frames can be triggered by various elements, such as language choices and different messengers and images. These communications elements, therefore, have a profound influence on decision outcomes."[173]

Creating a frame requires answers to the following questions:

- Who is the audience?
- What is the issue?
- What contributes to the problem?
- What contributes to the solution?

Framing begins with an understanding of the target audience. The targets might include those who face the problem of galvanizing grassroots support for action. At the other end of the spectrum of target audiences are policymakers who have the authority to make change. In the middle might be the media which can serve as support or opposition to the desired outcome.

Explaining the nature of the issue comes next. What is a one- or two-word name for the issue? This will become the sound-bite moniker so it must convey substance and emotion all in one short phrase. In deciding on the name, consider whether the framing seeks to address a high level, general issue or a specific, targeted single concern.

Next, a fact-based narrative with supporting data and appropriate visuals is needed to provide a description of the issue. If done successfully, the audience will say: "Ah, I get it! ... Wow, this is a real issue that needs attention."

Finally, the framing should offer strategies for resolving the problem. Solutions might involve education and information sharing, provision of resources, aligning incentives or government regulation.

The FrameWorks Institute's Framing Public Issues offers a variety of tactical considerations when framing. Highlights are:[174]

- Context – link current information to long-term needs, use facts and data to make the issue real to the audience, provide ideas on solutions.
- Numbers – limit the use of numbers, explain their importance before providing the data, focus data to amplify strategic aspects of the issue (e.g. the magnitude of the problem or the cost of inaction).
- Messengers – select a messenger who conveys authority, is trustworthy, has substantive expertise, and is not a distraction from the issue.
- Visuals – select pictures that support the message of the frame and link cause and effect and trends where possible.
- Metaphors and Analogs – use to simplify and/or make tangible more abstract concepts and use to help tell the narrative of the issue.

In developing the frame, understand that the audience is likely to already have a set of beliefs regarding the issue. Also, framing is interactive. While you are framing, others are as well and the external context may be evolving. Thus, the frame must resonate with existing viewpoints and attitudes. This caution is especially important in the public policy space, as most issues have already been frames to greater (or lesser) degree. Therefore, the lobbyist must build on frames that support his or her views or try to reframe the issues to better suit his or her policy goals.

> **Notable Quote**
> Reframing is social change.
> - George Lakoff
> Berry et al 2007)

There are powerful examples of successful reframing. Antismoking activists successfully reframed a number of existing tobacco industry frames as shown in Exhibit 6-4. Another area where there has been active reframing regards abortion. Policies concerning abortion are some of the most controversial in public discourse. Those in favor of late-term abortions cast the procedure as "intact dilation and extraction", the medical description of the process. This framing seeks to keep the debate in "sterile" medical terms. The antiabortion supporters, however, have reframed the issue by referring to the process as "partial birth abortion." They seek to emotionalize the issue using the words "partial birth."

Exhibit 6-4
Examples of Reframing the Smoking Debate

From: "Smoking is a matter of personal choice."
To: "People smoke because they are addicted."

From: "Smoking bans discriminate against smokers."
To: "Non-smokers have the right to breathe clean air."

From: "Tobacco is just one of many presumed health hazards. Why don't we regulate fat?"
To: "Tobacco is the only legal product that when used as intended, kills."

Source: Community Toolbox, Chapter 32, Section 5. Reframing the Issue, University of Kansas

---

While there are examples of success in reframing, there are also cases where reframing has been difficult to achieve. The environmental movement seeking to reduce carbon emissions was initially framed as global warming. While science supports the claims of long-term warming, season-to-season variation in weather (local short term conditions) does not always imply warming.

In 2010, Washington D.C. had a very cold and snowy winter. Senator James M. Inhofe, a passionate opponent of the global warming thesis, built an igloo in his front yard dubbing it "Al Gore's New Home."[175] The environmental community has recognized that the real impact

> **Food For Thought**
> What could the environmental community do to shift the framing from global warming to climate change?

of increasing amounts of carbon in the air is "climate change," which involves more extremes in weather patterns. The climate change terminology is more accurate and resonates more easily with the public, but reframing has been very difficult. Those opposed to carbon regulations are loath to move from the global warming framing which is easier to challenge.

Washington: The Real No-Spin Zone examines reframing specifically in a lobbying context. The authors study a random selection of 98 active policy areas. They identify the lobbyists who are involved in these issues and interview them to understand the

> **Fun Fact**
> While 30% of issue areas experienced policy change, only 5% were reframed.
> (Berry et al 2007)

current framing of the issue. The researchers re-interview the respondents 18-24 months later to understand how the framing of the issue has change. Their surprise finding is that only four of the 98 issues were reframed.

The authors offer several explanations for the paucity of reframing. First, there are resource constraints. Reframing requires resources and it is likely that the opposition will resist the reframing; therefore requiring even more resources. Fear of a "reframing spending race" limits willingness to attempt change of the frame. Second, there are political realities. Reframing can only take place if an issue is salient. Moreover, the media must be interested in participating in the reframing as print, broadcast and online outlets are the most effective venue for changing public perception of policy issues. The third explanation is that reframing must be consistent with prior positions and beliefs. Recall Cialdini's persuasion model: Lobbyists, politicians and the media must be consistent to maintain creditability.

In sum, frames are a very important vehicle for lobbyists to build support for their position. Framing and reframing efforts at the margins are often successful but wholesale reframing is rare.

Resources, Venue and Intensity. A core strategic question for lobbyists is what **resources** should be brought to bear in a lobbying campaign. A wide array of resources can be used to support a policy position. The most obvious is money for research, public relations, travel, campaign financing, etc. A second resource is access to meet with key policymakers. A third is time to work on the issue. A fourth resource is coalition participants. More partners bring more resources. Social proof is another lobbying resource. Recall that Cialdini argues people are influenced by evidence that others support your position. Influential people from politicians to journalist to academics to celebrities represent a powerful form of social proof. Numbers do as well. Public demonstrations of support with hundreds or thousands of supporters or petitions with thousands or even millions of signatures are strong persuasive forces.

One more resource is grassroots lobbying. In contrast to direct lobbying, the focus of this book, grassroots lobbying is where advocates state their perspective to the general public and ask those people to contact their legislators or other officials to support the desired policy position. Such lobbying has the potential to mobilize hundreds, thousands or even millions of people to support a lobbying goal.

A resource inventory, such as Exhibit 6-5, helps track lobbying assets.

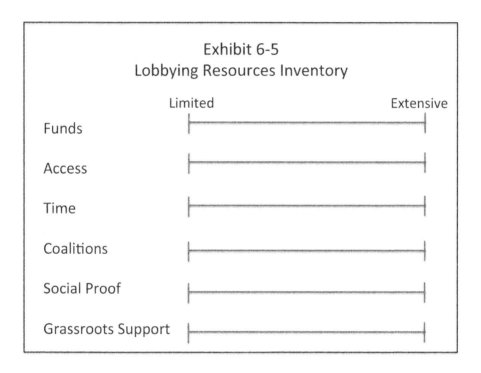

Where the campaign will be waged, **venue** is also a conscious decision. Lobbying takes place at a wide array of locations and with various lobbyees. Exhibit 6-6 illustrates venue options as a decision tree. The first decision is whether to lobby at the federal or state level. Next, what branch of government will be targeted - legislative, administrative or regulatory? Finally, the target within the branch is determined. For example if the place is Congress, the right level could be lobbying with rank and file members, committee members or chairs, or senior leadership.

```
┌─────────────────────────────────────────────────────────────┐
│                                                               │
│                        Exhibit 6-6                            │
│              Venue Options Decision Framework                 │
│                                                               │
│                                                               │
│   **Level**: Federal or State                                 │
│                                                               │
│                                                               │
│   **Branch**: Congress, White House, Departments, regulators  │
│                                                               │
│   **Target**:                                                 │
│    - Legislature: Member, Committee Chair, Leadership         │
│    - Executive Branch: Technocrat, Leadership                 │
│    - Independent Regulators: Technocrat, Leadership           │
│                                                               │
│                                                               │
└─────────────────────────────────────────────────────────────┘
```

Decision #1: Lobbying at the federal or state level is typically a function of the topic and where it is ripe. Some issues are dominantly federal such as trade policy and international relations. Others, for example school curricula and insurance, are largely driven at the state level. Still other policies are made at either or both Congress and state legislatures. Immigration policy is illustrative. Conceptually immigration policy is a federal issue; however, lack of action in Congress led states to take action and fill the vacuum. This in turn has spurred Congress to consider the issue. Another example of the migration from Federal to state venues is the Affordable Care Act which was debated and passed by Congress but is implemented, in large part, at the state level.

Decision #2: The right branch is generally where:

- The organization that has the <u>authority to act</u> – For proposed legislation, Congress is the primary venue. If the issue is implementation of legislation or associated rule-making, the authority may lie with administrative departments or regulatory bodies. Authority can be nuanced. When there is gridlock in Congress, presidential action can drive policy decisions. President Barack Obama's frustration with lack of Congressional action on raising the minimum wage led him to raise the minimum wage for federal contractors to $10.10 by executive order.[176]

- The organization is <u>likely to act</u>. Finding a body that is likely to take action, especially for new policy, is difficult. "The public agenda is finite so that problems compete for attention with policymakers and organizational advocates."[177] Of the 9,000 bills introduced in the 106/107th Congress only 765 were passed.[178] Therefore, lobbyists consider alternatives to Congressional action such as White House executive orders and/or executive departments and regulatory agency rulemaking.

- The lobbyist has good <u>access and insight</u> - The lobbyist may have better access to one branch versus another. Former members of Congress or their senior staff are likely to have better access to lawmakers than to regulators or agency heads. Lobbyists create value by understanding issues and processes. Those with greater knowledge of the workings of the White House might achieve better results at that venue. Of course, the preference is to lobby where the issue is relevant, where the action is taking place.

- The lobbyist enjoys strong <u>coalition support</u> - Thomas Holyoke while at George Washington University examined the how lobbyists select venues or "battlegrounds" as he refers to them.[179] Focusing on banking and finance policy, he interviewed interest group representatives to learn how they chose venues for lobbying. He found that having a coalition in a venue significantly increased the probability of lobbying in that venue.

- The <u>opposition is limited</u> – Multiple parties lobby on most issues of consequence. Therefore the venue decision must leverage not only the lobbyist's strengths and weaknesses but also reflect the capabilities of the opposition (Exhibit 6-7). Holyoke also found that lobbyists avoid venues where the opposition is strong. If there is a need to advocate in that venue, low-cost lobbying tactics are used.

Exhibit 6-7
Venue Selection Based on Opposition

		Weak	Strong
Opposition	Strong	Unattractive Seek Alternatives	Important But Expensive
	Weak	Ignore	Ideal Venue

Your Position

Source: Choosing Battlegrounds: Interest Group Lobbying Across Multiple Venue, Thomas Holyoke, Political Research Quarterly, Vol. 56, No. 3 September 2003.

The target branch is apt to change over time. Congress is the focus for advocacy for legislative proposals. Once passed, attention shifts to the responsible administrative agencies or regulatory bodies. The Securities and Exchange Commission (SEC) was tasked with rulemaking to address 90 provisions of the Wall Street Reform and Consumer Protection Act (Dodd-Frank). Lobbyists representing investment banks, depository institutions, hedge funds, pension funds and investors among others have been actively lobbying the SEC to shape the rules in their favor.

Decision #3: The third venue decision centers on determining who specifically to lobby. The target can be the policymaker, his or her staff or an indirect influencer. A practical reality guides the decision between policy maker and staff. Time with members of congress or department/agency heads and the president is very scarce. Working with staff is the right answer in almost all cases as they have the time, analysis is their job and the policymaker will rely on them for direction. Lobbying with a third party as a means of reaching a policymaker is appropriate when the lobbyist does not have access to the target. Using an intermediary is an additional strategy.

> **Fun Fact**
> Lobbyists report spending 80% of their time with staff v. 20% with members.
> (Fagan interviews)

Venue is rarely singular. Lobbyists often engage at multiple venues. For example, Congress is most appropriate if the issue is pending in proposed legislation. Nevertheless, the White House, executive departments and agencies can be important stakeholders in these matters. Moreover, there are times when lobbying at the state level helps to progress issues in Washington.

Lobbying the regulators is yet another venue. Making a case to regulators is often more challenging than lobbying Congress or the White House. First, regulators are not elected. Therefore, campaign finance for reciprocity is completely off the table. Along those same lines, regulators do not have constituents that can apply leverage. Second, regulators are often career bureaucrats with distinctive expertise. President John F. Kennedy's argument that lobbyists provide technical expertise is less a factor in this environment. Therefore information is less valuable and/or the level of sophistication required is much higher. Lobbyists must be careful to avoid implying that the regulator does not know the issues. Third, regulators fear lawsuits from failing to follow procedures. Any hint of unfair access or influence is avoided. Therefore, lobbying will likely include lobbying at multiple venues; although the intensity will be a function of stakeholder priorities and influence.

In addition to understanding resource availability and venues, lobbying strategy must address the **intensity** of advocacy, the amount and pacing of resources used. Is the strategy an all-out blitz or is it a slow war of attrition? The answer is in large part determined by the specific context faced. Contextual factors include:

- The likelihood of policy action – Will the issue be addressed by policymakers?
- The probability the policy outcome will be achieved. The importance of the issue to the client – Is this a need or want?
- Maintaining or changing the status quo – change requires significantly more resources.
- The strength of the opposition – Will they oppose? What resources do they have? How much will they use?
- The resources available to tackle this issue.
- The opportunity cost of using the resources on this issue rather than on other matters.

Exhibit 6-8 illustrates a graphical way of considering these factors. The "art" of lobbying strategy is determining how to use the information to make an appropriate decision on resource commitment. Experience is likely the best teacher.

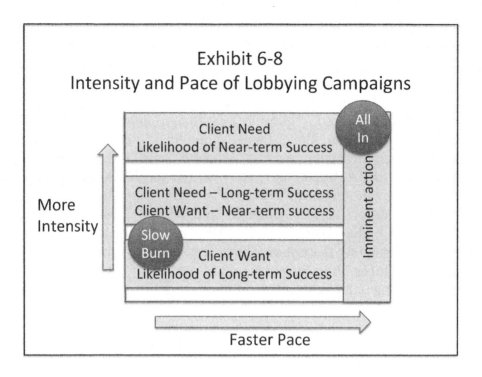

Exhibit 6-8
Intensity and Pace of Lobbying Campaigns

Substantive Content. The heart of every lobbying campaign is a strong substantive argument for the proposed policy. Comprehensive and fact-based research is the starting point. What are policymakers, academics, the media and other lobbyists saying on both sides of the issue? Prior policy debates often provide insights. Public opinion polls are also an important source of information. It may be appropriate to conduct your own primary research (e.g. surveys, interviews, focus groups) to truly understand stakeholder positions.

A strong fact-base enables the development of the lobbying message. Leverage Cialdini and Gardner insights to make the message clear, concise, compelling and memorable. Redescription, providing the message in a variety of formats, increases the accessibility of the message to stakeholders with a variety of learning styles. Focus groups are also an effective means for testing messages. The materials must describe the other side as well as your own. Doing so makes sure you really understand the other side. Also, the lobbyee expects to hear all sides of the issue from the lobbyist. Moreover, this is your opportunity to articulate why the other side's arguments should be dismissed in a credible way.

> Food For Through
> What would be your pitch for a friend to read one of your favorite books? Can you do it in 60 seconds?

The substantive information should be packaged into at least three forms. First is an elevator pitch. You meet the lobbyee in an elevator and in the time it takes to get from the lobby to her floor (about 60 seconds) you can give the target enough of the message that she will ask for more. Whether the encounter is in an elevator, fundraiser, softball game or at the member's office, a crisp message is valued. The content needs to include the issue and why it is important, your proposed solution and rationale, and an ask. Second, draft a one-page summary that you can leave with the lobbyee or his staff that summarizes the issue as well as your position and rationale. A small leave-behind increases your ability for structured follow-up. It may be appropriate to have customized versions of the pitch and one-pager for different targets. Exhibit 6-9 provides some guidelines. Finally, a more comprehensive whitepaper should be available that comprehensively and convincing lays out the case for your policy position. Increasingly, there is also a need for a social media format.

Exhibit 6-9
Customizing the Message

Audience	Message Design
Policymaker	The Bottom Line
Policymaker Staff	Specific and detailed
Interested Parties	Simple with key insights
General Public	Sound bites

Source: Based on Guideline on Lobbying and Advocacy, ICCO, June 2010, p. 37.

Beyond these outputs, the substantive work should be customized to the unique aspects of a lobbying meeting. First, lobbying meetings are short – expect 10-15 minutes but be prepared for it to be less than five minutes. Second, the lobbyist often has only 120 seconds to share information before the listening phase begins. Understanding the member's views and answering questions will likely consume most of the meeting time. The last 120 seconds is owned by the lobbyist to wrap up and make an ask. This compressed timeframe puts a premium on the lobbyist's ability to effectively communicate the message.

Implementation, Monitoring and Refinement. With the substance of the strategy defined, it is time to implement the effort. Implementing a lobbying strategy is no different than any other plan: The tasks, timeframe and accountabilities are defined, resources and materials are assembled, and the actions are undertaken.

Whether the strategy is classical, adaptive, shaping or visionary; lobbyists continually monitor the progress of their program and adjust it as necessary. Monitoring centers on the following questions:

- Is the reaction to the pitch as expected? Does it resonate with targets, the media, the public?
- Are the targets agreeing to the "ask" and following through on their commitments?
- Is the opposition responding as expected?
- Is the issue actionable?
- Are resources available and is the expenditure rate as planned?

Based on the answers to those questions, refinements might be necessary including identifying new targets, re-crafting messages and potentially suspending or abandoning the campaign.

Putting it All Together

The following examples illustrate how the process described above is woven into a comprehensive strategy. The first example is drawn from the lobbying strategy of the Irish Hemophilia Society to help its member organizations create a sustained lobbying campaign. The second is a strategy prepared by the American Legislative Exchange Council (ALEC) to help organizations repeal the Affordable Care Act.

Irish Hemophilia Society. The World Federation of Hemophilia (WFH) provides its member organizations with materials to "help hemophilia society leaders, staff and volunteers develop the skills necessary to effectively represent the interests of people with hemophilia."[180] WFH recognizes the importance of favorable public policy in achieving its objectives and therefore prepared a whitepaper, Developing and Sustaining an Effective Lobbying Campaign, to aid its members' advocacy efforts. The document details a seven-step process for building and executing a lobbying campaign (Exhibit 6-10). The approach consists of a series of planning and executing actions. The planning phase begins with defining objectives, detailing the campaign and preparing materials.

The execution phase involves meeting with policymakers, building and maintaining momentum, and leveraging grassroots efforts.

Exhibit 6-10
World Federation of Hemophilia:
Lobbying Process

Step 1: Defining Objectives
Step 2: Planning the Campaign
Step 3: Preparing the Materials
Step 4: Meeting with Targets
Step 5: Creating Momentum
Step 6: Maintaining Momentum
Step 7: Leveraging Elections

Source: Developing and Sustaining an Effective Lobbying Campaign, Brian O'Mahony, World Federation of Hemophilia, 2006. .

The application of these concepts enabled the Hemophilia Federation of New Zealand (HFNZ) to obtain government funds for treatment and financial compensation for individuals who contracted Hepatitis C from contaminated blood or other therapeutic

> **Fun Fact**
> HFNZ lobbied for 13 years before securing funding for their members.
> (World Federation of Hemophilia 2007)

products. In 1992, the media was abuzz with the "Bad Blood Scandal." Despite the attention focused on the issue, the campaign to receive government compensation lasted more than a decade. The group attributes five core elements to achieving access:

- Researching the Facts: The facts were compelling but few people knew them. Thus, the first priority was developing the evidence base to prove the damages and support the claim for funding. The group effectively leveraged investigative journalists to support their internal efforts.
- Mobilizing Members: Member engagement provided a flow of personal narratives on the dire conditions of those affected.
- Distilling Information: The vast material gathered from the research and personal narratives was boiled down to five points that resonated with the media and general public.

- Targeting the Right People/Institutions: The team determined the three targets necessary to engage. The first was Parliament, especially members from the smaller parties with the swing votes. Detailed information sharing also took place with the Minister of Health. Finally, the media was continuously appraised of new developments to keep the issue fresh and in the public eye.
- Managing Timing: The effort intensified as the election neared.

The author of this case study offers the following lessons learned which are broadly applicable in most lobbying efforts:[181]
- Uncover the facts and use them.
- Sound bites are more powerful than whitepapers.
- Politicians, the media and other stakeholders contribute to shaping the debate.
- Understand your members' needs and wants.
- Always maintain professionalism.
- Periodically reassess the strategy, otherwise stick to the script.
- Understand downstream implications (e.g. the organization's reputation was enhanced with the success of the lobbying campaign).

American Legislative Exchange Council. The passage of the Affordable Care Act of 2010 (ACA) was one of the most contentious legislative battles in recent memory. The controversy was accompanied by a sizable lobbying effort. Those for and against the legislation spent more than $500 million lobbying for their interests.[182] Even after passage, advocates continued the battle in state and federal courts and the court of public opinion.

One group that advocated against the legislation and subsequently for its repeal was the American Legislative Exchange Council (ALEC). The organization is "the nation's largest nonpartisan individual membership association of state legislators, with nearly 2,000 members across the nation and more than 100 alumni members in Congress. ALEC's mission is to promote free markets, limited government, individual liberty and federalism through its model legislation in the states."[183] A core vehicle for achieving their objectives is drafting model-legislation that can be adopted by state legislators and provide state-to-state consistency.

Regarding healthcare, the group's view is "the best healthcare is patient-driven not government-driven."[184] After the passage of the ACA and its subsequent affirmation by the Supreme Court, the group launched a lobbying campaign to stymie the implementation of the Act. The centerpiece of this effort is their whitepaper, *The State Legislators Guide to Repealing ObamaCare*, which was used as a way to educate state lawmakers about the negative aspects of the ACA and provide a game plan for negating its impact. The report opens with details of the adverse consequences of the Act – overburdening Medicaid programs, higher taxes, harmful individual mandates and job-killing individual mandates.[185] The paper goes onto specific actions state legislators can take to forestall or prevent the implementation of the Act.

ALEC facilitates this by offering model legislation entitled, 'Freedom of Choice in Healthcare Act'. "The legislation—which can be introduced as a statute or a constitutional amendment—prohibits any person, employer, or health-care provider from being compelled to purchase or provide health insurance; protects the right of a person or employer to pay directly for lawful healthcare services; protects the right of a health care provider to accept direct payment for lawful healthcare services, and protects the existence of a private health insurance market." [186] ALEC suggests convincing others to support the legislation by reframing the healthcare debate to focus on the opportunity of states to opt-out of the ACA where permitted by the Supreme Court and thus avoid the adverse consequences of the ACA.

Critics of ALEC argue that the organization is supporting the healthcare insurance industry's desire to "do exactly what they have been doing". According to Wendell Potter, a senior fellow on healthcare at the Center for Media and Democracy, this means "underwriting health risks in ways that make health insurance far too expensive for

> **Notable Quote**
> They spend considerable time coming up with titles for these model laws that are anything but what the title says.
> - Wendell Potter, Center for Media and Democracy
> (Center for Media and Democracy)

people who've been sick in the past and for people as they get older, and in many cases enabling insurance companies to refuse to sell coverage to people at any price because of preexisting conditions."[187] Who funds ALEC? The Center for Media and Democracy reports that the majority of funding for ALEC comes from large corporations, corporate foundations and industry trade associations.[188]

Notwithstanding the criticism, ALEC's model legislation has been proposed in a majority of states and enacted in several.[189]

ALEC adopted a number of elements of effective lobbying in responding to the Affordable Care Act.

- <u>Unambiguous Objective</u>: Slow or stop the implementation of the ACA.
- <u>Clear Target for its Advocacy</u>: State legislators because they have the power to enact opt-out laws.
- <u>Right Venue</u>: ALEC focused on the state level where much of the implementation takes place and where there are more sympathetic

policymakers.

- <u>Powerful Substantive Materials</u>: The whitepaper provides a data-driven explanation of the negative impacts of the ACA. It is also easy to read and understand. Moreover, the whitepaper offers ready-to-file legislation.
- <u>Reframing</u>: ALEC positions the ACA as a costly federal imposition that can be avoided though opt-out legislation.

Regardless of your views on ACA, ALEC's lobbying strategy provides a model of how advocacy can impact outcomes.

Challenge: Counteracting ALEC's Lobbying
Develop a lobbying strategy to counteract the efforts of ALEC. Specifically identify how you could offset the strengths of its campaign.

Strategy Synthesis
- Lobbying is typically a campaign – a connected series of actions to achieve the desired outcome.
- Strategy answers three core questions: Who is the target(s)? What is being "sold?" What enables the sale?
- Lobbying strategy is closely akin to business strategy; Porter's Five Forces model is applicable, but substitute "policy" for "product."
- The predictability and malleability of the policymaking environment dictates the strategy model to be employed from classical to adaptive to shaping.
- Strategy development is a continuous process: Whether the strategy is classical and updated annually or shaping and therefore in a constant state of flux, strategies must be reviewed and refined.
- Strategy begins with short-term and long-term objectives that are measurable, time-bound and energizing.
- Map stakeholder needs and wants (Who/What matrix) to gauge alignment of interests and identify coalition members.
- Frame the issue to build support with policymakers, the media and the general public. Most issues have an existing frame and reframing is difficult.
- Select the venue(s) based on which policymakers have the authority to act, will likely take action, where the lobbyist has access and insights. Also, select the venue where the opposition (or resistance) is lower.
- The amount and timing of resources applied to the campaign are a function of resources available, probability of success, strength of opposition and opportunity cost of using the resources on this issue versus others.

- Take time to develop substantive materials, which include an elevator pitch, a one-page handout and a comprehensive whitepaper.
- Progress of the strategy should be monitored over time and adjusted as necessary.

Learning by Doing

Hydraulic fracturing uses water, sand and chemicals to "crack" the shale and release the gas. The chemicals used in this process have been a point of contention between the pro- and anti-fracking advocates. The companies undertaking the fracking refuse to provide a detailed list of the chemicals used and in what quantities. They consider this information a trade secret. They argue that the mix of chemicals impact the amount of gas recovered and must remain proprietary. Those opposed to fracking are concerned that the chemicals used are causing environmental damage to aquifers. They argue, in the absence knowing the chemicals and the quantities used, regulators cannot assess the potential for damage until it has already occurred. The Environmental Protection Agency (EPA) is also concerned about the identity of the fracking chemicals and has proposed a rule to require disclosure.

Choose a side for or against the disclosure rule and identify a specific entity to represent. Do some research on the organization and then develop a lobbying strategy to advocate your position. The strategy should include:

- Your objectives for the campaign.
- A stakeholder map, lobbying targets and coalition members.
- A brief explanation on how you will frame the issue.
- The resource level and timing you will commit.
- The venues where you will lobby.
- Highlights of your substantive arguments.

Bibliography Chapter 6

Berry, Jeffrey M., Frank R. Baumgartner, Marie Hojnacki, David C. Kimball, and
    Beth L. Leech. "Washington: The Real No-Spin Zone." Chicago, Illinois, 2007.

"Campaign." *Merriam-Webster*. An Encyclopedia Britannica Company, n.d.
    http://www.merriam-webster.com/dictionary/campaign.

"Executive Order -- Minimum Wage for Contractors." *The White House: Office of
    the Press Secretary*, February 12, 2014. http://www.whitehouse.gov/the-
    press-office/2014/02/12/executive-order-minimum-wage-contractors.

Fang, Lee. "Demonstrations Test Turkey's Lobbying Clout in Washington." *The
    Nation.* June 5, 2013.
    http://www.thenation.com/blog/174672/demonstrations-test-turkeys-
    lobbying-clout-washington.

Feeney, Lauren. "ALEC's Attempts to Thwart Obamacare." *Moyers & Company*.
    Accessed August 3, 2014. http://billmoyers.com/2013/08/13/alecs-
    attempts-to-thwart-obamacare/.

Framing Public Issues. Washington D.C.: FrameWorks Institute, April 2005.
    http://www.frameworksinstitute.org/assets/files/PDF/FramingPublicIssue
    sfinal.pdf.

Frei, Frances X. "The Four Things a Service Business Must Get Right." *Harvard
    Business Review*. Accessed August 3, 2014. http://hbr.org/2008/04/the-
    four-things-a-service-business-must-get-right/ar/1.

Hojnacki, Marie, Frank R. Baumgartner, Jeffrey M. Berry, David C. Kimball, and
    Beth L. Leech. "Goals, Salience, and the Nature of Advocacy." *American
    Political Science Review*, August 31, 2006.
    http://www.unc.edu/~fbaum/papers/APSA06_lobby.pdf.

Holyoke, Thomas T. "Choosing Battlegrounds: Interest Group Lobbying Across
    Multiple Venues." *Political Research Quarterly* 56, no. 3 (September 1, 2003):
    325–36. doi:10.1177/106591290305600307.

"Influence: Influence & Lobbying: Ranked Sectors." *OpenSecrets*. Accessed May
    27, 2014.
    http://www.opensecrets.org/lobby/top.php?showYear=2010&indexType=c
    .

Markides, Constantinos Costas. "What Is Strategy and How Do You Know If You
    Have One?" 2004. doi:10.1111/j.0955-6419.2004.00306.x.

Mintzberg, Henry. "The Strategy Concept I: Five Ps For Strategy." *California
    Management Review* 30, no. 1 (Fall 1987): 11.

Nair, Smita. "Apple's Premium Pricing Strategy and Product Differentiation."
    Yahoo Finance. Jan. 28, 2014. Accessed August 3, 2014.
    http://finance.yahoo.com/news/apple-premium-pricing-strategy-product-
    191247308.html.

Neefus, Christopher. "Sen. Inhofe's Family Builds Igloo for Global Warming
    Spokesman Al Gore in Snow-Laden D.C." *CNS News*, February 9, 2010.

http://www.cnsnews.com/news/article/sen-inhofe-s-family-builds-igloo-global-warming-spokesman-al-gore-snow-laden-dc.

O'Mahony, Brian. *Developing and Sustaining an Effective Lobbying Campaign.* Irish Haemophilia Society, 2006. http://www1.wfh.org/publication/files/pdf-1255.pdf.

Porter, Michael E. "What Is Strategy?" *Harvard Business Review.* Accessed August 3, 2014. http://hbr.org/1996/11/what-is-strategy/ar/1.

Reeves, Martin, Claire Love, and Philipp Tillmanns. "Your Strategy Needs a Strategy." *Harvard Business Review.* Accessed August 3, 2014. http://hbr.org/2012/09/your-strategy-needs-a-strategy/ar/1.

Seitz, Patrick. "Sorry, Cheapskates, Apple iPhones to Remain Pricey." *Investor's Business Daily*, February 26, 2014. http://news.investors.com/SiteAds/Sponsorship.aspx?page=/NewsAndAnalysis/Article.aspx&position=sponsorbtn1&identifier=click&tile=2&ord=7364171220064911.

"State Legislators Guide to Repealing ObamaCare." *ALEC - American Legislative Exchange Council.* Accessed August 3, 2014. http://www.alec.org/publications/the-state-legislators-guide-to-repealing-obamacare/.

Tuttle, Brad. "Southwest Airlines: We're Not Really About Cheap Flights Anymore." *Time*, March 26, 2013. http://business.time.com/2013/03/26/southwest-airlines-were-not-really-about-cheap-flights-anymore/.

Chapter 7: Lobbying By Foreign Interests

The focus of this book so far has been on United States businesses, interest groups and individual citizens lobbying the federal government. Foreign interests also lobby the US government extensively. The goal of these efforts mirrors that of domestic lobbyists – to influence public policy decisions. While the goal may be the same, the context is decidedly different. Foreign interests are often not US citizens, do not pay taxes, or have First Amendment protections. Moreover,

> **Fun Fact**
> Foreign agents made 10,700 congressional contacts in 2008
> (Sunlight Foundation)

their interests may be in direct conflict with those who are US citizens, corporations, and taxpayers. This chapter explores the rationale for foreign lobbying, the restrictions on this practice, and the current state of advocacy by non-US interests.

The Rationale for Foreign Lobbying

The lobbying efforts of foreign interests can be categorized into four primary categories – aid, trade, foreign policy and reputation.

In lobbying for aid, the potential reward is high: The federal government provided approximately $50 billion in military and economic assistance annually from 2008 to 2011. More than 170 countries received assistance; forty of which received more than $100 million each.[190] These funds were distributed by 19 federal agencies; although Department of State, USAID, and the Department of Treasury accounted for the lion's share of disbursements. The funds are distributed to foster economic development, aid recovery from war, and align with US strategic interests. The top ten foreign governments lobbying in Washington spent $42 and $32 million respectively in 2008 and 2009.[191]

A second focus of foreign government lobbying is trade policy. Countries court Congress and the Executive Branch for more favorable trade treatment through comprehensive agreements such as the North American Free Trade Agreement (NAFTA) and country-specific actions. Lobbying is often a key component of a country's campaign to achieve improved trade status with the United States. Peru, for example, lobbied Washington for Congressional approval of an extension and enhancement of its trade pact. Negotiators reached agreement on a revised Andean Trade Promotion and Drug Eradication Act in 2006 and The Peruvian government ratified it that year. Congress took up the matter in 2007; it was implemented in February 2009. Between the signing, ratification, and implementation of the trade agreement; the Peruvian government actively lobbied in Washington. The government of Peru, working through the lobbying firm Fiece, Isakowitz & Blalock, initiated 142 contacts subject to disclosure.[192] The vast majority were discussions "in regard to passage of the Peru FTA, ATPA and implementation of FTA."[193] In 2008, the Peruvian embassy in the US hired Patton Boggs to assist on the same issue. The embassy paid the lobbying firm $150,000 for their efforts.[194] The contacts made during this period were with members of congress including Harry Reid, Jay Rockefeller, Charles Grassley, Mitch McConnell, Roy Blunt, Jerry Weller and Max Baucus.

Foreign governments also lobby regarding United States foreign policy. Morocco spent $2.8 million in 2010 alone, hiring LeClairRyan and Gabriel Co. to win Congressional support in its dispute over Western Saharan territory.[195] The Republic of Congo engaged several lobbying firms to help the country fight "vulture funds", private equity companies that acquire distressed sovereign debt for pennies on the dollar and bring law suits to recover as close to the face value of the debt as possible. The Congo government sought US legislation that would prohibit US courts from hearing these cases and bar US nationals from investing in the vulture firms.[196]

Foreign governments may also lobby to improve Congress's perception of a country's policies. According to ProPublica, Dubai spent a portion of its multi-million dollar lobbying budget to enhance the country's reputation with Congress (and the American public).[197]

Does it Pay? Foreign interests spend an estimated $60-$85 million annually lobbying in Washington. A logical question is: Does it pay? As with the return on investment of domestic lobbying, the answer is hard to determine. However, there is ample anecdotal and some analytical evidence that says "yes."

The following examples are representative of the anecdotal evidence. Following the Congressional outcry over Dubai Port World's acquisition of US port operators which was viewed as a threat to national security, the Dubai government retained the services of several US lobbying firms to improve the county's image in Congress. A year later, the Dubai Aerospace acquired US operators at airports without controversy.[198] Countries often lobby to secure military aid. The Japanese government lobbied Congress to continue funding the F-22 Raptor fighter jet with the goal of acquiring these aircrafts.[199] Turkey has been one of the most active lobbyists in Washington. A multiyear lobbying campaign to improve the image of Turkey on the Hill and prevent a resolution labeling the 1915 slaughter of Armenians as "genocide" is credited with providing collateral benefits when

> **Fun Fact**
> "The presence of an organized foreign lobby lowers tariffs in that industry by 6%."
> (Gawande et al 2004)

the Turkish government aggressively quelled demonstrations in 2013 and Congressional condemnation was largely absent.[200]

In their 2004 study "Foreign Lobbies and Trade Policies", Kishore Gawande, Pravin Krishna and Michael Robbins provide analytical evidence supporting the success of foreign lobbying, focusing on trade. They conclude that the presence of a foreign lobbying effort has almost equal impact in reducing trade barriers for imports as domestic company lobbying has on increasing barriers. [201] (Note that the data set examined is from 1978-1982 and the work has not been updated with more recent information.)

> **Fun Fact**
> A one standard deviation increase in lobbying reports is associated with a 15% increase in foreign aid.
> (Pevehouse Vabulas 2012)

A more recent study of the impact of foreign lobbying indicates a strong positive return on advocacy investment. In a 2012 paper, Jon Pevehouse and Felicity Vabulas answer the question: "Is US Assistance for Sale?"[202] Their analysis focuses on the relationship between the extent of foreign government lobbying and the amount of foreign aid the country receives. They hypothesize that lobbying by foreign governments provides congressional members with information that enables members to act in support of ethnic ties of constituents and/or enhance the member's reputation as a foreign policy expert. This argument builds on the Hall and Deardorff legislative subsidy model. Examining Foreign Agents Registration Act (FARA) filings over many years, they find a strong positive relationship between lobbying by foreign governments and the amount of foreign economic aid they receive. A one standard deviation increase in lobbying expenditures is associated with at 15 percent increase in aid.[203] The amount of lobbying effort, as measured by number of lobbying reports, yields similar results.

The Controversy. The idea that foreign aid and, by extension, foreign policy is for sale is disconcerting to many Americans. This concern is not new. Lobbying by foreigners has been steeped in controversy since the early years of the United States. In Federalist Paper #22, Alexander Hamilton writes: "One of the weak sides of republics ... is that they afford too easy an inlet to foreign corruption ... history furnishes us with so many mortifying examples of the prevalence of foreign corruption in republican governments."[204] More than two hundred years later, the same concerns exist. Newspaper and magazine articles with titles such as "Why Are We Still Sending Aid to Pakistan? Meet the Lobbyists Paid to Defend the Money" (The Blaze), "The Lobbyists Watching Egypt's Back: Tony Podesta helped Mubarak keep US aid flowing" (*Business Week*) and "How Foreign Governments Make Sure You Don't Know They're Lobbying You" (Buzzfeed) are emblematic.

The media has highlighted an array of specific concerns with lobbying by foreign interests, but there are credible explanations. A primary concern is that foreign governments can use lobbying to gain at the expense of the US citizenry. Trade is one area where this concern is centered: Critics say that foreign governments lobby Congress and the administration for trade advantages that harm US producers. Kishore Gawande and his coauthors offer this conceptual response: "*If* the policy outcome absent any involvement by foreigners is characterized by welfare-reducing trade barriers, lobbying by foreigners for reductions in such barriers may in fact shift trade policy in a direction that improves domestic consumer surplus (and possibly welfare.)".[205]

Critics are also concerned that foreign lobbying gives non-citizens/non-taxpayers a seat at the US policy table. Foreign representatives respond to the seat-at-the-table critique by arguing that the US exerts its political will with hard and soft power all over the world. Foreign lobbying is simply leveling the playing field.

Moreover, there is the argument that lobbying by foreign interests is unnecessary since that is the role of the foreign government's embassy. Embassies clearly serve a function in advocating for foreign interests. For example, embassy staff representing Mexico, El Salvador and other countries have advocated with members of Congress and the Administration about immigration reform. Representative Xavier Becerra (D-CA) defended his decision to meet with embassy personnel on immigration by saying that he is open to listening to anyone with good ideas.[206] Embassies are an important resource that foreign governments use to reach US policymakers; however, lobbying is often a more direct and sometimes a more politically-savvy means of communicating with policymakers as lobbyists may have a stronger network of contacts and better understand the policy making process.

Restrictions On Foreign Lobbying

Despite the negative consequences of foreign lobbying highlighted by Alexander Hamilton, the US did not regulate lobbying by foreign interests until 1938. The motivation for enacting restrictions was not commercial; rather, it was concern about Nazi propaganda. The legislative response was the Foreign Agents Registration Act. The purpose of the Act (as amended in 1942) is "to protect the national defense, internal security, and foreign relations of the United States by requiring public disclosure by persons engaging in propaganda activities and other activities for or on behalf of foreign governments, foreign political parties, and other foreign principals." The intention of the Act is to keep the government and its citizenry informed of the identity of foreign lobbyists so that they may understand and evaluate their influence."[207]

It is important to note that the Act does not censor speech by foreign interests. Rather, it seeks to ensure that such advocacy is clearly identified. This is accomplished through mandatory registration and disclosure.

The Act has been amended several times since its passage. Changes in the language of the Act were made in 1942 "to shield the U.S. Congress and the President from foreign-influenced grassroots lobbying shaping policy, legislation and lawmaking."[208] Responsibility for enforcing the Act was also shifted from the Department of State to the Department of Justice (DOJ). Perhaps the most important were the 1966 amendments, which changed the Act's focus from monitoring propaganda to regulating business and political lobbying by foreign companies and governments. Under the Act, an agent, anyone who works on behalf of a foreign principal (a foreign country's government, political party, individual or business), must register within 10 days of becoming an agent and undertaking activities related to lobbying that are listed in the Act. Registration statements are filed with the Counterespionage Section, National Security Division of the Justice Department.

Disclosures are required every six months. The disclosure requirements center on the registrant, their foreign principal, the activities they undertake and their finances. Agreements between foreign principals and their agents must be provided along with copies of advocacy materials. Exhibit 7-1 details the filing requirements. The Act imposes penalties for willfully failing to register and accurately report listed activities; a fine of not more than $10,000 or imprisonment of not more than five years.[209] An alien found guilty of willful violation of the stature can be deported. The level of information required and the criminal sanctions are a higher standard than those required by the LDA. The rationale for the greater burden is the concern that the interests of foreign governments may not align with those of the US citizenry.

Exhibit 7-1
Foreign Agents Registration Act
Disclosure Requirements

I. Registrant – name, address, nationality, organization, partners, ownership, employees and services

II. Foreign Principal – name and address

III. Activities – full description of actions

IV. Financial Information – receipts, disbursements, political contributions,

V. Informational Materials – budget, language, dissemination vehicles, target groups, actual materials

Source: Registration Statement, OMB NO. 1124-0001

After passage of the Lobbying Disclosure Act of 1995 (LDA), businesses, interest groups and individuals not working directly on behalf of foreign government or a political party were allowed to register under LDA. LDA registration and disclosure is less burdensome.

FARA set the groundwork for the foreign and domestics lobbying regulations in place today. A variety of concerns with its effectiveness remain despite the numerous amendments to the original act. These are detailed below.

Concern #1: Transparency. First is the lack of transparency of foreign lobbying activity owing to the difficulty of sorting and analyzing the filings. Registrant forms, paper or digital, are uploaded to the DOJ's FARA database. The Quick Search function provides access to active and terminated registrants and foreign principals. The Document Search feature provides access to all document types from registration and supplemental statements to dissemination reports. These are searchable by registrant name or number. While the raw materials are available, there is no handy means for sorting or information analysis. Moreover, privacy issues limit the Internet access to some filings. The Sunlight Foundation and ProPublica created a searchable database of FARA filings called the Foreign Lobbying Influence Tracker to facilitate information analysis; however, there is a significant delay in making the data available.

Concern #2: Outside US Contacts. A second concern is that only contacts made in the US are covered by FARA. The law does not cover lobbying with US officials abroad. Members of Congress and the Administration routinely travel abroad to learn firsthand about foreign issues in other countries. During these visits foreign government officials and/or their agents are able to petition the US officials and these activities are not covered by FARA.

Concern #3: Bypass. A frequent critique is that the registration and disclosure provisions of FARA can be easily circumvented. United States citizens advocating on behalf of the interests of a foreign government, but not engaged by the foreign country, can lobby outside of FARA. The most common form of bypass is advocacy undertaken by American grassroots NGOs.

The American Israel Public Affairs Committee (AIPAC) is widely regarded as a very powerful voice in Washington for the interests of the State of Israel. AIPAC is organized and funded by 100,000 Americans who seek "to strengthen, protect and promote the U.S.-Israel relationship in ways that enhance the security of Israel and the United States" by building relationships with their members of congress and educating decision makers "about the bonds that unite the United States and Israel and how it is in America's best interest to help ensure that the

Jewish state is safe, strong and secure." AIPAC's work is credited for the sizable US aid provided to Israel. AIPAC is not registered under FARA as it is an American non-profit interest group and does not directly represent or receive funds from the government of Israel. The organization does register and disclose its lobbying activities under the LDA. Some argue the tie between AIPAC and Israel is so strong that the organization really does represent the interest of the Israeli government and therefore should register under FARA.

AIPAC is one of many such advocacy groups that seek to influence US foreign policy. Another example is the United States India Political Action Committee (USIPAC). This group is credited with leveraging its domestic resources to secure the U.S.-Indian agreement to provide nuclear fuel to India. The group actively lobbied by framing "the issue in a way that emphasized the positive

> ### Food For Thought
> Should organizations such as USIPAC and AIPAC be required to register under FARA rather than LDA?

linkages to other goals" such as climate change and fighting terrorism.[210] These efforts overcame early opposition to the measure and helped to secure its passage. In the case of USIPAC, the Indian government has acknowledged the importance of the organization's lobbying work, which "constitutes an invaluable asset in strengthening India's relationship with the world's only superpower."[211] Comments like these lead some critics to argue that USIPAC should register under FARA.

Concern #4: "Foreign" Campaign Contributions. Federal election laws prohibit foreign nationals from contributing to US elections. However, some have expressed concern over the possibility of lobbyists for foreign actors donating personally to election campaigns of Congressional targets and/or presidential candidates. The Center for Investigative Reporting and ABCNews.com examined the links between the presidential candidates and lobbyists for foreign interests during the 2008 election. They found that key fundraisers for candidate Hillary Clinton were also active lobbyists for foreign governments including Dubai, Turkey, Taiwan and Ethiopia. John McCain campaign financiers represented Saudi Arabia, Peru, Dubai and Columbia. In the words of the Executive Director of the Center for Responsive Politics, foreign governments seek lobbyists with strong ties to presidential candidates because "you always want someone who is well-connected, someone who is going to be greeted with open arms" when you have an issue needing attention.[212] Professor James Thurber of American University captures the importance of transparency when it comes to lobbyist fundraisers' ties to election campaigns: "[scrutiny is] even more critical because it has such an impact on relations between nations... the fundraiser is certainly going to be welcome in the White House, more so than people they don't know, to pitch for a specific interest."[213]

Concern #5: Lack of Enforcement. FARA was enacted prior to World War II to deter the dissemination of propaganda by requiring the registration and disclosure of such activities. The Department of Justice (DOJ) was tasked with enforcing compliance with the Act. Prior to and during the War, the Act was used to successfully prosecute 23 criminal cases.[214] In the intervening 50 years, only 3 indictments were handed down for FARA violations, none were successfully prosecuted.

Compliance with the Act has been largely "self-policed, such that it requires the lobbyists themselves to take the initiative to learn which types of activities necessitate disclosures and when disclosures must be filed."[215] DOJ is expected to ensure those who need to register and disclose do so and that the filings are correct and comprehensive. The Government Accounting Office (GAO) examined the robustness of FARA enforcement several times. In 1974, in response to questions about the impact of the 1966 amendments, the GAO reported that 67 percent of required statements and exhibits were not filed on time and 70 percent of supplemental statements were incomplete. Based on their analysis, the GAO concluded: "Late, incomplete or uninformative registration materials does not meet the full and adequate public disclosure requirements of the act and related regulations."[216] The GAO recommended that the Attorney General establish a system to ensure timely and complete filings. The GAO returned to the issue of FARA enforcement in 2008. The findings showed little change since the 1974 assessment. DOJ attributed its inaction to lack of resources and uncertainty about the legal authority of the agency to inspect records of potential registrants. While GAO suggested Congress grant this authority, no action on the matter has been forthcoming.

> **Notable Quote**
> But nobody wants to be a foreign agent. With its sinister ring, draconian enforcement requirements...
> -Buzzfeed
> (Rosie Gray 2013)

Current State of Foreign Advocacy

The current size and scale of lobbying by foreign governments is not known with certainty, owing to the lack of a comprehensive and accessible database noted above. Sunlight Foundation gathered and analyzed FARA disclosure documents in 2007-2010 which gives a more in-depth picture of foreign lobbying. There's no reason to think it's dramatically different today. Based on the data from 2009, more than 300 foreign entities lobbied the federal government, making more than 17,000 contacts with congressional officials including 2,900 meetings. They spent roughly $85 million in 2008 and $60 million in 2009.[217] The decline may well be a post-election year retreat.

The Spenders. The countries that were most active during this period were United Arab Emirates, the Cayman Islands, United Kingdom, Japan, Iraq, Turkey and Morocco. The expenditures of these countries are shown in Exhibit 7-2. Several, such as Turkey and Morocco, are big spenders in both years. The United Arab Emirates (UAE), mainly Dubai, paid lobbyists more than $10 million in 2008 in response to concerns relating to its image in the US. For example, Senator Charles Schumer (D-NY) stated that Dubai "has a very strong nexus with terrorism" during the debate over Dubai's port operations acquisitions in the US. [218] In response, Dubai hired three prominent lobbying and communications firms in Washington to improve the country's image.

Another active lobbyist was the Cayman Islands, which retained lobbying assistance to keep abreast of legislative activities that could impact the ability of United States individuals and companies to do business on the Islands. In one FARA filing, the lobbyist reported it would "correct any misinformation or misconceptions" about the Cayman Islands.[219] The country's concern stems from the attractive tax environment it offers. The Republic of Congo was a sizable lobbyer in 2009. The focus of their advocacy was on proposed legislation to protect debtor nations from "vulture funds," as described earlier. Lobbying is also used to facilitate inter-governmental meetings and relationship building. The Democratic Party of Albania spent $120,000 in 2009 with for-hire lobbying firm BKSH & Associates to arrange for meetings for the Albanian Prime Minister and/or the Albanian Parliament Speaker with Nancy Pelosi, Dan Burton, Lindsey Graham, and John McCain among others.[220] The forgoing examples are illustrative of the range of lobbying goals of foreign governments.

Exhibit 7-2
Top Foreign Principals
Lobbying the Federal Government
(millions of dollars)

Principal	2008	Principal	2009
United Arab Emirates	$10.9	Cayman Islands	$7.9
United Kingdom	6.1	United Arab Emirates	5.4
Japan	4.2	Republic of Congo	3.9
Iraq	3.7	Morocco	3.1
Turkey	3.5	Bahamas	2.6
Morocco	3.3	Brazil	2.5
Saudi Arabia	3.3	Serbia	2.2
South Korea	2.9	Turkey	1.7
Netherlands	2.7	Vanuatu	1.6

Source: Sunlight Foundation, Anupama Narayanswamy and Luke Rosiak and ProPublica, Jennifer LaFleur, 8/18/2009 and 12/2/2010

The Lobbyees. The targets of the lobbying are members of Congress especially those on the Senate Foreign Relations Committee and the House Foreign Affairs Committee as well as the Congressional leadership. Robert Wexler (D-FL) had 173 contacts in 2008. Roy Blunt (R-MO) and Dan Burton (R-IN) had 105 and 100 contacts respectively. That year Nancy Pelosi (D-CA) and John Boehner (R-OH) each had more than 80 contacts. Of note, both sides of the political aisle are lobbied intensively.

The Lobbyers. The lobbying is done by hundreds of firms. The major K Street firms participate in advocacy for foreign entities include Akin Gump, APCO Worldwide, Barbour, Griffith & Rogers, Cassidy & Associates, DLA piper, Gephardt Group, among others. There are also scores of niche lobbying firms representing foreign governments. A number of registrants are not formal lobbying firms, rather they are entities that advocate with an eye toward building the foreign country's image in the US rather than directly impacting public policy. Examples include the Cayman Islands and Bermuda departments of tourism, and VisitSweden.

The Anatomy of a Foreign Lobbying Campaign. Perhaps the best way to paint the picture of lobbying by foreign interests is to profile a year of lobbying by a foreign government. Panama actively sought a free trade agreement with the US in the mid-2000s. An agreement was reached in 2006 but required ratification in both Panama and the US. Panama approved the pact in 2007. Beginning in 2007, the Panamanian government launched a multi-year lobbying campaign in Washington for US approval of the agreement. Ratification was especially controversial, as the newly elected President of the National Assembly had been indicted by a US grand jury for murder. Additional concerns surrounded allegations that Panama served as a safe haven for tax evaders. Finally, there were general concerns that the agreement would result in the loss of US jobs.

Between 2007 and 2010, the Republic of Panama, The Ministry of Foreign Relations of Panama and the Embassy of Panama actively lobbied in Washington. Hundreds of contacts were made with US officials by eight lobbying firms. The vast majority was with members of Congress or their staff members in support of the free trade agreement. The $1.8 million spent for these efforts paid off; the US ratified the agreement in October 2011.

Outlook For Foreign Lobbying

The desire of foreign entities to influence US policymakers will continue. If anything, globalization will increase

> **Notable Quote**
> "If they want to take foreign clients, they must be willing to claim them."
> - Sen. Claire McCaskill
> (New York Times, 6/12/2008)

lobbying activity. Based on the number of countries and the investment they make in lobbying in Washington, foreign interests must believe they earn an attractive return on their lobbying investment. While individual country efforts will wax and wane based on specific issues at any point in time (e.g. trade agreements, need for reputational enhancement, emergency aid), the law of large numbers ensures that every year there will be a number of countries actively lobbying Congress and the Administration.

Do not expect any change in the core regulatory framework for foreign lobbying. FARA will continue to be the law of the land for lobbying by foreign governments; LDA will continue to be available for foreign businesses. Notwithstanding the numerous concerns about the effectiveness of FARA, Congressional action to enhance the measure is unlikely. Representative Marcy Kaptur (D-OH) introduced legislation in 2013 titled Ethics in the Foreign Lobbying Act of 2013 to prohibit campaign contributions from political action committees by foreign-owned corporations; the bill is unlikely to be reported out of committee. [221] One change that can be anticipated is more active enforcement of FARA by the DOJ. In the past several years, the Department increased its proactive audit of firm filings and has been "…more diligent into looking for firms that should have filed but haven't."[222] In response, reports that were late have been filed and supplementary information has been forthcoming. Given the stiff penalties for failure to register and disclose, increased DOJ action might be the most effective means of Americans knowing which foreign governments are lobbying their own.

Foreign Lobbying Fast Facts

- Foreign interests (governments, political parties, businesses, NGOs and individuals) actively lobby in Washington.
- They lobby on the full spectrum of issues from trade to aid to foreign policy. Many also lobby to enhance their reputation among US policymakers.
- Annually foreign interests spend tens of millions of dollars lobbying and make thousands of contacts with Congress and the Administration.
- Based on the consistency of lobbying efforts and both anecdotal and analytic evidence, their lobbying efforts pay off.
- Lobbying by foreigners has long been controversial. The controversy centers on the risk that foreign interests gain at the expense of US citizens; the belief that non-taxpayers/voters should not have a seat at the policy table, and the idea that lobbying is a duplication of embassy activities and therefore not necessary.
- Foreign lobbying is regulated via registration and disclosure; the underlying philosophy is transparency rather than suppression.
- The Foreign Agents Registration Act (FARA) empowers the Department of Justice to enforce registration and disclosure with criminal sanctions.
- FARA has been criticized for lack of transparency, ease of bypass and inadequate enforcement.
- There is little appetite to change FARA although the DOJ has increased its enforcement.
- Foreign interests will continue to lobby Washington and, if anything, activity will likely increase due to globalization.

Learning by Doing

Foreign governments have a strong interest in the extent of fracking in the US. Major gas importing countries are eager for the US to continue its drilling activities and want the US to export its gas as this will increase global supply and reduce world prices. In contrast, gas-exporting countries seek to limit the amount of US gas and certainly desire to prevent the gas from flowing offshore. Pick a country on either side of the issue and develop a lobbying campaign for them. Specifically, address: (1) the policy actions desired; (2) how to advocate for that outcome; (3) who will lobby for the effort; and (4) how the lobbying will be done to meet the spirit and letter of FARA.

Chapter 7 Bibliography

"2062 Foreign Agents Registration Act Enforcement." *United States Attorneys' Manual*, 1997. http://www.justice.gov/usao/eousa/foia_reading_room/usam/title9/crm02062.htm.

Atieh, Jahad. "Foreign Agents: Updating FRA to Protect American Democracy." *University of Pennsylvania, Journal of International Law* 31, no. 4 (2010).

Bogardus, Kevin. "Justice amps up enforcement of law on foreign advocacy." *The Hill*, October 28, 2011. http://thehill.com/business-a-lobbying/190379-officials-turn-up-enforcement-of-foreign-lobby-law.

Evans, Will, and Avni Patel. "Lobbyists for Foreign Governments Raise Money, Get Clinton, McCain Meetings." *ABC News*, February 1, 2008. http://abcnews.go.com/Blotter/story?id=4228113&page=1.

Fang, Lee. "Demonstrations Test Turkey's Lobbying Clout in Washington." *The Nation*. June 5, 2013. http://www.thenation.com/blog/174672/demonstrations-test-turkeys-lobbying-clout-washington.

"FARA - Enforcement." *The United States Department of Justice*. Accessed August 6, 2014. http://www.fara.gov/enforcement.html.

"Foreign Assistance Fast Facts: FY2012." *U.S. Overseas Loans and Grants: USAID*. Accessed August 3, 2014. http://gbk.eads.usaidallnet.gov/data/fast-facts.html.

"Foreign Influence Explorer, Client Profile: Country of Peru." *Sunlight Foundation*. Accessed August 3, 2014. http://foreign.influenceexplorer.com/client-profile/129990.

"Foreign Influence Explorer, Client Profile: Democratic Party of Albania." *Sunlight Foundation*. Accessed August 6, 2014. http://foreign.influenceexplorer.com.

"Foreign Influence Explorer: Government of the Kingdom of Morocco." *Sunlight Foundation*. Accessed August 3, 2014. http://foreign.influenceexplorer.com/client-profile/129964.

Gawande, Kishore, Pravin Krishna, and Michael J. Robbins. *Foreign Lobbies and US Trade Policy*. Working Paper. National Bureau of Economic Research, January 2004. http://www.nber.org/papers/w10205.

Hamilton, Alexander. "The Federalist Papers: No. 22." *The Avalon Project*, December 14, 1787. http://avalon.law.yale.edu/18th_century/fed22.asp.

Helfrich, Jesse. "Foreign governments lobbying hard in favor of immigration reform." *The Hill*, February 7, 2013. http://thehill.com/policy/international/281605-foreign-governments-lobby-hard-in-favor-of-immigration-reform.

"Justice and Law Enforcement: Effectiveness of the Foreign Agents Registration Act of 1938, as Amended, and Its Administration by the Department of Justice," March 13, 1974. http://www.gao.gov/products/B-177551.

Narayanswamy, Anupama, Luke Rosiak, and Jennifer LaFleur. "Adding It up: The Top Players in Foreign Agent Lobbying." *Sunlight Foundation*, August 18, 2009.

http://sunlightfoundation.com/blog/2009/08/18/adding-it-top-players-foreign-agent-lobbying/.

Narayanswamy, Anu. "International Influence: Agents of Foreign Clients Report Thousands of Lobbying Contacts, Millions in Fees." *Sunlight Foundation*, December 2, 2010. http://sunlightfoundation.com/blog/2010/12/02/top-players-2009/.

"Notes on 22 U.S.C. § 611 : US Code - Notes." *Findlaw*. Accessed August 6, 2014. http://codes.lp.findlaw.com/uscode/22/11/II/611/notes.

"Sidley Austin Lobbying for Cayman Islands." *The Blog of LegalTimes*, March 25, 2010. http://legaltimes.typepad.com/blt/2010/05/sidley-austin-lobbying-for-cayman-islands.html.

Vabulas, Felicity, and Jon Pevehouse. *The Role of Informational Lobbying in US Foreign Aid: Is US Assistance for Sale?* Charlottesville, VA: International Political Economy Society Conference, November 2012. https://ncgg.princeton.edu/IPES/2012/papers/S300_rm1.pdf.

Chapter 8: Intergovernmental Lobbying

The lobbying explored thus far is largely done by private groups – corporations, associations, NGOs, individual citizens. Governmental units also lobby other governmental organizations. The terms "public lobbying" or "intergovernmental lobbying" refer to these efforts. There are three primary intergovernmental lobbying efforts. The largest is state and local governments lobbying the federal government. The second is local governments lobbying their own state legislators and executives. The third is lobbying of the federal government conducted by entities without direct representation such as Puerto Rico and the Virgin Islands.

Recalling the general definition of lobbying as contact with government officials to influence policymaking; there is a variety of reasons why governments lobby other governments. The first mirrors a primary reason for private lobbying: State and local governments seek to gain a part of federal government funding. With the growth of federal earmarks in the 1980s and 1990s, state and local governments have use used lobbying to increase their capture of federal funds. For example, Galena, a small Alaskan town of 470 people, spent $60,000 ($127.00 per capita) to lobby the federal government for funds to upgrade its infrastructure after the Air Force departed the city. The $1.5 million in capital for repairing utilities from Washington saved the city from financial failure. In the words of the city manager, "Without the lobbying, the city would have been unincorporated."[223]

State and local governments also lobby other government organizations to influence policy that will impact how they spend their own money. For example, the growing influence of the federal government during the 1970s and 1980s lead to a number of federally-mandated programs that state governments were required to adopt. Many such as the Clean Air Act and Americans with Disabilities Act were underfunded or unfunded: States were required to undertake the programs but federal funds were not provided to cover the full costs of the program. Frustration with this federal control led to the Unfunded Mandates Reform Act of 1995, which aimed to limit such programs.

Nevertheless, underfunded programs continue. In 2001, the No Child Left Behind Act passed, which required states that accept federal money for schools fund programs to meet the threshold requirements of the act. Today, one of the largest federal mandates is Medicaid, providing healthcare for the poor. The program is required by the federal government, but funding from Washington only covers about half the cost. State and local government must fund the rest themselves. State governments attempt to impact such mandates through lobbying. Nevada, for example, combined a for-hire lobbying firm with the state's Senate Delegation to "successfully oppose an amendment that would have cost the state $75 million in federal Medicaid revenue."[224]

A final explanation is the lack of direct representation. Puerto Rico and the Virgin Islands actively lobby in Washington in lieu of having voting power. Puerto Rico spent $1.5 million in 2013, more than any individual state. Puerto Rico has been a consistent lobbyer. Since 1998, the Commonwealth spent $40 million, although the spending level has been declining. The primary and continual focus of their lobbying has been on taxes, economic development and crime/law enforcement. They have also advocated about transportation, immigration and agricultural policy but on an episodic basis. Puerto Rico primarily lobbies Congressional members, but also lobbies the Department of Transportation, the Coast Guard, Customs Service and Homeland Security. In 2013 Puerto Rico relied on more than 20 lobbyists including those from Miller & Chevalier, Podesta Group, Prime Policy Group and Smith, Dawson & Andrews. [225]

The US Virgin Islands is also an active lobbyist of the federal government. While not at the scale of Puerto Rico, the Virgin Islands consistently spent $600,000 to $1 million annually on federal lobbying over the past 10 years. Taxes, immigration and transportation are the focal issues for the Virgin Islands. As with Puerto Rico, they focus their lobbying efforts on Congress. Lobbyists firms hired by the Virgin Islands include Callwood Associates and Winston & Strawn. [226]

States Lobbying the Federal Government

State governments and their affiliates spent $2.8 million in 2012 lobbying the federal government. This expenditure represented a decline from 2011, continuing a downward trend that began in 2005 when spending exceeded $10 million. Prior to that time, spending by state governments increased at a strong and steady clip as shown in Exhibit 8-1. (This contrasts with overall lobbying spending which continued to increase until 2010 and has since plateaued.) The long period of increasing lobbying expenditures can be attributed largely to the growing awareness of the ability of lobbyists to successfully place earmarks into legislation. During this period, the number of intergovernmental lobbying clients increased and the expenditures of those already lobbying also grew. The post-2005 decline has not been rigorously analyzed but might be ascribed to (1) the completion of some major policy actions such as the military base closure process (2) intransigence in Congress and (3) the federal ban on earmarks.

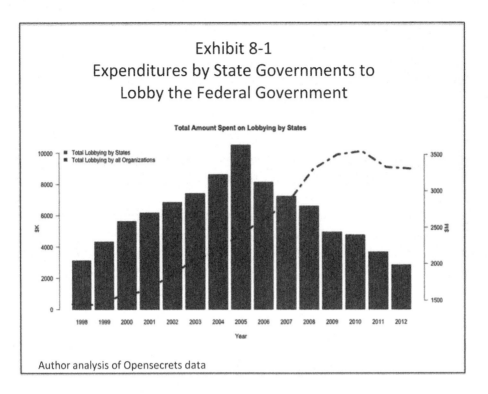

Exhibit 8-1
Expenditures by State Governments to
Lobby the Federal Government

Total Amount Spent on Lobbying by States

Author analysis of Opensecrets data

The States That Lobby. Almost all of the 50 states engaged in lobbying the federal government in at least one year during the 1998-2012 period. However, there is a strong concentration in spending among a select few. Exhibit 8-2 shows the states that do most of the lobbying and their level of expenditures. The lobbying states include those that are politically liberal and conservative, large and small, urban and rural. They are also geographically dispersed – from East Coast to Midwest to West Coast. Pennsylvania, which spent almost $18 million between 1998 and 2013, was the largest lobbyist over that time period. New York, Nevada and Hawaii each spent more than $5 million lobbying. At the other end of the spectrum, 11 states including Massachusetts, South Dakota, Michigan and Tennessee each spent less than $250,000 over the past 16 years. Between these extremes, we find 30 states that are moderate spenders, at $500,000 to $1.5 million.

> **Fun Fact**
> 48 of 50 states lobbied in at least one year from 1998-2013
> (OpenSecrets)

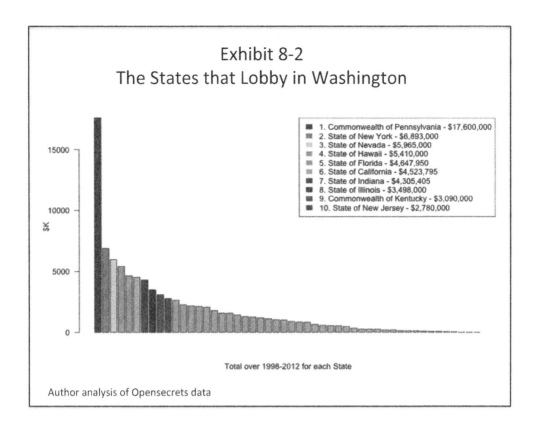

Exhibit 8-2
The States that Lobby in Washington

1. Commonwealth of Pennsylvania - $17,600,000
2. State of New York - $6,893,000
3. State of Nevada - $5,965,000
4. State of Hawaii - $5,410,000
5. State of Florida - $4,647,950
6. State of California - $4,523,795
7. State of Indiana - $4,305,405
8. State of Illinois - $3,498,000
9. Commonwealth of Kentucky - $3,090,000
10. State of New Jersey - $2,780,000

Total over 1998-2012 for each State

Author analysis of Opensecrets data

The states that spent the most money lobbying between 1998 and 2013 were also persistent advocates over that time period. Seven of the top spenders lobbied in each of the 16 years examined. The remaining three states lobbied in at least 11 of the 16 years. The states that spent the least on lobbying generally lobbied in only two or three of the past 16 years. The moderate spenders (the majority of states) typically lobbied in half of the years. This lobbying pattern is similar to that of foreign governments lobbying in the US.

State Lobbying: The Issues States lobby on a wide array of issues. Four issues dominate the lobbying efforts of states in Washington – budget and appropriations, transportation, defense spending and education. A total of 31 states engaged in lobbying on issues related to the federal budget and appropriations between 1998 and 2013, collectively spending $20 million of the $93 million states spent on lobbying. Almost the same amount of money was spent by a comparable number of states lobbying on transportation. Exhibit 8-3 illustrates that while budget and appropriations is a consistent focus for lobbying, transportation is more sporadic. Transportation spending rose dramatically from 1998 to 2005 and then fell. This pattern is consistent with the transportation appropriations process and the passage of a major transportation spending bill in 2005.[227] The exhibit also shows the rapid buildup and equally precipitous decline of lobbying on defense. Defense lobbying was largely driven by the military base closures effort that the

Pentagon undertook that culminated in a 2005 report by the Defense Base Closure and Realignment Commission.[228] The remaining spending is highly diffused across more than a dozen issue areas. The activity appears directly linked to specific context/issues faced by individual states. For example, Hawaii spent $3 million lobbying on issues related to Native Americans.

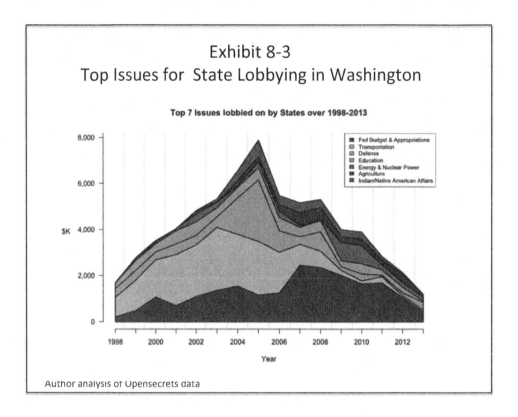

Exhibit 8-3
Top Issues for State Lobbying in Washington

Top 7 Issues lobbied on by States over 1998-2013

Author analysis of Opensecrets data

Lobbying Targets. As with business lobbying, most of the state lobbying contacts are with members of Congress. However, states also actively lobby the White House and executive branch departments such as the Departments of Transportation and Defense.

Role of For-Hire Lobbyists. Many states have a Washington office to advocate on behalf of the state and support their Congressional delegation. While some of the office employees are registered lobbyists, states rely extensively on for-hire lobbying firms. States spent more than $90 million with for-hire lobbyists between 1998 and 2013. While a handful of larger firms work for multiple states; lobbying services are also provided by a wide array of smaller firms focused on a single state. The firms that support Pennsylvania's federal lobbying efforts are typical of states that actively lobby. (Exhibit 8-4) Pennsylvania relies on between two and eleven lobbyists each year and there is often a pattern of persistence. In other words, the same firms work for the state for several years at a time.

Exhibit 8-4
Pennsylvania's Lobbyists

Pennsylvania
Sum of Amount (in thousands)

Lobbying firm	1998	1999	2000	2001	2002	2003	2004	2005	2006	2007	2008	2009	2010	2011	2012	2013	Grand Total
American Continental Group	40	80	80	80	80	180	200	240	340	680	600	120	120				2,840
Blank Rome LLP								325	640	650	730	720	720				3,785
Pennsylvania Higher Educ Assistance Agcy											220	430	440	440	440	220	2,190
Borski Assoc						120	240	240	240	360	350	240	240				2,030
Miller, Scott E		100	100	220	280	280	280	20		100							1,540
Baker, Donelson et al	120	170	160	160	140	160	180	120	160								1,390
Peyser Assoc						650	413	263									1,325
Stevens & Lee		110						250	270	260	100						990
LG Strategies														180	240	120	540
Capitol Assoc	50	80	40	40	40	40	40	40	40	20							430
B&D Sagamore						80	80	140									300
Hill Solutions				40	40	40	40	20									240
B&D Consulting									120	10							130
Fleishman-Hillard Inc				90													90
Buchanan, Ingersoll & Rooney							80										80
Renberg Strategies		20															20
Wolf, Block et al						20											20

Author analysis of Opensecrets data

Explaining State Lobbying Patterns. What explains why some states are active lobbyists and others are not? On the surface, all states should have similar motivations for lobbying – increase their share of largess directly though discretionary funds and indirectly via favorable policies. The determinative characteristics that explain lobbying by the private sector (comparatively large organizations, facing regulation, and impacted by federal policy[229]) do not have a direct analog for intergovernmental lobbying.

Rather, state level lobbying is largely ad hoc and issue driven. When the base closure issue became salient, states lobbied to maintain their military installations. When a transportation funding bill is in debate, states become more active lobbyists. While the forgoing issues periodically arise, the majority of issues lobbied by states are of the moment. For example, when Massachusetts was working with one of its Native American tribes on a gaming compact, the state engaged a for-hire lobbyist to help with the legal and political issues associated with the arrangement.

The issue orientation explains when and why most lobbying takes place; however, it does not explain why a handful of states lobby consistently over many years. On the surface, there is no clear reason why Pennsylvania, California, Nevada and Arizona would lobby each year of the past 16, and Massachusetts, Mississippi, Virginia and Ohio would not. An examination of the state level lobbying finds no correlation between state lobbying and demographics, political ideology, legislative sophistication, economic base, reliance on federal funds and Congressional power.[230] Further research is needed to explain the phenomenon of why some states lobby on a more regular basis than others.

One hypothesis for the imbalance is that non-lobbying states may use substitutes for influencing public policy. For example, a state in which the Congressional delegation includes ranking members of key committees might not see the need to lobby. State Chambers of Commerce are another means of lobbying a state's interests without directly engaging in intergovernmental lobbying. Large corporations with extensive federal lobbying activity might be another substitute.

State Lobbying "Return on Investment." The rationale for lobbying is a positive return on investment. Fagan, Perez and Tighe assess the return on investment by examining the aggregate lobbying dollars spent with federal funds flowing to the states. They find no statistically meaningful relationship. Moreover, the cohort of states that persistently lobby does no better in terms of federal dollars received. A possible explanation is the gains from lobbying are large compared to the money spent on advocacy yielding an attractive ROI but the gains are small in terms of overall federal funds and therefore do not have a measurable impact. Another is that lobbyists are great at sales as well as advocacy. Once hired, lobbyists are successful in convincing the state that persistence in lobbying pays off when that might not be the case. Rigorous analysis must be done to confirm or refute these suppositions.

Other Intergovernmental Lobbying

Individual counties, cities and towns also directly lobby the federal government. However, of the 30,000+ US counties, cities and towns, only a handful engages in federal lobbying. For example, between 1998 and 2008, 498 cities across 45 states lobbied.[231] The number of localities lobbying and their expenditures have been on the rise

> **Fun Fact**
> Texans pay their members of Congress salaries of $6 million annually and then another $2 million to lobbyists.
> (Texas Tribune, Nov. 11, 2010)

since the 1980s. One driver of this growth is the reduction in state aid flowing to municipalities and the subsequent search for federal funds to make up the difference. In the words of Randy Neugebauer, a member of Congress from

Texas, "The reality of the situation is that federal monies are currently available to cities [that] choose to utilize them."[232] The City Manager of Abilene, Texas summarizes the city's decision to spend hundreds of thousands of dollars this way: "Even though cites are creatures of the state, we get very little funding from the state for anything we do;" it is the lobbyists in Washington who are able to secure needed funding.[233] Another driving force is tough economic times. Researchers at Rice University found that "local economic distress is associated with an increased likelihood that a city will choose to retain a lobbyist in Washington, in an apparently counter-cyclical attempt to influence national policy."[234]

The question of whether these communities achieve an attractive return on investment has been answered as a qualified "yes," based on anecdotal evidence. Galena, Alaska is one example. The director of government relations in the City of Austin, Texas explains lobbying in Washington, saying: "We have gotten a lot of federal transportation

> ### Food for Thought
> Should your city lobby the federal government for funding to support roads, water, etc.?

dollars. We've gotten a lot of money to help wastewater projects. The airport was built essentially with federal dollars."[235] Twin Cities, Idaho invested $60,000 in lobbying and attributes $1.6 million in federal funds for a wastewater treatment plant and $100,000 for digitizing microfiche and historical records to the city's lobbying efforts.[236] The evidence is not universally positive. Plaquemines Parish, Louisiana has been an active lobbyist since Hurricane Katrina and the Deepwater Horizon oil spill but a city council member reported, "I don't see any strong results."[237]

The forgoing examples are of state and local governments lobbying at the federal level. Similar processes take place in each state as local governments seek to influence state actions. The size and scale of lobbying at the state level is

> ### Fun Fact
> Minnesota municipalities spent $7.8 million lobbying their own state.
> (Star Tribune, July 17, 2013)

significantly lower than in Washington but it is still material.

Intergovernmental Lobbying Strategies
Public lobbying by state and local governments takes place in a more transparent environment than private lobbying. State and local governments often require that decisions take place in open meetings and with the input of the public. The result is that lobbying strategies are more transparent. Moreover, the approach is often subject to public comment that can alter lobbying strategies and delay their implementation. A positive aspect of citizen

involvement in public lobbying is that it may make grassroots mobilization to support a lobbying effort easier to accomplish.

The toolkit for lobbying by state and local lobbyists is similar to that used by private lobbyists with one critical exception. Public lobbyists are generally prohibited from making campaign contributions to elected officials. Thus, campaign financing based access and influence is not available for public lobbyists. As a result, public lobbyists gain access largely through a strong network of contacts and a reputation for outstanding knowledge of the issues and excellent packaging and communications skills. These lobbyists also leverage the legitimacy afforded to governmental entities.

Intergovernmental Lobbying Bottom-line

Governments lobby other governments for the same reasons private lobbying takes place, they seek to obtain funds and/or policies that add value for their constituents. There is powerful anecdotal evidence of success of intergovernmental lobbying but they are just examples. Rigorous analytical evidence explaining why some states and local governments lobby and others do not is yet to be undertaken. The same is true for proof that there is a strong return on investment for intergovernmental lobbying.

Intergovernmental Insights

- Some government bodies lobby other government organizations for public gain – more funding, favorable policies, etc.
- Puerto Rico and the US Virgin Islands actively lobby Washington as a substitute for direct representation.
- 48 of 50 states have lobbied the federal government in at least one of the past 16 years; only a handful have lobbied consistently over this period.
- Appropriations, transportation and defense are the most frequently lobbied policy areas.
- Lobbying expenditures peaked in 2005 and have been declining since; the level is now similar to that in 1998.
- Neither demographics, political ideology, legislative professionalism, economic activity, nor reliance on federal funds correlate with states' lobbying activity and/or spending.
- Lobbying by states appears tied to issues and lobbyists are used for distinctive expertise on such issues.
- Evidence of an attractive return on investment for intergovernmental lobbying is mixed. There is some anecdotal evidence, especially for municipalities. However, a more rigorous analytical analysis is needed.
- Localities also actively lobby state governments, but not to the extent that states lobby the federal government.
- Intergovernmental lobbying strategies are similar to those used by business and NGO interests; although intergovernmental activities are often more transparent.
- Intergovernmental lobbying does lack one of the key tools of private lobbying – campaign funding.

Learning by Doing

State governments have lined up in support of and against fracking. Representatives of both camps are interested in the role of the federal government in regulating fracking. For example, does the Clean Water Act impact the fracking process? Should the EPA regulate the chemicals used in the fracking process? Are the greenhouse gasses that are emitted during fracking covered by the Clean Air Act?

Take on the role of a governor/government affairs office of a pro- or anti-fracking state and write an Op-ed for the *Washington Post* articulating why the federal government should support your position.

Chapter 8 Bibliography

"Defense Base Closure and Realignment Commission," 2005. www.brac.gov.

Hallman, Tristan. "Cities, Counties Spend Millions to Lobby in D.C." Texas Tribune, November 11, 2010.

"Lobbying Database." OpenSecrets.org Center for Responsive Politics, n.d. https://www.opensecrets.org/lobby/.

"Lobbying Industry: Transportation." *OpenSecrets.org Center for Responsive Politics.* Accessed August 6, 2014. https://www.opensecrets.org/lobby/background.php?id=M&year=2013.

The Lobbying Manual, William Luneburg and Thomas Susman, ABA, 3rd Edition, p.329

Loftis, Matt, and Jaclyn J. Kettler. "Lobbying from inside the System: Why Local Governments Pay for Representation," *Rice University.* August 14, 2013.

Newkirk, Zachary. "Tiny Towns Spend Big Bucks on Lobbyists to Reap Federal Government Riches." *OpenSecrets Blog*, May 4, 2011. https://www.opensecrets.org/news/2011/05/tiny-towns-spend-big-on-lobbyists-to-reap-federal-government-riches/.

Nixon, Ron. "In Post-Earmark Era, Small Cites Step Up Lobbying to Fight for Federal Funds." *The New York Times.* February 2, 2012.

Regan v. Taxation With Representation, 461 U.S. 540 (U.S. Supreme Court 1983).

Whaley, Sean. "Nevada Tops List On Federal Lobbyist Spending, Near Bottom On Returns," July 20, 2010. http://www.nevadanewsbureau.com/2010/07/20/nevada-tops-list-on-federal-lobbyist-spending-near-bottom-on-returns/.

Chapter 9: Lobbying by Charitable Organizations

More than one million charitable organizations operate in the United States. These organizations, which include religious, educational, healthcare and social actions groups, provide a valuable service to civil society. In exchange for this service that increases social welfare, the government grants them tax-exempt status. Funds donated to these groups are tax deductible for the donor and the charitable organization does not pay taxes on the receipts. Such organizations are known by the section of the tax code that covers them, "501(c) 3".

Many of these groups are involved in advocacy work, lobbying policymakers on behalf of their constituents. However, charitable organizations face special limitations regarding lobbying. In exchange for tax-exempt status, essentially a subsidy from the government, these organizations may not be an "action organization." In other words, they may not attempt to influence legislation as a substantial part of their activities and they may not participate in any campaign activity for or against political

> **Fun Fact**
> 73% of nonprofits sampled report some level of advocacy during a year period.
> (Nonprofit America: A Force or Democracy 2008)

candidates.[238] The limitation is driven by the idea that the government should not provide an unlimited subsidy to charitable organizations in their quest to impact government policy. [239] Charitable organizations that want an unfettered means for advocating about government policy should register as a 501(c)4. Such organizations may lobby without restriction and retain their tax-exempt status for their own revenues; however, donors' contributions to the organization are not tax-deductible.

This chapter details the lobbying regulations that face 501(c)3 and 501(c)4 organizations. It moves on to profile a few charitable entities that engage in lobbying. The chapter concludes by considering the impact of the Internet on the lobbying efforts.

Regulation of Charitable Organization Lobbying

Limitations on Lobbying. IRS regulations unambiguously prohibit 501(c)3 organizations from participating in political campaigning. These organizations are not allowed to raise funds for candidates nor are they permitted to make written or oral statements for or against a candidate for public office. Violations of this probation may lead to revocation of tax-exempt status and the imposition of excise taxes. Organizations registered as 501(c)3s also face limitations on lobbying, although these are less concrete. "In general, no organization may qualify for section 501(c)(3) status if a substantial part of its activities is attempting to influence legislation (commonly known as *lobbying*). A 501(c)(3) organization may engage in some lobbying, but too much lobbying activity risks loss of tax-exempt status", according to the Internal Revenue Code.[240]

The limitation on lobbying was incorporated into the IRS code in 1934. As with the Foreign Agents Registration Act, the motivation for action was based on concerns that such organizations would disseminate propaganda to influence legislation. "Influencing legislation" is clearly defined in the Internal Revenue Code: "An organization will be regarded as attempting to influence legislation if it contacts, or urges the public to contact, members or employees of a legislative body for the purpose of proposing, supporting, or opposing legislation, or if the organization advocates the adoption or rejection of legislation."[241] The scope of activity covered includes lobbying on bills and resolutions adopted by Congress and lobbying of state and local governments as well as referenda.

There are important differences between the IRS's definition of direct lobbying and that of the Lobbying Disclosure Act. On one hand, the IRS considers a request to the members of a charitable organization to contact legislators in support or opposition of a particular legislative initiative as direct lobbying. Media advertisements funded by a charitable organization that calls for a specific outcome of pending legislation can also be considered direct lobbying. On the other hand, nonpartisan analysis, studies and research (as long as they do not refer to specific legislative proposals or take a position on the legislation) are not considered direct lobbying. Charitable organizations are also permitted to communicate with legislators to protect their own interests. As explained by William Luneburg and Thomas Susman in *The Lobbying Manual,* the "self-defense" exception allows an organization "to lobby on matters relating to its powers, existence, duties, tax-exempt status, or the tax treatment of contributions to the organization…",.[242]

The Five Percent Threshold. The prohibition on influencing legislations is not an outright ban. Rather, the charitable organization is not permitted to have a "substantial portion" of their activities devoted to advocacy. What constitutes a "substantial" part has not been defined. Over the years, the IRS and courts have provided some parameters around substantial lobbying. First, the determination is largely based on the specific facts at issue. In *Christian Echoes v. U.S.*, the court held that "the political [e.g. legislative] activities of an organization must be balanced in the context in the objectives and circumstances of the organization to determine whether a substantial part of its activities was to influence or attempt to influence legislation."[243] Second, the IRS will take into account the percentage of time (including staff and volunteers) as well as expenditures that the organization devotes to lobbying in establishing whether substantial lobbying has taken place.[244] However, many gray areas persist. In *Seasongood v. Comm'r* (227 F2d 907, 1955) 5 percent of activity was suggested as not violating the substantial standard. While this level was never codified as an acceptable limit, it does provide a benchmark that is used in practice.

The Expenditure Test. In response to the ambiguity of substantial lobbying, the IRS introduced the Expenditure Test in 1976. Under the Code, a nonprofit charity could be an "H Elector" signifying the organization's acceptance of proscribed lobbying expenditure limits and associated reporting requirements. The Expenditure Test defines two types of lobbying – direct and grassroots. Direct lobbying is communications with legislative officials (or other government employees who participate in the legislative process) with the intent of influencing the outcome of a specific legislative proposal. In contrast, grassroots lobbying is directed at the general public with the intent of having the recipient contact their legislator to share a perspective on the issue. A "call to action" exists if the organization: (1) suggests contacting a specific legislator; (2) provides contact information to reach the legislator; (3) includes a petition to be sent to the legislator; or (4) identifies the names of legislator(s) opposed to the position of the organization.

The actual amount of permitted lobbying spending is set as a percentage of annual income. The percentage is a sliding scale beginning with 20 percent of the first $500,000 of an organization's revenues. For the next $500,000, the organization may spend 15 percent on lobbying and 10 percent on the next $500,000. Above $1.5 million, 5 percent of expenses may be used for lobbying up to a total lobbying expenditure of $1 million. An additional 25 percent of the lobbying budget can be spent to support grassroots lobbying.

The charitable organization can select the Expenditure Test or substantial part option annually. The election of the Expenditures Test requires only information such as name of the organization, address of the organization, signature of the entity's official and checking the box. Despite the clarity of the Expenditure Test option and the simplicity of opting for it, very few charities choose this option. The need to maintain

> **Fun Fact**
> Only 2% of 501(c)3s opt for the Expenditures Test
> (Non Profit Law – Galston)

and make public expenditure records as well as concerns about the allocation of shared costs help to explain the limited use of the Expenditures Test.

Legal Challenges to the Limitations. A number of organizations have challenged the constitutionality of the lobbying restriction for charitable organizations based on First Amendment grounds. The Supreme Court has consistently upheld the IRS Code's limitations on lobbying. In *Cammarano v. United States,* a unanimous Supreme Court decision rejected the contention that denial of tax deductibility of lobbying expenses was a violation of the First Amendment. Justice John M. Harlan delivered the opinion of the Court:

"Petitioners are not being denied a tax deduction because they engage in constitutionally protected activities, but are simply required to pay for those activities entirely out of their own pockets, as everyone else engaging in similar activities are required to do in the provisions of the Internal Revenue Code."[245]

While *Cammarano* addresses the tax deductibility of lobbying expenses in general, the Supreme Court dealt with the tax-exempt status specifically of charitable organizations in *Regan v. Taxation with Representation of Washington.*

> **Notable Quote**
> Congress "is not required by the First Amendment to subsidize lobbying"
> - Supreme Court
> (Regan v. Taxation With Representation of Washington)

Taxation with Representation of Washington (TRW) was a non-profit corporation that advocated for what it termed the "public interest" regarding tax policy in Washington. The IRS denied TRW's application for 501(c)3 status because it appeared that the organization would devote a substantial part of its activities to influencing tax policy and legislation. TRW brought suit against the IRS, basing their case on a violation of First Amendment rights and the equal protection afforded by the Fifth Amendment (veterans organizations are allowed to engage in unlimited lobbying). Interestingly, the organization was formed from two 501(c)4 entities that were able to engage in unrestricted lobbying, but their donors did not benefit from tax deductible contributions. Leaders of the new organization wanted the benefit of advocating with tax-deductible donations.

The Supreme Court dispatched the First Amendment challenge: "The Code does not deny TWR the right to receive deductible contributions to support its non-lobbying activity, nor does it deny TWR any independent benefit on account of its intention to lobby. Congress has merely refused to pay for the lobbying out of public moneys. This Court has never held that Congress must grant a benefit such as TWR claims here to a person who wishes to exercise a constitutional right."[246]

The Court also dismissed the Fifth Amendment cause for action: "Although TWR does not have as much money as it wants, and thus cannot exercise its freedom of speech as much as it would like, the Constitution does not confer an entitlement to such funds as may be necessary to realize all the advantages of that freedom." The Court added: "It is also not irrational for Congress to decide that, even though it will not subsidize substantial lobbying by charities generally, it will subsidize lobbying by veterans' organizations." Veterans have "been obliged to drop their own affairs to take up the burdens of the nation, subjecting themselves to the mental and physical hazards as well as the economic and family detriments which are peculiar to military service and which do not exist in normal civil life."[247]

Lobbying Disclosure Act Applicability. With these decisions, the courts have set the legal framework for lobbying by charitable organizations from the IRS perspective. These organizations are also subject to the Lobbying Disclosure Act requirements if they meet the reporting threshold. For-hire lobbyists working on behalf of charitable organizations must also register and disclose their activities.

Challenge: Lobbying by Tax Exempt Organizations

United States political thought and law limit the role of lobbying by charitable organizations in exchange for their tax-exempt status. The Europeans take a very different view of lobbying by these groups. The EU encourages the active participation of NGOs in the policymaking process. In fact, they subsidize the lobbying activities of some charitable organizations. The EU logic is that policymaking needs the input of all stakeholders and NGOs, with generally fewer resources than business interests, should have every opportunity to be heard. Write an op-ed in support or opposition to unlimited lobbying by charitable organizations in the US.

Lobbying By Charitable Organizations

Many charitable organizations engage in lobbying notwithstanding the constraints of the IRS regulatory environment. They seek to impact policies that support their mission through both direct (grasstops) and grassroots advocacy. Their efforts raise public awareness of their issue and support increased funding (or at least prevents the loss of government-funded programs). Nonprofits, foundations and philanthropists have spent $35 to $45 million annually for lobbying in recent years reflecting a substantial increase over earlier year expenditures. (Exhibit 9-1) Those amounts understate the full lobbying expenditures as they only reflect the filings required under the Lobbying Disclosure Act (LDA). Although not ideal, the LDA reports provide insight into who is lobbying, what issues are addressed and who is doing the advocacy.

> **Notable Quote**
> Nonprofit lobbying is the right thing to do. It is about empowering individuals to make their collective voices heard on a wide range of human concerns.
> - Center for Lobbying in the Public Interest
> (Vaughan & Arsenault 2013)

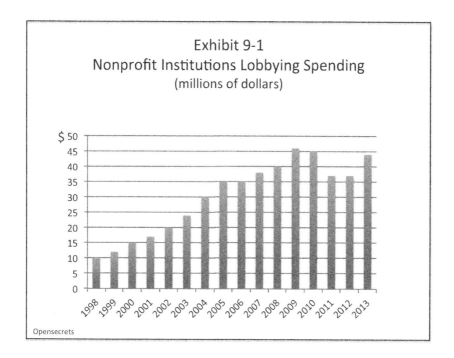

Exhibit 9-1
Nonprofit Institutions Lobbying Spending
(millions of dollars)

Opensecrets

Profile of LDA Lobbying. In 2012, nonprofits, foundations and philanthropists spent $37 million lobbying. More than 370 organizations lobbied that year. The spending was highly concentrated with 25 organizations accounting for 40 percent of the spending. Exhibit 9-2 shows the distribution of spending is focused on a few dozen organizations but there is a long tail.

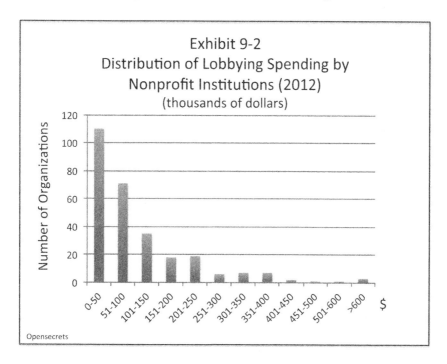

Exhibit 9-2
Distribution of Lobbying Spending by
Nonprofit Institutions (2012)
(thousands of dollars)

Opensecrets

The top 12 spenders and their primary issues are shown in Exhibit 9-3. The organizations include many organizations with "brand" recognition including the Pew Charitable Trusts, The Y, and Goodwill Industries. While some of the top spenders have a business orientation, such as the China-US Exchange Foundation and the National Quality Forum, scores of social welfare organizations are also lobbying. Federal Budget and Appropriations issues dominate the lobbying efforts. Yet, the range of issues is broad, from taxes to transportation, from foreign policy to healthcare, and from education to the workplace.

Exhibit 9-3 Largest Nonprofit Lobbyists and Issues (2012)		
Organization	Expenditure	Issues
Open Society Policy Center	$3,250	Foreign Relations/Civil Rights
Pew Charitable Trusts	2,440	Food/Energy/Environment
Bipartisan Policy Center	1,120	Budget and Appropriations
Local Initiatives Support	600	Budget and Appropriations
Self Help Credit Union	595	Banking
National Public Radio	570	Radio/TV Broadcasting
China-US Exchange Foundation	507	Foreign Relations
Goodwill Industries	474	Budget/Labor-Workplace
National Quality Forum	450	Healthcare
Southwest Research Institute	440	Defense
The Y	400	Budget/Health
RTI International	390	Agriculture

Opensecrets

Non-LDA Lobbying. Above and beyond the advocacy disclosed under LDA is lobbying that takes place but does not meet the threshold for disclosure. It is impossible to quantify this activity. Taken individually, the amounts are likely small. However, the sheer number of such organizations implies that – in aggregate – it is likely substantial. What is the nature of this lobbying? Beth Leech in her book *Lobbyists at Work* profiles a number of advocates for charitable organizations. The following interview with the President of Families Against Mandatory Minimums captures the flavor of the non-LDA lobbying:

In response to the question, do you consider yourself a lobbyist? The president responded: "Well, technically, I'm not. I have not registered as a lobbyist, although our government affairs counsel has. When I started FAMM, I knew nothing about lobbying. I just knew that what I needed to do was introduce members of Congress to the kinds of people who were going to prison under the laws they passed. When probed about whether being a policy advocate made her a lobbyist she responded: "Yes. I'm a lobbyist in the sense that I try to persuade legislators to adopt my perspective."[248]

Researchers at Johns Hopkins University's Center for Policy Studies in collaboration with the Center for Lobbying in the Public Interest surveyed 872 nonprofits on their advocacy efforts and views. Almost three quarters of the respondents indicated that their organization undertook policy advocacy or lobbying in the prior year. Larger and more established organizations are more likely to lobby. Of the organizations that do lobby, most have signed letters to policymakers and visited/called government officials. Typically, two thirds of the lobbying took place at the state or local level. The organization's executive director is the dominant lobbyer. Eighty nine percent of survey respondents report working with coalitions to increase the impact of their advocacy efforts. Finally, most nonprofits report they expect the same level of lobbying or an increase in the future.[249] Highlights of the report are provided in Exhibit 9-4.

Exhibit 9-4
Nonprofit Lobbying Survey Highlights

Engage in advocacy or lobbying	73%
Engage 1 or more time per month	61%
Signed correspondence to government official	97%
Visited a government official	86%
Devoted more than 2% of budget to lobbying	11%
Devoted >10% of lobbying spend to grassroots	23%
Motivation for action – impact programs	92%
Motivation for action – impact service populations	92%
Participation in coalitions	89%
Significant/somewhat involved – executive director	71%
Significant/somewhat involved – others	40%

Nonprofit America: A Force for Democracy?, Lester Salamon and Stephanie Lessans Geller, Johns Hopkins University Listening Post Project, 2008.

The "Missing" Lobbyists. Concerns about violating the Substantial Lobbying prohibition as well as tracking and allocating costs associated with the Expenditures Test keep many charitable organizations from lobbying at all. Jeffrey Berry of Tufts University analyzed the lobbying practices of 501(c)3 organizations. He discovered that these organizations' leaders did not understand the details of lobbying regulation. "Sadly, this general ignorance of the law has profound consequences for the behavior of nonprofit groups ... this misunderstanding has led to lower levels of advocacy before government."[250] He concludes: "Nonprofit groups should no longer use federal law as an excuse for inaction. It's legal to lobby and it's legal to lobby extensively. And lobbying is necessary because nonprofit groups must give voice to those who can't speak for themselves."[251] Berry's findings are corroborated by the Aspen Institute's Strengthening Nonprofit Advocacy Project, which found more than half of respondents infrequently or never lobbied on legislation.[252]

> **Notable Quote**
> "Lobbying today is a must. Any organization that does not lobby ... is almost certainly to get left out"
> - Charity Lobbying in the Public Interest
> (Land Trust Alliances and Practices 2004)

Lack of familiarity with the IRS lobbying regulations is certainly part of why charitable organizations do not lobby. However, there are other factors including a lack of time and requisite skills for effective lobbying as well as a reliance on coalition members to advocate on their behalf. Seventy-two percent of nonprofits participating in Johns Hopkins' Listening Post Project reported that a lack of staff time was a barrier to more active lobbying. Insufficient skills and reliance on coalitions were the barriers identified by 41 percent and 50 percent respectively.[253]

Another significant barrier is the negative connotation associated with the term lobbying. Nonprofit leadership fears the reputation risk and the potential loss of funding associated with lobbying. Skepticism among their supporters also keeps many from directly advocating policymakers. In a study of the language of advocacy, researchers confirmed the negative perception of lobbying. Their study participants "asserted that nonprofits need to maintain an image that is beyond reproach, and being associated with lobbying could potentially hinder their reputations."[254]

What are ways to increase the advocacy of charitable organizations? First, nonprofits would benefit from basic education on the rules of lobbying. The Listening Post Project revealed that nonprofits spent only 2 percent of their budgets on advocacy.[255] There is, therefore, ample room to increase spending without concerns about violating the substantial portion limitation. Second, rebranding "lobbying" to "education" and "advocacy" may encourage more charitable organizations to engage with elected representatives. Third, nonprofits would be more involved with the legislative process if they were able to build lobbying capacity. The strategy section below is a starting point for effective nonprofit lobbying.

Strategy Nuances. The lobbying strategies of NGOs and charitable organizations look much like those used by the business sector detailed in Chapter 6. There are, however, several nuances associated with lobbying strategies for charitable organizations. First, charitable organizations usually advocate on behalf of multiple constituencies – their members, the clients and civil society. Care must be taken to ensure lobbying efforts for one constituency do not undermine another. Second, nonprofits generally have very limited resources for advocacy; therefore, their strategies often focus on highly targeted initiatives where the issue is highly salient in terms of importance to the organization's mission and ripe from the perspective of policy action. Resource limitations also encourage participation in coalitions to drive advocacy synergies among other nonprofits and business interests. Third, charitable organizations that deliver social value have a level of legitimacy that other lobbying organizations do not. Thus, strategies are designed to highlight this factor.

Finally, nonprofit strategies are increasingly incorporating power and cost effectiveness of the Internet and social media to share messages and motivate advocacy. However, the use of digital technology presents unique concerns for charitable organizations as detailed in the next section.

The Impact of the Internet on Charitable Organization Lobbying
The advent of the Internet and social media greatly enhance the ability of charitable organizations to execute the lobbying strategies outlined above. Digital medium are a low cost means of connecting with members, enhancing participation, augmenting fundraising and reaching policymakers. In many ways the cost effectiveness of web/social media enable charitable organizations to level the advocacy playing field with other voices in the policymaking process.

An effective web presence and use of social media have become the norm for most charitable organizations to communicate their primary mission and lobby decision makers. However, Internet activism also introduces the risk of violating the prohibition on political campaigning and limitation on substantial lobbying.

Risk #1: Political Campaign Violation. The IRS prohibits 501(c)3s from engaging in political campaigning. What happens if a charity hosts a blog and on that blog a supporter posts an entry explicitly endorsing a candidate for election? Is the organization obligated to proactively monitor its blogs and message boards for such content and remove it? Another concern is if a link to or from the tax-exempt organization's Web site contains a political endorsement.

Risk #2: Excessive Lobbying. Charitable organizations track their lobbying expenses to ensure they do not violate the Substantial Portion requirement or expenditure limits of the IRS Code. They routinely allocate personnel and overhead expenses to lobbying and non-lobbying activities. However, the advent of the Internet has made the allocation much more complex. If a charity posts an advertisement in a newspaper supporting a legislative proposal, the cost of this lobbying effort is clear – the cost of the advertisement and the staff time needed to develop and place the ad. If the same request is made via a posting on the charity's Web site, what is the cost? The staff time to write and upload the posting is a lobbying expense. But what portion of the cost of developing and hosting the Web site should be allocated? The answer is not well defined. The IRS also uses factors including the dissemination of advocacy material in making a substantial portion determination. How is this calculated in the Internet context? A magazine advertisement's reach can be estimated by the periodical's circulation. There is no direct measurement with the Internet. Moreover, digital media is far easier to pass on to others than hard copy.

The IRS Response. The IRS issued a Request for Comments concerning the need for greater clarity around the lobbying via the Internet in 2000. The request solicited comments on a range of issues including: "[1] Does a Web site constitute a single publication or communication? [2] When allocating expenses for a Web site, what methodology is appropriate? [3] To what extent and by what means should an exempt organization maintain the information from prior versions of the organization's Web site? [4] To what extent are statements made by subscribers to a forum, such as a listserv or newsgroup, attribute to an exempt organization that maintains the forum? [5] Does the publication of a webpage on the internet ... constitute an appearance in the mass media?"[256] Notwithstanding the request, the IRS has yet to offer any clarifications vis-à-vis the impact of Internet lobbying on charitable organization tax exempt status.

> ### Food For Thought
> Why does the IRS leave the Internet impact rules ambiguous?

Practical Advice. The Alliance for Justice offers some practical advice: "1. Treat most communication on the Internet the same as you would any other communication to the general public. Thus, unless an organization takes steps to make sure that only the organization's members receive the communication, online lobbying by 501(c)(3)s will be grassroots lobbying... 2. Beware of how the Internet can change the context of your message and create unexpected consequences. For example, legislative information that a 501(c)(3) posts on its Web site can become lobbying if the site also includes a link to allow users to e-mail their legislators."[257] The Alliance of Justice also offers suggestions on the allocation of costs associated with Internet lobbying: "The basic rule is that allocation methods must represent a good-faith attempt to reflect costs and must be consistently applied."[258] They recommend documenting the rationale for the allocation method; For example the number of web pages devoted to lobbying as a percentage of total web pages.

The low cost of digital communications makes the Expenditures Test more attractive. While under that Substantial Portion Test the ambiguity surrounding the number and type of people reached via the Internet and social media is of concern, under the Expenditures Test only the cost to create and distribute the material is relevant. Good accounting eliminates the risk.

After an initial flurry of concern about the risks to tax exempt organizations of lobbying via the Internet, there have been few instances of problematic Internet lobbying. Consequently, charities adopting a prudent approach and good bookkeeping can maximize the power of the Internet in achieving their goals.

501(c)3 Finale

- There are more than one million tax-exempt charitable organizations in the US; the majority engages in some level of advocacy for their organization or clients.
- In exchange for tax-deductible donations, charitable organizations are prohibited from engaging in "substantial lobbying."
- The IRS has not defined 'substantial lobbying'; such a determination is situation specific and a function of the nature and extent of the lobbying (who does it, who is targeted and the means used).
- The IRS does provide an alternative, the Expenditure Test, which offers a clear-cut limit. However, few organizations select this option because of concerns about cost allocation and record keeping.
- Independent of the IRS, charitable organizations are also subject to the Lobbying Disclosure Act if they meet the threshold for registration and disclosure.
- Nonprofits (including charitable organizations, foundations and philanthropists) spend a collective $35-$45 million annually to lobby.
- Additional lobbying does occur, but fails to reach the threshold for disclosure. The full amount is unknown and, while small for each organization, is likely large in total.
- An opportunity for greater advocacy clearly exists – only 2 percent of nonprofit budgets are used to lobby.
- The cost effectiveness and potential reach of the Internet and social media make these advocacy tools especially powerful for charitable organizations; however, care must be used to avoid inadvertently violating IRS rules.
- Greater understanding of the effectiveness of lobbying and strategies to limit reputational risk as well as more funds, time, and skills are needed to increase the advocacy of charitable organizations.

Learning by Doing[1]

Save Our Water (SOW) and Energy Independence (EI) are both 501(c)3 organizations with missions to educate the general populace about fracking. Both are focused on national regulation of fracking and have annual donations amounting to $550,000. SOW seeks legislation that directly regulates the chemicals used in the hydraulic fracturing process, the treatment of water after the process, and protection of aquifers. SOW would also like EPA supervision of the regulations and proposes a new sub-agency to inspect compliance with the requirements. EI's objectives are to keep the federal government out of the fracking regulation arena. The organization's leadership believes state regulation is effective and there is no need for federal action. Moreover, they see federal involvement as a barrier to their core objective, encouraging fracking as a means to US energy independence.

Both organizations seek to influence public policy about fracking; they also do not want to risk their tax-exempt status. Your task is to serve as a consultant to one of the above organizations and help them develop a lobbying campaign in support of their position. Specifically, (1) map the stakeholder interests; (2) determine your objectives; (3) frame your position; (4) outline the elements of the lobbying campaign; (5) prepare a budget for the effort; and (6) demonstrate that the campaign will not jeopardize the organization's tax-exempt status.

---

[1] The organizations and events described are fictitious and are illustrative for teaching purposes only.

Chapter 9 Bibliography

Announcement 2000-84. Internal Revenue Service. *Request for Comments Regarding Need for Guidance Clarifying Application of the Internal Revenue Code to Use of the Internet by Exempt Organizations*, October 16, 2000.

Berry, Jeffrey M. "Nonprofit Groups Shouldn't Be Afraid to Lobby." *The Chronicle of Philanthropy*, November 27, 2003. http://philanthropy.com/article/Nonprofit-Groups-Shouldnt-Be/61998/.

Cammarano v. United States, 358 U.S. 498 (U.S. Supreme Court 1959).

"Charities & Non-Profits." *Internal Revenue Service.* Accessed August 7, 2014. http://www.irs.gov/Charities-&-Non-Profits.

"Christian Echoes National Ministry Inc. v. United States." United States Court of Appeals Tenth Circuit. F2d, no. 470 (December 18, 1972). http://openjurist.org/470/f2d/849/christian-echoes-national-ministry-inc-v-united-states.

Kingsley, Elizabeth, Gail Harmon, John Pomeranz, and Kay Guinane. "E-Advocacy: Using the Internet for Lobbying and Other Political Activities." *The Grantsmanship Center*, 2001. http://www.tgci.com/sites/default/files/pdf/E%20advocacy_0.pdf.

Leech, Beth L. *Lobbyists at Work.* First edition. Berkeley, CA; New York: Apress, 2013.

Luneburg, William V., Thomas M. Susman, and Rebecca H. Gordon. *The Lobbying Manual: A Complete Guide to Federal Lobbying Law and Practice.* American Bar Association, 2009.

Pamela O'Kane Foter, Looking on the Internet and the Internal Revenue Code's Regulation of Charitable Organizations, 43 N.Y.L. SCH. L. REV. 567 (1999).

Salamon, Lester M., Stephanie Lessans Geller, and Susan C. Lorentz. *Nonprofit America: A Force for Democracy.* Johns Hopkins University: Center for Civil Society Studies Institute for Policy Studies, 2008.

Taliaferro, Jocelyn D., and Nicole Ruggiano. "The 'L' Word: Nonprofits, Language, and Lobbying." *Journal of Sociology & Social Welfare* XL (June 2013).

Chapter 10: Lobbying Around the Globe

Lobbying has existed in the United States since the founding of the country. Over the past 200 years, lobbying has become professionalized and pervasive. With regard to size, scope and sophistication; the United States is viewed as the "leader" in lobbying. However, in the broader context of advocacy, lobbying takes place in many other countries. This chapter profiles lobbying activities, regulation and structure on four continents. The term "lobbying" is used throughout this section; although, "advocacy" is a more acceptable term in many places. Regardless of the nomenclature, the practices described are in fact lobbying as we have come to understand it in the first few chapters of this book.

The starting point for understanding the global view of lobbying is the European Union. Although lobbying in the EU is a comparatively new phenomenon, Brussels is now a close second to Washington in terms of lobbying activity and influence. The continuing evolution of the Union and its laws and regulations drive the desire for organizations to impact policymaking. We then move on to lobbying in China because of the impact the country's policies have on the world at large and the increasing desire of non-governmental actors to impact policy decision-making. While minimal today, China has the potential to be a locus for lobbying in the future. The next stop on the global tour of lobbying is Mexico, where the impact of adjacency (the geographic proximity to the United States) is driving the development of a professional lobby. The US is Mexico's largest trading partner, the flow of immigrants between the countries is a source of policy debate, and the countries are neighbors sharing a 1,900 mile border. The final destination is Argentina, a country with a long history of military and civilian dictators where corruption continues to be problematic. Post-WWII, Argentina has bounced back and forth between elected governments and military juntas. Charges of corruption have accompanied both forms of rule. Against this history, is there a role for lobbying?

Lobbying in the European Union

Lobbying in Europe is rapidly mirroring the size, scope and scale of advocacy in the United States. The epicenter for lobbying in Europe is now Brussels, as the European Union (EU) establishes laws and regulations to support unification.

The roots of lobbying in Europe extend back centuries. The Magna Carta offers the right to petition the government and some argue that the term "lobbying" itself is a reference to private actors influencing public policy in the halls of Westminster. Notwithstanding the longstanding precedent, lobbying was not a major influence on policymaking in European countries for most of the 20th Century. There were pockets of direct policy advocacy (lobbying in the context of this book) by private parties such as in the United Kingdom and Germany, but these efforts were limited in scope and impact compared to lobbying in the US. The limited role of lobbying was in part a function of the negative connotation of this activity: "Lobbying confers an unfair advantage on those that can afford to carry it out and therefore runs counter to the notion of democracy."[259] In recent years, the term 'lobbying' has become more accepted; a less problematic term is "interest representation," a word to describe advocacy which puts more emphasis on information exchange and fair representation of particular ideas.

Growth in EU Lobbying

The creation and continual expansion of the European Union, however, changed the advocacy dynamic. Brussels has become the locus for a burgeoning lobbying industry in Europe. Several factors contributed to the growing importance of lobbying in the EU. First, the evolution of the Union as a primary policymaker created an interest by parties to influence the outcome of laws and regulations in the burgeoning union. In 1988, then-European Union Commission President Jacques Delors stated: "In 10 years, 80 percent of legislation related to economics, maybe also to taxes and social affairs, will be of Community, rather than individual country, origin."[260] Fifteen years later, the Dutch Secretary of State for European Affairs reported that 60 percent of laws and regulations in the Netherlands had their roots in Brussels.[261] While more recent analysis of the data show a much smaller direct tie, EU policymaking is having a substantial impact on the nation states. Each policy creates winners and losers; organizations increasingly are using lobbyists to generate favorable outcomes. The steady growth in countries included in the EU further increases the stakes for incumbents and new admittees.

Growth Driver #1: EU Policy Expansion. As was seen in the US, the growth of government influence is driving the increase in lobbying in Brussels. The EU budget increased from €93 billion to €140 billion between 2000 in 2012.[262] This 50 percent increase understates the growing importance of EU policymaking as the reach of EU actions is significantly beyond the budget. The EU's non-budget purview now extends to trade policy, financial regulation, education and more.

Growth Driver #2: Multiple Access Points. The second factor driving the growth in EU lobbying is the structure of the policymaking process, which includes multiple entry points for advocates. Policymaking engages three EU institutions:

- The European Commission (EC) is responsible for setting the legislative and regulatory agenda. The EC also drafts legislation; a most important responsibility from the perspective of interest groups. Additionally, the EC is responsible for the supervision and implementation of EU policies. The Commission is staffed by technocrats and is the "bureaucracy" of the

EU. Given its portfolio, this group has been the primary target of lobbyists. The extent of lobbying activity is shown in Exhibit 10-1.

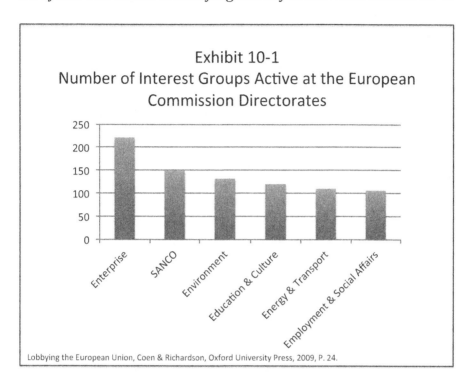

Exhibit 10-1
Number of Interest Groups Active at the European Commission Directorates

Lobbying the European Union, Coen & Richardson, Oxford University Press, 2009, P. 24.

- The <u>European Parliament (EP)</u> was initially a consultative body, tasked with reviewing and revising Commission proposals based on a European perspective. Until recently, lobbyists gave this body low priority because of its lack of legislative initiative. Lobbyists also struggled with how to advocate to this group as the Parliament was thought to have less interest in the lobbyists' primary product: information. However, through a series of treaty changes, the European Parliament's reach has been extended. Today, the Parliament has co-decision making authority in 80 policy areas ranging from agriculture to immigration to justice. In response to this increased authority, lobbying to the EP has increased as advocates realize EP's review process is an opportunity for shaping policy. Parliamentarians are becoming eager consumers of the information lobbyists provide since the information reduces the dependence of Parliament on other institutions. [263] Moreover, the involvement and expertise provided by interest groups gives Parliament additional political legitimacy, as they are considering the will of constituents and stakeholders.[264]

- The <u>Counsel of Ministers (CM)</u> also plays a role in the EU legislative process. This body represents the interests of the 28 member states and enacts the legislative proposals made by the Commission and the Parliament. The Counsel has even more authority in the areas of taxation and foreign policy. The CM is viewed as the least accessible of the EU institutions for lobbyists. Fiona Hayes-Renshaw, an Irish academic and visiting professor at the College of Europe, offers five reasons: (1) lack of process transparency; (2) complex decision making process including multiple layers and fragmentation; (3) a limited number of permanent staff; (4) decision-making driven by both treaty obligations and informal norms that have evolved over many years; and (5) less interest in lobbyists' information exchange.[265]

Growth Driver #3: Consultation Philosophy. The expansion of lobbying in the EU is also driven by the key role of consultation in policymaking. The Commission and Parliament have formal processes for interest group engagement. The Commission actually funds some interest groups, the majority of which are citizen and youth/education organizations. Yet, some funding extends to trade and professional entities. (Exhibit 10-2) Each directorate-general (D-G) offers consultation, the extensiveness is a function of overall activity in an area and the number and interest of external stakeholders. While taxation averages two to four consultations per year, transportation and environment each average 10-15 annually.[266]

> Food For Thought
>
> Should a government use its resources to fund lobbying by selected groups?

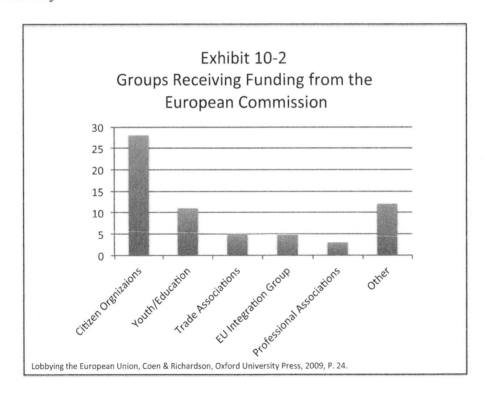

Exhibit 10-2
Groups Receiving Funding from the European Commission

Lobbying the European Union, Coen & Richardson, Oxford University Press, 2009, P. 24.

Civil Society Dialog is the mechanism for engaging the views of stakeholders. D-G officials organize and attend meetings with civil actors to better understand civil society positions, exchange viewpoints and share best practices. Stakeholders are encouraged to submit position papers to the D-G. Since 2008, the D-G has held 20-30 meetings annually. More than 300 representatives attended at least one session in 2013.[267]

Growth Driver #4: Economic Impact. A final key driver of lobbying growth in the EU, especially from the business community, is the economic impact of the Union – the largest economy in the world. Many European and international corporations have a vital interest in impacting policy in the EU. A prime example is corporate interest in the EU's framework for financial regulation. Another important issue is data privacy. This issue has brought Silicon Valley companies to Brussels arguing for less restrictive privacy regulations. Privacy activists in Europe are actively lobbying the other side of this "titanic clash" as named by the chairman of Friends of Privacy.[268]

Lobbyist Registration

David Coen, writing on behalf of the European Parliament, captures the important role of lobbying in EU policymaking: "Nowhere is this truer than in the European public policy process where some 15,000 commission and European parliamentary officials face some 20,000 lobbyists on a daily basis."[269] Beyond these general statistics, there is only partial information about who lobbies, on what issues, and with what resources. The EU has introduced a transparency register to provide citizens with insight into who is interacting with the EU institutions to impact policymaking. The register has been developed and is maintained by the European Parliament and European Commission. It serves as a single source of information for who is lobbying and how much they are spending.

All parties who lobby, both organizations and individuals, are expected to register. For the purposes of registration, lobbyists are those who conduct "activities carried out with the objective of directly or indirectly influencing the formulation or implementation of policy and decision-making processes of EU institutions."[270] Activities include meeting with members, preparing positioning materials and organizing events with the intent of influencing policymaking. The information required for registration includes the name and address of the lobbyist; the organization's goals; the number of people in the organization required to register; the revenues earned from lobbying activities, individual clients and associated revenues; and funds – if any – received from EU institutions.

Registration is, however, voluntary. What incentives are provided to registrants? Very few. Registrants do receive expedited access cards to the

European Parliament's buildings. They can also receive e-mail alerts on consultations conducted by the Commission. Finally, when the Commission publishes contributions for public consultation, only those organizations who have registered are given recognition for their contribution to the policy discussion. Registration does not infer accreditation or endorsement nor are there any privileges associated with registration.

The information contained in the register is fully transparent. The register was established in 2008 by the Commission and re-launched jointly by the Commission and Parliament with renewed emphasis in 2011. Since the re-launch, almost 6,000 lobbyists have registered (Exhibit 10-3). The first 12 months saw a significant enrollment; registrations have increased at a much slower pace during the past year. The rationale for registration appears to be the legitimacy it confers to the lobbyist in the eyes of policymakers. While some view this benefit as worth the effort to register, clearly many do not.

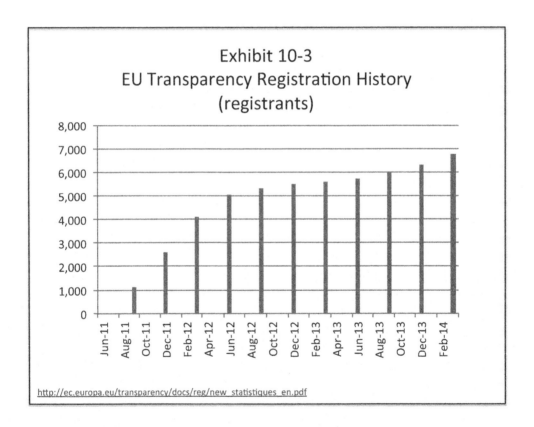

The Transparency Register has been strongly criticized for failing to reflect the true picture of lobbying in the EU. The Alliance for Lobbying Transparency and Ethics Regulation (ALTER-EU) has been campaigning to make the register mandatory and accurate. This coalition of civic society organizations, trade union, academics and policy think tanks actively campaigns for greater transparency in lobbying via mandatory registration, limiting the impact of the revolving door, and enhancing the code of ethics for Europe's policymakers. In an analysis titled 'Rescue the Register,' ALTER-EU documents that many major lobbying organizations are not included in the register. "We have identified over 100 unregistered companies with a representative office in Brussels or known to have been lobbying the EU."[271] The list includes major banks, technology companies, defense contractors, and consumer products manufacturers.

This finding is not surprising. There are few incentives for business interests to register. Moreover, a major disincentive is that registration can bring undesired attention to the organization. Law firms have largely refused to register because identifying clients would be a violation of their confidentiality agreements. Registration of non-business interests, on the other hand, is likely to be more comprehensive as registration creates legitimacy for these organizations.

Based on filings to the Register, annual lobbying expenditures have been about €350 million. Concerns about the accuracy of the database abound. The Association of Accredited Pubic Policy Advocates to the European Union states: "This list should be considered with a great deal of caution."[272] Not only are the number of lobbyists underreported, but the Register is widely believed to significantly underestimate spending and misclassify registrants. ALTER-EU examined the largest lobbying spender in the database and found that the firm was a medium size French insurance and pension company that spent €54 million and retained 500 lobbyists. However, the firm's entire staff is shown as 500. Other firms in the top spender list are equally questionable.

Composition of the Registrants

Understanding the inaccuracies in reporting, consider the insights that emerge for an examination of the Register. The business lobby dominates advocacy in the EU. (Exhibit 10-4) About half of the registrants are in-house lobbyists and trade/professional associations that represent business interests. Moreover, there are about 700 for-hire consultancies, law firms and independent lobbyists which also support the business sector. The majority of corporations lobbying in Brussels are European entities, but United States firms have a strong presence as well.

> **Fun Fact**
> The annual compensation for a senior lobbyist in the EU can top €400,000.
> (Wall Street Journal 9/17/2010)

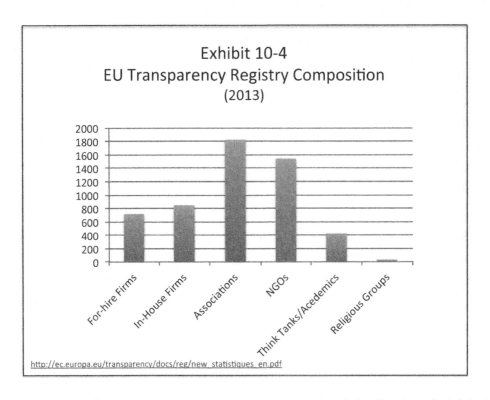

Exhibit 10-4
EU Transparency Registry Composition
(2013)

Nongovernmental organizations comprise a quarter of the Register's lobbyists. Civil society lobbyists provide legitimacy. According to Justin Greenwood, a professor of European Public Policy and an author of many articles on the lobby in the EU, these interest groups "bring much-needed resources to policymaking, implementation, and monitoring. In some accounts of how European integration develops, they help the EU to acquire more policy competencies by bringing your irresistible demands to member state doorsteps, and assist in the popular identification with the European Union."[273]

EU Lobbying Model

The relationship described by Greenwood can best be described as an exchange model. Lobbyists provide information and, in some cases legitimacy, in exchange for access and the opportunity to share perspectives with policymakers. (Information is the currency of exchange in the EU; in contrast to campaign contributions plus information in the US.) The specific nature of the exchange is a function of the institution being lobbied. The Commission seeks expert technical knowledge, as it is responsible for initiating and drafting legislation, and places a premium on technical expertise. Its collaborative approach to policymaking makes the Commission the easiest institution to access and thus the most common place to lobby. Parliament has historically been most interested in the views of European and national stakeholders, consistent with their role as commentator on proposed legislation. As Parliament's role expands into more policy creation, technical expertise is also desired. The Council, to the limited extent they engage in exchange with lobbyists, is interested in understanding the views of the national constituencies.

The EU lobbyist community can be segmented into individual firm actors, associations and consultants. Individual firms typically have a narrow focus, but also a more profound expertise. These individual firms are further segmented by size: large, medium and small. Large firms with substantial advocacy resources have become very professional in their delivery of information to the European institutions. This sophistication results in greater access. Associations often deal with a broader range of issues which limits their depth of knowledge on any particular topic. The need to form consensus positions among the membership may reduce the impact of associations. Some argue that their multilayer organizational structure inhibits their ability to understand the preferences of their constituents.[274] Their comparative advantage is the breadth of citizenry they represent and the legitimacy they provide through their sheer size. Third-party lobbyists (i.e. consultants) can provide distinctive expertise on individual issues but tend not to carry as much credibility as the aforementioned groups.

EU Lobbying Strategies
EU lobbying strategies mirror those used in the US. Success factors are also similar. As in the US, access is the first requirement. The ability to meet with policymakers in the EU is easier than in the United States. Pieter Bouwen, a university professor and a staff member of the European Commission, wrote, "EU institutions are eager to interact because they need close contacts with the private sector in order to fulfill their institutional role."[275] The consultative philosophy described above supports a more open-door approach. Policymakers are also under staffed, therefore the "subsidy" provided by lobbyists is an essential resource boost for the Commission and Parliament. Notwithstanding the need for expertise, the lobbyist's network is still required for access. Greenwood writes, "Brussels can be an insider's town, where operating effectively depends upon a dense network of interpersonal and intra-organizational links, and where it is very difficult for outsiders to arrive, win the day through persuasion, and go home again."[276] Who gets access? Bouwen analyzed comparative access at the European Parliament, Commission and Counsel in 2004. Associations have the greatest access at all three institutions. Associations' access is greatest at Parliament and least at the Council.[277]

Second, is reliable information. Bouwen observed that organizations that provide the best information have the best access.[278] Because of the multiple sources of information available to the European institutions, misinformation and/or too much spin are readily detected. Reputational risk, therefore, provides a strong incentive for lobbyists to provide reliable information.

Lobbying is the primary means of stakeholders influencing policy in the EU; however, litigation is an important secondary option. The European Court of Justice (ECJ) oversees questions of legislative constitutionality. Individuals, as well as national governments, have the ability to bring challenges to the Court. However, this is a pricey option as bringing a suit at the ECJ can cost €40,000 just to get started and the process often takes a year or more.[279] Bouwen and Margaret McCown conducted case studies examining the lobby versus litigation decision-making process. They conclude the ECJ is the more attractive avenue for policy impact if the legislative path is blocked. Parties considering the litigation approach should note that the Court has a bias toward supporting integration and liberal economic theory.[280]

Conflicts of Interest

One stark contrast between lobbying in the EU and US is attitude toward conflicts of interest. In the US, there is a strong desire to avoid conflicts associated with lobbying. The greatest concern is conflicts arising from the revolving door. The Lobbying Disclosure Act of 1995 and the Honest Leadership and Open Government Act of 2007 require a one to two year cooling off period as lobbyists enter government or policymakers become lobbyists to ensure that their prior position does not provide them with undue influence with government decision makers. Having lobbyists who are also simultaneously policymakers would be unthinkable.

Not so in the EU, where members of the European Parliament also have "second jobs" where their work objectives could easily influence their policymaking. An example highlighted in a Reuters Special Report profiled Klaus-Heiner Lehne who is a member of the European Parliament and also a partner in the German law firm Taylor

> **Noteable Quote**
> It is not the case that everything that comes from the lobby is per se bad.
> - Klaus-Heiner Lehne
> (Reuters 3/18/2011)

Wessing. As a parliamentarian, Lehne has helped to write the EU's business laws covering mergers, accounting requirements, and shareholder rights. As a member of the law firm, he advised corporations on the same issues. Lehne does not see a problem with his dual responsibilities: "It would be a lie to say that I don't profit professionally from the fact that I have been active in politics over a long period of time." He goes on to say that working in both government and private practice is beneficial. "It strengthens independence," he says, "by securing him a job after politics." If a proposal desired by one of his private sector clients comes before Parliament, Luhne states: "I would look at the proposal just as I would every other. I would decide if it was good or bad. Why should I reject it on principle? That would be nonsense."[281] ALTER-EU does not agree; its mission includes the objective of reducing conflicts of interest.

The push for greater transparency and stronger ethics regulations took on a more populist approach with the Worst EU Lobbying Awards. Founded by a group of environmental and consumer activists in 2005, the awards were used to highlight the "[t]housands of corporate lobbyists roam[ing] the corridors of power in Brussels. Operating out of the spotlight, many of them do not hesitate to employ improper methods: pretending to be concerned environmentalists, scaremongering the EU into inaction, or securing privileged access to EU decision-makers. These underhanded tactics have allowed corporate lobbyists to continue for-profit lobbying at the expense of more climate- and consumer-friendly regulation; putting profits before people and the planet."[282] Past recipients include RWE, Goldman Sachs, and ISDA. They were "honored" with a public award ceremony held on the sidewalk outside one of the company's offices. Green Party member Turmes put the need for transparency more colorfully: "Lobbying is a bit like prostitution – it will always exist, and if you try to forbid it, then you would get a black market. I'm interested in all the actors' views, but we have to do this in a transparent way."[283]

While attitudes toward conflicts of interest are less stringent than those in the US, registration in the EU requires agreement to a code of conduct; a step the US has not taken. The rules include honestly representing yourself and your interests, obtaining information appropriately, providing up-to-date and accurate information and abiding by rules that govern EU institutions and officials. In the EU, there is a process for reporting and investigating ethics violations as well as for enforcing sanctions. The sanctions range from temporary suspension to exclusion from the register to withdrawal of access cards to the European Parliament, depending on the severity of the violation.

Despite the Code of Conduct and the more relaxed view of conflicts of interest, the EU has seen its share of scandals. The most jarring was in 2011 when *The Sunday Times* reporters posed as lobbyists and asked members of the European Parliament to offer amendments to legislation in

> **Notable Quote**
> The scandal was an accident waiting to happen.
> - Andy Rowell
> (ALTER-EU)

exchange for cash payments of up to €100,000. Sixty members were approached, 14 indicated a willingness to do so, and four agreed.[284] While this scandal was not "Abramoff-size" it was a very vivid reminder of the potential for abuse. The parliamentarians accused in the sting denied wrongdoing. In one case, the court did not agree. Ernst Stasser, an Austrian member of the European Parliament, was sentenced to a four-year prison term. According to an article in EurActive, an alternative media source covering European affairs, "The judge said that the court had no doubt the Stasser illegally demanded money in 2011 in exchange for influencing the legislative procedure."[285] Release of the *Times* journalists' video tape of him asking for the money and a

€12,000 invoice for "consulting services" were more than enough evidence to support the conviction. The reporters testified that Stasser wanted €100,000 per year for his services.

As with all scandals, the response among European politicians was one of outrage. Many called for reform. Parliament President Jerzy Buzek declared: "We are determined to practice zero tolerance of the kind of actions that led to the resignation of our colleagues."[286] He called for a more rigorous code of conduct for the members and to make it legally binding. ALTER-EU used the scandal to renew calls for transparency and ethics reforms: "This scandal was an accident waiting to happen. The politicians in Brussels – who are responsible for making the laws - enjoy far too cozy a relationship with industry lobbyists. It is a surprise that the MEPs found it so easy to act on behalf of the fake lobbyists. This scandal could be merely the tip of the iceberg."[287] Despite the outrage, few concrete actions have been taken thus far.

Future of EU Lobbying

EU lobbying is likely to be a growth industry for the foreseeable future. First, the EU continues to introduce, debate, and enact legislation to unify the union. Moreover, each round of expansion brings more issues and viewpoints to the table. Second, the Treaty of Lisbon (2007) expands the application of Qualified Majority Voting (QMV) where member states' votes are approximately proportional to their populations. It is generally thought that this system makes passing legislation easier and thus the amount of legislation enacted is expected to increase. The Lisbon Treaty extends QMV to policy areas ranging from defense to energy to intellectual property.[288] If these assumptions hold true, the demand for information exchange with lobbyists will increase from both demand and supply perspectives. Demand will increase as policymakers are faced with a larger agenda and no additional staff to handle the increased volume. Lobbyists are likely to increase the supply of services as they have more opportunities to influence legislative and regulatory outcomes. Third, the epicenter for advocacy is now the EU institutions, not the national capitals. Brussels has become a magnet for interests, as its policy agenda has grown. That shift, still underway, shows no signs of abating. Lobbyists and their clients seek to make sure their voices are heard as the EU institutions make policy.

Challenge: US v. EU Lobbying Firm

The US and EU are the primary markets for lobbyists. Consider the Strengths, Weaknesses, Opportunities, and Threats (SWOT) of the two geographies to decide where you would want to set up a lobbying firm.

Lobbying in China

Lobbying in China provides a strong contrast to the US and EU. China has a different historical context for lobbying. The earliest historical records of the practice date back to the Spring and Autumn Warring States Period (770-221 B.C.E.) when kings hosted "dining guests" or "persuaders" to hear various perspectives. One such lobbyist was Su Qin who advised multiple kings on political and military affairs. He is noted for coalescing multiple kingdoms to oppose another. These early lobbyists had the independence and self-preservation traits seen in today's lobbyists as revealed in the following quote from Qiang Yan's 'Bandwagoning, Balancing, and the Unification of Seven Countries in China': "These [early] lobbyists, however, were definitely not patriots of their national states. What they really cared [about] was their personal interests due to their coupling activities among the seven states. Therefore, these lobbyists might occasionally change their political standings when it was applicable."[289]

Despite the very old lobbying tradition, modern China does not have a foundation of the right to petition the government. Lobbying is a recent outgrowth of efforts to facilitate the rise of private business and participation in the global economy. Although it is a new facet of policy making, lobbying has had a strong uptake in China. Today, lobbying is an integral part of policymaking but the philosophy, strategies and process has a distinctly Chinese flavor.

Lobbying in China – Business Advocacy

Lobbying in China is largely synonymous with business advocacy, as civil society lobbying is still in its infancy. The development of business lobbying has two driving forces. First, private enterprise seeks to shape the legislative and regulatory environment in which they operate. "China may not yet have "rule of law," writes Scott Kennedy in his book 'The Business of Lobbying in China,' "but it assuredly has rules by the thousands that touch upon every aspect of business," providing ample incentive for lobbying.[290] Second, policymakers need insight into how their programs will impact economic growth. As Kennedy writes, "firms have gained policy leverage because they are central to accomplishing government objectives such as growing the economy, stable prices, high employment, and expanding tax receipts." The combination of these forces leads to a wonderful symbiosis captured in the following: "a business 'educates' officials to viewing problems from the companies' perspective, all the while showing how the firms' preferred outcome can also benefit the government and the country as a whole."[291]

The business lobby in China consists of two key segments – firm direct and association indirect lobbying. Firms acting with internal employees or through for-hire lobbying firms advocate directly with policymakers. Firms that directly lobby are large enterprises with the resources to build or buy lobbying capabilities. Direct lobbying is most commonly used when the issue at hand has a significant impact on the organization and the policy desired can be addressed by the lobbyee. Associations are used independently or in conjunction with direct lobbying. The advantage of associations is the critical mass they bring to an issue. The disadvantage is that the "ask" is often generic in order to garner broad membership support.

Over the past decade, the number of lobbying organizations has grown rapidly. *The Washington Post* offered this description as Beijing prepared for the 2007 Party Congress: "Armies of lobbyists are descending on the Chinese capital in anticipation of the 17th Communist Party Congress." [292] The entourage included leading international lobbying companies. Public relations and law firms include APCO, Ogilvy, Burson-Marstella, Hogan & Hartson, and Jones

> **Notable Quote**
> China learns fast every trick in the business world, and the art of lobbying is no exception
> - Globalization Monitor
> (Globalization Monitor Limited 2010)

Day to name a few. Domestically, there are about 400 National industry associations and thousands more at the provincial and local level. The associations often have close ties to the government or may even be funded by the government. There are also Chinese lobbying firms. Global Public Relations Company was one of the first formed in 1985 by a government news agency. Today, an unknown – yet, predictably large – number of domestic lobbying firms provide advocacy for private clients.

The issue areas lobbied in China are business focused yet broad; covering the gamut from antidumping policies encouraged by the steel industry to more favorable tax treatment for consumer electronics companies.

Lobbying Strategies in China

What is the core strategy for lobbying in China? In a word ... *Guanxi*, which literally translates as relationship. The more common understanding of the term is connections. In the context of lobbying, *Guanxi* is using your network to access and influence policymaking. It is a very personal one-to-one relationship. The power of this

> **Fun Fact**
> 70 percent agree "*guanxi* is the key to influencing public policy"
> - Guosheng and Kennedy
> (2009)

concept is that once a *Guanxi* relationship exists between an advocate and policymaker there is an obligation to attempt to accommodate the request. The obligatory nature of the relationship means that *Guanxi* is not easily achieved. A sustained period of interpersonal relationship building is required often involving social invitations, gifts and even helping relations find jobs. In addition, at the firm level, businesses hire former government officials directly or as consultants, fund government-sponsored think tanks, and engage in philanthropy. "The importance of Guanxi in navigating the bureaucracy in China cannot be overstated, and in recent years it has become a commodity that is increasingly for sale," writes Scott Seligman, in his book, 'Chinese Business Etiquette: A Guide to Protocol, Manners, and Culture in the People's Republic of China'. "Many of the sons and daughters of high ranking [officials], in particular, have set up 'consulting shops' or 'service' companies and offered the ability to mobilize their own [network of connections] and those of their parents, to the highest bidder."[293]

Guanxi remains a central lobbying strategy, but China is also developing a version of the exchange model. In China, the exchange often goes beyond basic information exchange for access as seen in the US and EU. As Scott Kennedy describes: "Officials provide entrepreneurs access to scarce goods, credit, government and overseas markets, and protection from onerous regulations. Entrepreneurs, in return, provide officials with payoffs and gifts, employment, and business partnership."[294] The exchange model can be broadened to the concept of win-win outcomes in China. The idea is well captured by the following by Kennedy and Guosheng: "Business may seek to educate officials to view problems from their perspective, all the while showing how their preferred outcome can also benefit the government and the country as a whole."[295]

Beyond information, businesses also provide training and research projects in exchange for access and influence. For example, BP launched a project on climate control and global warming. Separately, they invested $10 million in a joint venture with Chinese academic institutions to leverage clean energy technology.[296] General Electric has offered training programs to the Central Organization Department, the group responsible for selecting senior government officials.[297]

Lobbyists in China rely on influencing the media to bolster their advocacy efforts. The rationale for focusing on the media is that a good public image can attract the attention and support of officials."[298] There is a history of providing reporters with "red envelopes" containing cash to come to press conferences and for good coverage. While this practice is understood by all participants, lobbying firms actively leverage the media. Guosheng and Kennedy found that 90 percent of firms that lobby hold press conferences where policy is discussed. Sixty percent hold training sessions for the press.[299] The same percent of firms submit at least two articles per year to the media. As in the US, issue advocacy is more often a long campaign than a request that results in immediate action. The media can help to keep an issue on a policymaker's priority list.

Legal and Regulatory Framework

There is little legal and regulatory framework to govern lobbying activities in China. Unlike the US where lobbying is transparent and the EU where it is translucent; in China, lobbying is opaque. Lobbyists do not register and/or disclose their clients, activities or expenditures. Lobbyists and lobbyees are, however, subject to public anti-corruption laws. China has been a signatory to the United Nations Convention against Corruption since 2006. Since that time, the government has adopted a number of measures to prevent corruption. Current law criminalizes both active and passive corruption, extortion and money laundering and makes it illegal for a public official to abuse his or her position for private gains.[300] The threshold for a criminal investigation of bribery is less than $2,000. The Second Five-year Anti-corruption Plan, adopted in 2013, includes a new code of ethics intended to stymie problematic behavior. Punishment has been the primary deterrent in the past; however, increasingly the government is focused on prevention through education and supervision. With regards to lobbying, there are some practices that could be interpreted as corruption. One commentator bluntly described the issue: "Chinese consultancy companies do more than regular business lobbying. Their chief mission is to cultivate *guanxi* and, in many instances, this involves bribery..."[301] Thus far these concerns do not appear to have inhibited lobbying. As lobbying's visibility continues to grow, this could be a concern in the future.

Audience For Lobbying

There are multiple audiences for lobbying efforts in China. China's governance structure is provided in Exhibit 10-5. At the national level, lobbying centers on the ministries and commissions under the State Council agencies. The State Council "exercises the power of administrative legislation, the power to submit proposals, the power of administrative leadership, the power of economic management, the power of diplomatic administration, the power of social administration, and other powers..."[302] These agencies of the Council are the workhorse of the Chinese national government. They include ministries and commissions, administrative offices and state administrations and bureaus. These groups are responsible for the full array of government activities from the Ministry of Finance to the State Administration for Industry and Commerce to the State Intellectual Property Office. Given these responsibilities, the officials that run these bureaucracies benefit the most from business information and have the most direct impact on business activities. Both companies and associations lobby here.

> **Notable Quote**
> The government and the Party may be a distinction without a difference.
> - Scott Kennedy
> (2008)

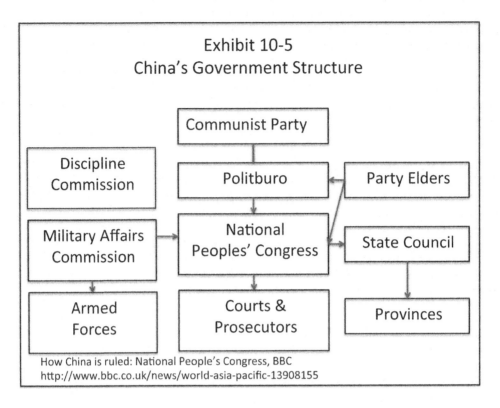

Exhibit 10-5
China's Government Structure

How China is ruled: National People's Congress, BBC
http://www.bbc.co.uk/news/world-asia-pacific-13908155

There is also lobbying with the National People's Congress (NPC), China's national legislature. Officially, the NPC enacts laws, oversees government operations and elects key government officials. The NPC drafts legislation and is a forum for discussing legislative proposals. Some observers question whether the NPC fulfills this mission or largely confirms the decisions made by the ruling elite and/or the Communist Party. As the BBC reported in 2012 "what actually tends to happen, therefore, is that the party drafts most new legislation and passes it to the NPC for 'consideration.'"[303] Members are also facilitators; in the words of one delegate, "I act as a bridge, which means I help the government promote its policies to the people and relay peoples' opinion back to the government."[304] There is recent evidence that the NPC is taking a more proactive role. The People's Political Consultative Conference is also a target audience for lobbyists but to a much lesser degree as it serves an advisory role. With the right *guanxi*, a member of the Chinese Communist Party can be lobbied. Finally, there is extensive lobbying at the local level.

There are no formal assessments of lobbying results in China. Anecdotal evidence points to positive impact. Amway, the US-based firm providing health, beauty and home products through multi-level sales direct to customers, succeeded in relaxing the ban on direct sales in 1998. In 2007 *The Washington Post* reported: "In June, foreign companies successfully lobbied Chinese officials to remove conditions on hiring temporary workers in a new labor law that they said would make it prohibitively expensive to do business in China. Likewise in

August they were able to persuade China to remove some language in early drafts of the anti-monopoly law that seemed to discriminate against foreign companies..."[305] The Chinese lobbying firm Global Public Relations highlights several lobbying success stories on its webpage ranging from arranging key meetings to preparing materials for the media.[306]

A study of firms and associations that lobby in China conducted by Scott Kennedy revealed a very interesting finding about the impact of lobbying: Firms tend to downplay the impact they have on policymaking. Only 5 percent of company respondents said they "successfully influenced a central or local government policy." In contrast, 67 percent of associations said they had successfully influenced policy.[307] What accounts for the contrasting views? Firms likely understate their impact for fear of showing too much power, thus attracting attention and scrutiny. Associations are incented to overstate their influence because without impact there would be no reason for them to exist.

Future of Lobbying in China
Looking to the future, lobbying in China is a growth industry. The potential for gains are high and the costs of entering the fray are relatively low, especially for those with strong networks. Associations will continue to advocate on behalf of their members. It is unlikely that this sector will exhibit substantial growth, as hundreds of associations are already established and active. Firm-level lobbying will likely be the focus for expanded lobbying in China. Domestic and foreign firms will be drawn to lobby as business laws and regulations continue to evolve and more companies see the ability to impact outcomes. Lobbying strategies will likely continue to center on *guanxi* for access and credibility as well as information exchange as the "currency" for the access. Win-win solutions that create value for firms and policymakers will remain the goal. As Scott Kennedy describes: "The growth of business lobbying, no matter how imperfectly structured, has brought certain benefits. By taking into account the views of those to be regulated, greater information is available to decision-makers, and it is more likely that adopted policies will be acceptable to those being regulated, and hence, more implementable over the short and long term."[308] Business is delighted to provide information as this provides them with a seat at the policy setting table.

Lobbying in Mexico

There are several reasons to suspect that lobbying in Mexico would mirror lobbying in the US. First, the Mexican Constitution is based on the US Constitution. The Mexican federal government consists of legislative, executive and judicial branches. The legislature is bi-cameral with a House of Deputies and Senate. Moreover, the right to lobby is constitutionally guaranteed in the rights to assemble, petition, and speak.[309] Second, the Mexican government itself is a lobbyer in the US. For example, the Mexico Ministry of Tourism has lobbied in the US. Third, the proximity and tight economic, geographic, and social ties between the countries could be expected to yield a "spillover effect" from the US.

Despite the similarities in the foundational aspects of the countries' governments, lobbying in Mexico is much less robust than in the US. One key explanation is the relatively recent need for legislative lobbying. From the establishment of the constitution in 1921 until the 1990s, the ruling party, the PRI, maintained a super majority in the House and therefore policy debates at the legislative level were less robust. However, in 1997 the PRI lost its decades long control in the House and, as a result, the House became a more powerful policymaker.[310] A second factor is that legislators do not stand for reelection. After the three-year term for Deputies and six-years for Senators, their legislative service is complete. The single-term limit restricts the time available to build relationships and leverage those relationships to create a return on investment for the lobbyist.

Since the late 1990s, lobbying in Mexico has become part, albeit a small part, of policymaking in Mexico. Several hundred lobbyists have registered with the House of Deputies. They consist of independent, for-hire consultants as well as in-house advocates who represent corporations such as Philip Morris, Monsanto and Grupo Modelo.[311] Their approach to lobbying is similar to their counterparts in the US. The exchange model is the primary approach with lobbyists providing legislators with information and analysis in exchange for the opportunity to be heard. Javier Medina, legislative director for Grupo Salinas captured the role of business lobbying this way: corporations have a need and an "obligation to participate increasingly in the public policies of the country" to ensure economic growth and prosperity.[312]

A cadre of professional lobbyists belong to Procab, the National Association of Professional Lobbying in Mexico. The objectives of the group are threefold. First, they promote the ethical practice of lobbying among its members. Second, Procab promotes public recognition of lobbying as a contributing factor to the democratic life of the country. Finally, the group monitors and evaluates the mechanisms intended to regulate lobbying at the federal level.

Members agree to abide by a code of ethics which requires adhering to legal rules, avoiding conflicts, being open and honest about the nature of their work, and "respect[ing] the integrity and honesty of our partners in the public service and legislative representation, avoiding any action that might mean a private benefit for them."[313]

Despite the increasing professionalism of lobbying and the Procab's code of ethics, there have been frequent calls for greater regulation over the past decade. Between 2002 and 2008 there were more than 20 efforts in the House or Senate to regulate lobbying; none were successful. In 2010 the House adopted Article 263 which requires lobbyists to register, publish lobbying documents and it forbids Deputies from accepting gifts and other benefits from lobbyists. The Senate passed Article 298 which requires reporting of lobbying contacts and prohibits accepting gifts or cash from lobbyists. Notwithstanding these efforts, concerns about corruption and influencing peddling remain. A senator of the PDR party captured the need for regulation this way: Lobbying practices "produce much suspicion and mistrust because there is nothing regulating it. We live with them, hear them, but [there is] no transparency." He goes on to highlight the importance of transparent regulation: Lobbying should be "a tool for civil society, to enrich democracy, and not as an agent of gossip."[314]

The lobbying outlook in Mexico is one of continued growth and increasing professionalism. Business interests will continue to dominate lobbying activity. For sustained expansion regulation and transparency will be required.

Lobbying in Argentina

Argentina is a federal republic with 23 provinces. The president is head of state and is elected to a four-year term and can be reelected for a second term. The legislature is bicameral with a House of Deputies and Senate. Deputies serve a four-year term and are elected based on a closed list proportional representation system where the party determines the candidates and their order. Senators are elected for six-year terms. The party winning the most votes in each electoral district is awarded two seats and the second place party receives a third seat. Historically, the executive branch has held the reins of power for several reasons. First, this branch allocates the government's resources. Second, presidential decrees have been frequently used to bypass the legislature. Third, the legislators are determined by provincial party leaders based more on allegiance than expertise. Finally, legislators view this role as a stepping stone in the political hierarchy and are therefore beholden to their party leadership, not their constituents.

Lobbying in Argentina is in its infancy as pluralistic public policymaking is only now emerging in the country. For most of the 20th century, Argentina oscillated between democratically-elected governments and military rule. The lack of continued pluralistic politics limited the need for and value of lobbying. Moreover, the concept of advocacy is widely recognized but often with a very negative connotation. It is "portrayed as a perversion of democracy linked to corrupt practices. It is an activity often associated with secrecy, and the trafficking of influence."[315]

There are, however, countervailing forces supporting a professional lobby. A constitutional amendment in 1994 empowered citizens to offer bills in the House of Deputies. At about the same time, judges at the national Chamber of Civil Appeals ruled that political pressure per se is not bad or illegal; paying an official for influence is illegal. Transparency has been an important ingredient in legitimizing lobbying in other geographies and is foundational for Argentina, as it must overcome the shroud of corruption. Numerous bills were filed to require registration and greater transparency; none have passed. In 2003, President Cristina Fernández de Kirchner signed a decree, the Improvement of the Quality of Democracy and Its Institutions, establishing a framework for lobbying the executive branch. Lobbyists are required to report who they are, who they visit, the purpose of the meeting and a summary of the session. Do lobbyists abide by the regulations? There is scant evidence that the program is enforced.[316] Nevertheless the formal recognition of lobbying legitimizes its existence.

Lobbying strategies in Argentina mirror those in other countries. Advocates press their views with information and insights to legislators, the administration, and civil society. Lobbying by the tobacco industry to prevent anti-smoking regulations provides a powerful case example. The "tobacco industry effectively used direct lobbying, third party allies, public relations campaigns and scientific and medical consultants" to make their case, writes Diane Johnson in her article, 'Continuity and change in Argentine interest group activity and lobbying practices.'[317] For many years, the industry lobbied successfully to limit regulations. However, by 2005, popular demand for smoking bans was so strong the government enacted restrictions. As in the US and Europe, coalitions are often effectively employed in Argentina. An interesting coalition was formed to lobby the legislature for a freedom of information act consisting of the executive branch's Anticorruption Office and civil society. The group was successful in attaining House approval of the measure. However, an alliance of national intelligence service, the police and military interests prevented passage in the Senate. Both cases illustrate the importance and power of the lobby in Argentina, even if it is on a limited scale.

Lobbying is likely to remain a tangential force on public policymaking in Argentina. Pluralism is still taking hold in the country and its roots must be deepened and broadened for lobbying to become institutionalized.

International Insights
European Union

- Lobbying in the European Union is growing rapidly, mirroring the size and scale of lobbying in the US.
- The growth of lobbying is a function of new legislation, limited policymaking resources and a philosophy of consultation.
- There are multiple entry points for lobbyists in the EU, but the Commission is the primary target as it sets the legislative agenda and drafts laws and regulations.
- The exchange model best describes the lobbyist/lobbyee relationship – information is offered in exchange for access.
- Registration is voluntary with few incentives to do so.
- Conflicts of interest are a secondary concern in the EU; many EU parliamentarians have "second jobs" in the private sector.
- Lobbying in the EU is likely to continue to grow rapidly as the EU's scope expands and lobbying becomes more institutionalized.

China

- Lobbying in China is a modest but growing factor in policymaking as business interests seek to shape economic policies and lawmakers attempt to foster growth.
- Guanxi, relationships and connections, is the core lobbying strategy; the connections are used to share information with policymakers.
- Lobbyists also provide philanthropy and leverage the media to communicate their message.
- There is little legal/regulatory framework to govern lobbying; anticorruption laws put the onus on public officials to avoid corrupt practices.

Mexico/Argentina

- Lobbying in Mexico is in the early stages of professionalization and is following the US path in strategy and regulation.
- The negative connotation of lobbying and the only recent pluralistic policymaking combine to limit the importance of lobbying in Argentina.

Learning by Doing

Shale containing gas is also abundant in Britain and many countries in Europe. While the quantity of recoverable gas is subject to further test drilling, the amount could be substantial. The energy industry is eager to tap this gas through fracking. The availability of native gas is especially attractive as much of Europe is dependent on Russia for this energy source which has – at times – been problematic. Fracking proponents are using the energy independence argument along with the need to have competitively priced gas for manufacturing steel and chemicals to support their push for tapping shale gas.

Environmental concerns are front and center and anti-fracking forces are mounting a well-organized campaign to prevent hydraulic fracturing. Fracking has been banned in France and Bulgaria and parts of Spain. Other counties are studying the environmental impacts before allowing this form of gas extraction. Concerns center on aquifer contamination, water consumption and pollution, as well as noise. Moreover, the environmental community is skeptical of supporting the development of a fossil fuel, even if it has a lower carbon impact than coal.

The EU is attempting to establish a communitywide policy framework for fracking. In response to concerns of the environmental community, the European Parliament, in October 2013, voted in favor of requiring in-depth environmental studies before fracking. Supporters of fracking received a boost shortly after Parliament's action, when the EU environment commissioner rejected a comprehensive ban on fracking in the EU. The policy path forward remains to be established.

Take a side in the EU fracking debate and create a one-page outline of a lobbying campaign to achieve your objective in the EU.

Chapter 10 Bibliography

"ALTER-EU Reacts to MEP Lobbying Scandal." *Corporate Europe Observatory*, Accessed August 11, 2014. http://corporateeurope.org/2011/03/alter-eu-reacts-mep-lobbying-scandal.

Bouwen, Pieter. "Exchanging Access Goods for Access: A Comparative Study of Business Lobbying in the European Union Institutions." *European Journal of Political Research*, no. 43 (2004): 337–69.

Bouwen, Pieter, and Margaret Mccown. "Lobbying versus Litigation: Political and Legal Strategies of Interest Representation in the European Union." *Journal of European Public Policy* 14, no. 3 (n.d.): 422–43. doi:10.1080/13501760701243798.

Bristow, Michael. "How China Is Ruled: National People's Congress." *BBC News*, March 4, 2009. http://www.bbc.co.uk/news/world-asia-pacific-13908155.

Chang, Gordon G. "How To Lobby Beijing." *Forbes*, May 6, 2010. http://www.forbes.com/2010/05/06/china-business-government-opinions-columnists-gordon-chang.html.

Charrad, Kristina. "Lobbying the European Union." *Westfälische Wilhelms-Universität Münster Nachwuchsgruppe „Europäische Zivilgesellschaft Und Multilevel Governance*, n.d.

Coen, David. *Lobbying in the European Union*. Directorate General Internal Policies of the Union, November 2007.

Coen, David, and Jeremy Richardson, eds. *Lobbying the European Union: Institutions, Actors, and Issues*. Also available as: eBook, 2009.

"Constitucion Politica de Los Estados Unidos Mexicanos: Articulos 5,6,7," February 5, 1917. http://www.diputados.gob.mx/LeyesBiblio/htm/1.htm.

Ex-Austrian MEP imprisoned in lobbying scandal, January 15, 2013, euractiv.com.

"Financial Programming and Budget." *European Commission*. Accessed August 14, 2014. http://ec.europa.eu/budget/index_en.cfm.

Friedman, Ellen D. "Complicity, Campaigns, Collaboration, and Corruption: Strategies and Responses to European Corporations and Lobbyists in China." *Globalization Monitor Limited*, November 29, 2010. http://www.amrc.org.hk/node/1030/print.

Gonzalez, Susana. "Fortalecer El Cabildeo, Pide Directivo de Grupo Salinas." *La Jornada*, July 5, 2010.

Greenwood, Justin. *Interest Representation in the European Union*. Palgrave Macmillan, 2003.

Guosheng, Deng, and Kennedy, Scott. "Big Business and Industry Association Lobbying in China: The Paradox of Contrasting Styles." Indiana University, Indianapolis and Bloomington, Indiana, 2009.

Hauser, Henry. "European Union Lobbying Post-Lisbon: An Economic Analysis." *Berkeley Journal of International Law* 29, no. 2 (2011).

How China is ruled; National People's Congress, BBC News, October 8, 2012.

Johnson, Diane E. "Continuity and Change in Argentine Interest Group Activity and Lobbying Practices." *Journal of Public Affairs* 8, no. 1–2 (February 1, 2008): 83–97. doi:10.1002/pa.282.

Kennedy, Scott. "Comparing Formal and Informal Lobbying Practices in China the Capital's Ambivalent Embrace of Capitalists." *China Information* 23, no. 2 (July 1, 2009): 195–222. doi:10.1177/0920203X09105125.

Kennedy, Scott and Guosheng, Deng. "Big Business and Industry Association Lobbying in China: The Paradox of Contrasting Styles." *China Journal* 63 (2010): 101–25.

Lobbying Bonanza as Firms Try to Influence European Union, Lipton and Hakim, New York Times, October 18, 2013.

O'Donnell, John. "Special Report - How Lobbyists Rewrite Europe's Laws." *Reuters*, March 18, 2011.

Peter, Laurence. "Fourth Euro MP in Lobbying Probe." *BBC News*, March 28, 2011. http://www.bbc.com/news/world-europe-12880701.

PROCAB: Codigo de Etica. Accessed August 11, 2014. http://www.procab.org.mx/etica.aspx.

"Public Anti-Corruption Initiatives." *Business Anti-Corruption Portal: Global Advice Network*. Accessed August 11, 2014. http://www.business-anti-corruption.com/country-profiles/east-asia-the-pacific/china/initiatives/public-anti-corruption-initiatives.aspx.

Ramirez, Erika. "En Las Cámaras, 250 Grupos de Cabilderos Al Servicio de Trasnacionales." *Contralinea*, July 2, 2013.

"Rescue the Register! How to Make EU Lobby Transparency Credible and Reliable." *ALTER-EU: Europe's Campaign for Lobbying Transparency*, June 20, 2013. http://www.alter-eu.org/documents/2013/06/rescue-the-register.

Schultz, Teri. "Lobbying Scandal Shocks Europe; Members of the European Parliament Resign (VIDEO)." *GlobalPost*. Accessed August 11, 2014. http://www.globalpost.com/dispatch/news/regions/europe/110407/european-parliament-lobbying-scandal.

Silicon Valley Companies Lobbying Against Europe's Privacy Proposals, Kevin O'Brien, New York Times, January 25, 2013.

"The State Council." *The Central People's Government of the People's Republic of China*. Accessed August 11, 2014. www.gov.cn.

Thu, Christian. "EU Lobbying Top 100 Biggest Spending Organizations." *Association of Accredited Public Policy Advocates to the European Union*, September 26, 2013. http://www.aalep.eu/eu-lobbying-top-100-biggest-spending-organisations.

Toeller, Annette. "Claims That 80 per Cent of Laws Adopted in the EU Member States Originate in Brussels Actually Tell Us Very Little about the Impact of EU Policy-Making." *EUROPP*.

Accessed August 11, 2014.
http://blogs.lse.ac.uk/europpblog/2012/06/13/europeanization-of-public-policy/.

Transparency Register: Frequently Asked Questions. Joint Transparency Register Secretariat, October 4, 2012.

Warleigh, Alex, and Jenny Fairbrass. *Influence and Interests in the European Union: The New Politics of Persuasion and Advocacy.* Europa Publications, 2002.

"Worst EU Lobbying Awards 2010." Accessed August 11, 2014. http://www.worstlobby.eu/.

Chapter 11: The Future of Lobbying

Lobbying has been and continues to be in the public eye. On October 15, 17, 19, 20, and 24, 2013, *The New York Times* ran stories about lobbying with titles including: "Lobbyists Ready for a New Fight on US Spending" and "Lobbying Heats Up Before Farm Talks." Based on these and other media reports as well as the data reported via the Lobbying Disclosure Act, lobbying remains a major part of the policymaking process. The current state of affairs implies that the future of lobbying is secure. There are, however, some storm clouds on the horizon that could change the lobbying status quo. This chapter highlights the evolving environment for lobbying and offers insights into how lobbying might adapt to new conditions.

Basic Demand and Supply

The demand for and supply of lobbying services combine to offer a strong foundation for advocacy in the coming years. Not only is demand sustained through increasingly complex legislation that requires outside expertise to untangle, but there's a constant supply of lobbyists making their way to K Street each year. As much as we are uncomfortable with special interests buying their way into government processes, the profession remains constitutionally protected and Supreme Court justices continue to affirm the right to petition. However, there are evolving factors that may change lobbying as we know it in the near future.

Demand. Policymaking by Congress, administrative agencies and regulators is not going away. We have seen major legislation in the past few years including the Affordable Care Act and the Dodd-Frank financial reform legislation. There is no shortage of new legislative proposals, including issues ranging from immigration to privacy to climate change. Moreover, the fundamental reason why organizations lobby – to achieve desired policy outcomes for private and public gains – remains in tact. The government will continue to spend trillions of dollars annually and that alone provides ample reasons for lobbying. Public policy also impacts trade, tax and foreign policy, adding to the incentive for private businesses, nonprofits and local governments to advocate.

The rationale that supports the various models of lobbying – exchange, expertise and legislative subsidy – remains. The opportunity for exchange continues, as lobbyists who aid politicians' campaign finance efforts expect to have an open door to share their perspectives. The complexity of issues facing Congress and regulators will continue the need for well-researched and articulated information. The need for a legislative subsidy will remain strong, as there is little support for more Congressional and Executive department staff.

A final reason for continued lobbying is that it works: There is extensive anecdotal and mounting analytical evidence that lobbying provides a strong return on investment. Moreover, there is a perception that the risk of not lobbying is high. The risk concern might become more salient as pressures for budget cuts and smaller government reduce the size of the pie that lobbyists are vying for.

Business will continue to dominate lobbying as their potential private gains are great and they are well resourced. Even the most active companies that lobby spend significantly less than one percent of revenues on regulated advocacy. Thus, lobbying may be viewed as an inexpensive "insurance policy". Non-business interest group lobbying may see an increase as social media and the Internet reduce the cost of entering the advocacy arena.

Supply. The supply of lobbying services is holding stable. While the number of federally-registered lobbyists peaked in 2007 at 14,800, it has remained at about 12,000 since. Nevertheless, many Congressional members and senior staff continue to move to lobbying after they leave the government. The shift from the Hill to K Street is logical; it provides senior public officials an opportunity to monetize the "assets" (network, process knowledge, substantive expertise) they built while in public service.

Other Positive Factors
There are several additional factors that favor a positive outlook for lobbying. From increasing globalization to the rise of social media to the integration of public relations with lobbying, the advocacy business has a promising future.

Globalization. Lobbying is becoming a more accepted practice around the globe; although, often under the name "advocacy". The EU is rapidly matching the size, scale and strategies used in the US. This creates a new market and revenue opportunity for European and US lobbying firms. China is also a burgeoning market for lobbying. While the approach to and process for lobbying is decidedly Chinese, Western lobbying firms are participating in this emerging market. Moreover, globalization is continuing to bring foreign interests to lobby in the US.

Internet and Social Media. The Internet and social media have the potential to democratize lobbying. The Internet has become both a research tool and communications vehicle. A few clicks and most anyone can become an "expert" on any policy topic. Social media has become a powerful means for crowd-sourcing advocacy. The combination of the Internet and social media could democratize lobbying by offsetting the resource advantage of traditional business lobbying.

Growth Potential. – In *The Dynamics of Firm Lobbying*, William R. Kerr, William F. Lincoln and Prachi Mishra find only a small portion of corporations lobby. While those that lobby do so consistently, those that do not are equally persistent in not lobbying. The authors hypothesize that the reluctance to lobby is a function of the high cost of entry including learning the lobbying process, building relationships, understanding laws, setting an agenda, understanding opposition etc. The mounting evidence that lobbying provides an attractive return on investment combined with the Internet and social media reducing costs of entry may encourage more firms to lobby. Moreover, the leveling off of lobbying spending might encourage lobbying firms to more aggressively market to non-lobbying firms.

Related Services/Vertical Integration. Many lobbying firms have long been offering legal or public relations services as a complement to other advocacy efforts. Expansion into these areas will likely continue to diversify offerings and grow the business. Broadening services has the added benefit of reducing disclosure requirements as individuals are only required to disclose their lobbying activities if advocacy accounts for more than 20 percent of their activities.

Storm Clouds on the Horizon

The forgoing picture implies the future of lobbying is secure. However, there are countervailing forces ranging from increased polarization in Washington to *Citizens United* providing alternative ways to influence policymakers. These alternatives could fundamentally alter the lobbying industry with less costly and more accessible options.

Polarization. The first threat to the lobbying industry is the increasing polarization of the parties in Washington. Research confirms what most Americans perceive: Democrats and Republicans are becoming more divergent in their views and little compromise is taking place. Without compromise, new legislation is less likely to pass. Congressional gridlock also reduces the need for lobbying to protect the status quo. There is less opportunity for "educating" the opposition, especially the fence sitters, as positions are so extreme.

Citizens United. A second dark cloud on the lobbying horizon is the *Citizens United* decision. The Supreme Court ruling allows corporations to donate funds directly to candidates for election. While on the surface this does not impact lobbying, funding candidates directly provides businesses with an alternative path to influence those in office and the positions they support. In the 2012 election cycle, the *Citizens United* decision was in full effect. That year, lobbying spending declined for the first time, excluding the financial crisis. Might the decline support the argument that corporations are using this alternative path for advocacy? The answer awaits more time and analytical assessment.

Rising "Costs and Risks." An additional threat to lobbying is the rising costs of advocacy. The costs refer to reputational risks associated with a lobbyist gone bad such as Jack Abramoff. Another cost is adverse publicity related to reporting of lobbying data under the Lobbying Disclosure Act. *The Boston Globe* front-page exposé about the lobbying activities of Whirlpool that highlighted favorable tax and trade treatment was not the publicity the firm wanted. Lobbyists also face increased risks of violating LDA and HLOG regulations. Inadvertent miss-steps such as accepting tickets to the symphony can lead to violations. One clear trend is that harsher penalties are being meted out to those convicted of breaking lobbying laws. Former Speaker of the Massachusetts House Sal DiMasi was sent to prison for eight years after being convicted of seven counts of corruption including conspiracy to defraud the government, extortion and mail fraud.

A summary of the strengths, weaknesses, opportunities and threats facing the lobbying industry is provided in Exhibit 11-1.

Exhibit 11-1
SWOT Analysis of Lobbying Industry

Strengths	Weaknesses
• Long legal tradition • History of success • Entrenched function • Alignment of interests • World/issues getting more complex	• Ethics concerns and scandals • Win only 50% of the time • Negative public sentiment
Opportunities	**Threats**
• Globalization of lobbying • Small existing market share • Vertical integration	• Proliferation of media outlets • Rising costs and risks • *Citizens United* • Polarization of the discourse

What It All Means
Lobbying has been a part of American policymaking since the founding of the country. Over the years, lobbying has become professionalized and entwined with lawmaking, regulation and administration. Lobbying will remain an integral part of the American political process. Businesses will continue to

dominate the Washington advocacy scene. However, the Internet and social media will provide a stronger voice for non-business interests. Lobbyists will themselves become more polarized as their targets move apart. Nevertheless coalitions will continue be an important strategy and will often make for strange bedfellows.

For policymakers, the implications for the future of lobbying are threefold. First, lobbyists will continue to be an important source of information and insight for policymakers, especially members of Congress. The complexity of issues will only increase. However, the amount of legislative subsidy available to members and regulators may level off or diminish, given the alternative path that corporations have to influence policy created by way of the *Citizens United* decision. The decline in lobbying spending in 2012 and 2013 is early evidence of this impact. Finally, policymakers will need to pay more attention to social media-driven advocacy. Interest groups will continue to use this cost effective vehicle to make their voice heard. If policymakers fail to pay attention to campaigns conducted through this medium; they may be faced with an unhappy public.

Finally, there are implications for you and me, the general public. For us, the future of lobbying will likely positively and negatively impact our ability to influence public policy. Business interests will continue to dominate access to policymaking through both lobbying and campaign contributions. While these groups may not directly represent our interests, we do gain by having our better informed policymakers. Should we be concerned that legislators are only hearing from one side of the issue? Perhaps not, as one legislator relayed: If I am smart enough be elected to Congress, I am smart enough to know lobbyists spin their viewpoints. Therefore I solicit input from all sides of the issue. My value added is taking the range of lobbying and general public perspectives and reaching my own conclusions.

We too can have a virtual seat in the legislator's office by leveraging social media. From email to Twitter, to Facebook, to blogs we can reach our elected officials expeditiously and at minimal cost. But effective advocacy requires more than signing an online petition. Just as lobbyists do their homework and create a powerful narrative for their position, so must we. Again in the words of a legislator: A substantive argument from a constituent carries as much or more weight than that of a lobbyist. Equally important, a Massachusetts executive office Secretary shared that electronic petitions with thousands of signatures are largely discounted because they are too easy to submit. They do not demonstrate a real commitment to the issue; a customized letter does. Blogs have become a powerful voice in policy debates. Legislative staffers troll the blogosphere to both gauge public opinion and gain substantive insights.

We can amplify our voice by encouraging charitable organizations who share our perspective to become more active advocates. As detailed earlier in the book, charitable organizations routinely "under lobby" for fear of risking their chartable status. However, most are far from reaching that threshold. Educating these groups about their ability to lobby and supporting them with some expertise can go a long way to having legislators hear your views. Lawmakers are often very willing to provide access to charitable groups as it increases the legitimacy of their decision making.

Reaching out to regulators and administrators responsible to rule making and policy implementation is another, often overlooked avenue, for impact. Major legislation such as the Affordable Care Act and Dodd-Frank lead to dozens of rule-making actions by the implementers of these laws. Professional lobbyists are active at these venues; the public is often not. Increasingly electronic rule making is being used to solicit input. Key agencies publish opportunities for input on their webpage. With relatively little effort, you can find and comment on policies of interest. These organizations pride themselves on their professionalism and objectivity. Therefore they are often receptive to strong substantive arguments regardless of who submits them. Moreover, these policy makers not elected officials and therefore are not influenced by lobbyists' campaign contributions.

Finally, we need to take a page from the lobbyist's playbook –get face time with the member outside the office to build a relationship. Lobbyists routinely attend campaign fundraisers to gain access. Several lobbyists have shared with me they go to fund raisers with one objective in mind, to say a 30 second hello to the candidate. That connection says: I came out to support you. We can do the same. It will not be through attending $1000 a plate dinners, rather it comes from attending town halls and arranging for meetings with their members in the district. And yes, attending the $10 fundraiser picnic is also valuable. You can also build a relationship indirectly through the member's staff in the district. Access is free and easy. If you offer substance you will get a fair hearing.

All of the above takes effort. Yes, it takes time and grey matter to impact policy. Lobbyist work hard, you must as well.

Toward a More Perfect Lobby
Lobbying creates value by providing useful, quality, information to policymakers. Lobbying is a protected right; it will always be a part of policymaking. There are, however, several opportunities to improve the lobby. First and foremost is improving access for all voices, not just the well funded. The persistent criticism of lobbying is it provides an unfair advantage to those with resources and/or connections. Leveling the access and expertise playing field would greatly enhance the public value that lobbying creates. Two

strategies that could help to achieve this objective is (1) pro bono lobbying by in-house and for-hire lobbyists and (2) members setting aside time blocks for those who have a harder time gaining access.

The lobbying industry would also benefit from minimizing scandals through industry self-regulation and an enforceable code of ethics. Several approaches could be used to turn this concept into reality. First, the industry could not only establish a code of ethics, it could establish a review and verification protocol to ensure individual lobbyists comply with the code. Those that do would be awarded the equivalent of the "Good Housekeeping Seal of Approval." A second and more aggressive enforcement mechanism would be the creation of an independent ethics commission with enforcement powers. Much like the American Bar Association, this body would be a place to lodge complaints about lobbyist behavior and it would research and adjudicate such issues. Another idea is to divorce lobbyists from campaign finance. Campaign fundraising is undoubtedly linked to member access and potentially to policy influence. Under such a proposal federally-registered lobbyists would abstain from campaign financing activities. Clearly, this is fraught with First Amendment rights issues. A final idea to "clean up" lobbying is to establish a fiduciary relationship between lobbyist and client. Doing so would raise the level of obligation between the parties and hopefully prevent conflict of interest issues that plagued Abramoff's relationships with the various Native American tribes he represented.

These actions would enhance the practice of lobbying, but they are challenging to adopt. As a former member of the Boston City Council turned lobbyist put it: I'm not sure these would fly! While I share his skepticism, at the end of the day they may be essential to maintaining a robust lobbying industry that benefits all of us.

****

As you began this book you took a survey about your attitudes toward lobbying. Retake the test and see how, if at all, your beliefs have changed. I look forward to hearing from you about the results at mark_fagan@hks.harvard.edu.

Endnotes

[1] "Lobby." *Oxford Dictionaries*. Oxford University Press, 2013. http://oxforddictionaries.com/us/definition/american_english/lobby.

[2] "What Is Lobbying? Definition and Meaning." *BusinessDictionary.com*. Accessed July 18, 2013. http://www.businessdictionary.com/definition/lobbying.html#ixzz2Tz3y4A3l.

[3] "What Is Lobbying?" *The Law Dictionary*. Accessed July 18, 2013. http://thelawdictionary.org/lobbying/.

[4] Ostas, Daniel T., and Philosophy Documentation Center. "The Law and Ethics of K Street." Edited by Denis G. Arnold. *Business Ethics Quarterly* 17, no. 1 (2007): 33–63. doi:10.5840/beq200717113.

[5] Mayer, Lloyd Hitoshi. *What Is This "Lobbying" That We Are So Worried About?* SSRN Scholarly Paper. Rochester, NY: Social Science Research Network, January 1, 2008. http://papers.ssrn.com/abstract=1012334.

[6] Kollman, Ken. *Outside Lobbying: Public Opinion and Interest Group Strategies.* Princeton, N.J.: Princeton University Press, 1998.

[7] "DC Mythbusting: 'Lobbyist' Coined at Willard Hotel." *We Love DC*. Accessed July 18, 2013. http://www.welovedc.com/2009/06/09/dc-mythbusting-lobbyist-coined-at-willard-hotel/.

[8] "Tool Company V. Norris - 69 U.S. 45 (1864)." *Justia US Supreme Court Center*. Accessed July 18, 2013. http://supreme.justia.com/cases/federal/us/69/45/case.html.

[9] Byrd, Robert. "United States Senate." Government. *Lobbyists*, September 28, 1987. http://www.senate.gov/legislative/common/briefing/Byrd_History_Lobbying.htm.

[10] *Ibid.*

[11] *Ibid.*

[12] Jacob, Kathryn Allamong. "King of the Lobby." *Smithsonian* 32, no. 2 (May 2001): 122–131.

[13] *Ibid.*

[14] Kaiser, Robert G. "Citizen K Street." Newspaper. *Citizen K Street*. Accessed July 18, 2013. http://blog.washingtonpost.com/citizen-k-street/chapters/introduction/.

[15] Athena Jones, Political newcomers face high costs and difficult political odds, CNN http://www.cnn.com/2012/01/22/politics/newcomers-campaign-costs

[16] Jacob, Kathryn Allamong. "King of the Lobby." *Smithsonian* 32, no. 2 (May 2001): 122–131.

[17] "WGBH American Experience . Transcontinental Railroad | PBS." *American Experience*. Accessed July 18, 2013. http://www.pbs.org/wgbh/americanexperience/features/general-article/tcrr-scandal/.

[18] Byrd, Robert. "United States Senate." Government. *Lobbyists*, September 28, 1987. http://www.senate.gov/legislative/common/briefing/Byrd_History_Lobbying.htm.

[19] "Corporations Record Huge Returns from Tax Lobbying, as Gridlock in Congress Stalls Reform - The Boston Globe." *BostonGlobe.com*. Accessed July 19, 2013. http://www.bostonglobe.com/news/politics/2013/03/16/corporations-record-huge-returns-from-tax-lobbying-gridlock-congress-stalls-reform/omgZvDPa37DNlSqi0G95YK/story.html.

[20] Byrd, Robert. "United States Senate." Government. *Lobbyists*, September 28, 1987. http://www.senate.gov/legislative/common/briefing/Byrd_History_Lobbying.htm.

[21] Hall, Richard L., and Alan V. Deardorff. "Lobbying as Legislative Subsidy." *American Political Science Review* 100, no. 01 (2006): 69–84. doi:10.1017/S0003055406062010.

[22] *Ibid.*

[23] Baumgartner, Frank R. "Converting Expectations: New Emporical Evidence on Congressional Lobbying and Public Policy." *University of North Carlona at Chapel Hill* (2013).

[24] "To Keep the Lobbyist Within Bounds." *The New York Times Magazine*, February 19, 1956. Congressional Record, March 2, 1956, vol. 102, pp. 38023.

[25] "Government Relations and Lobbying." *Patton Boggs*. Accessed July 18, 2013. http://www.pattonboggs.com/practice/government-relations-and-lobbying.

[26] Hall, Richard L., and Alan V. Deardorff. "Lobbying as Legislative Subsidy." *American Political Science Review* 100, no. 01 (2006): 69–84. doi:10.1017/S0003055406062010.

[27] *Ibid.*

[28] "Lobbying Database." *OpenSecrets.org*. Accessed July 18, 2013. http://www.opensecrets.org/lobby/.

[29] Leech, Beth L., Frank R. Baumgartner, Timothy M. La Pira, and Nicholas A. Semanko. "Drawing Lobbyists to Washington: Government Activity and the Demand for Advocacy." *Political Research Quarterly* 58, no. 1 (March 1, 2005): 19–30. doi:10.1177/106591290505800102.

[30] Stolberg, Sheryl Gay. "How Tom Donohue Transformed the U.S. Chamber of Commerce." *The New York Times*, June 1, 2013, sec. Business Day.

[31] "American Medical Association Advocacy Topics." Accessed July 22, 2013. https://www.ama-assn.org/ama/pub/advocacy/topics.page?

[32] Baumgartner, Frank R., and Beth L. Leech. "Interest Niches and Policy Bandwagons: Patterns of Interest Group Involvement in National Politics." *Journal of Politics* 63, no. 4 (2001): 1191–1213. doi:10.1111/0022-3816.00106; 1195.

[33] *Ibid, 1197.*

[34] Kerr, William R., William F. Lincoln, and Prachi Mishra. *The Dynamics of Firm Lobbying*. Working Paper. National Bureau of Economic Research, November 2011. http://www.nber.org/papers/w17577.

[35] *Ibid.*

[36] Levine, Bertram J. *The Art of Lobbying: Building Trust and Selling Policy.* Washington, D.C.: CQ Press, 2009; 41.

[37] "Sunlight Foundation." *Sunlight Foundation*. Accessed July 22, 2013. http://sunlightfoundation.com/.

[38] Gura, David. No deluge of campaign cash after limits end. Marketplace, July 24, 2014.

[39] "Lobbyist Salary | Salary.com." *Salary.com*. Accessed July 22, 2013. http://www1.salary.com/Lobbyist-Salary.html.

[40] Richter, Brian Kelleher, Krislert Samphantharak, and Jeffrey F. Timmons. *Lobbying and Taxes*. SSRN Scholarly Paper. Rochester, NY: Social Science Research Network, October 22, 2008. http://papers.ssrn.com/abstract=1082146.

[41] "OpenCongress." *H.R.1148 STOCK Bill (STOCK Act)*. Accessed July 22, 2013. https://www.opencongress.org/bill/112-h1148/show.

[42] "Be Very Wary of the STOCK Act." *Sunlight Foundation*. Accessed July 22, 2013. http://sunlightfoundation.com/blog/2011/11/17/be-very-wary-of-the-stock-act/.

[43] "Texas Ethics Commission." *Lobbying in Texas: A Guide to the Texas Law.* Accessed July 22, 2013. http://www.ethics.state.tx.us/guides/LOBBY_guide.htm.

[44] "Texas Lobby Group." *A Full Service Lobbying and Government Relations Firm.* Accessed July 22, 2013. http://txlobby.com/.

[45] "Regan V. Taxation With Representation - 461 U.S. 540 (1983)." *Justia US Supreme Court Center*. Accessed July 28, 2013. http://supreme.justia.com/cases/federal/us/461/540/.

[46] "Eastern R. Conference V. Noerr Motors - 365 U.S. 127 (1961)." *Justia US Supreme Court Center*. Accessed July 28, 2013. http://supreme.justia.com/cases/federal/us/365/127/case.html.

[47] Fair Political Practices Com. v. Superior Court, Supreme Court of California (1979).

[48] ACLU of New Jersey v. New Jersey Election Law Enforcement Commission (United States District Court, District of New Jersey 1981).

[49] Marshall v. Baltimore and Ohio RR

[50] Senator Byrd, Lobbyists

[51] ACLU of New Jersey v. New Jersey Election Law Enforcement Commission (United States District Court, District of New Jersey 1981).

[52] Browne, Steven. "The Constitutionality of Lobby Reform: Implicating Associational Privacy and the Right to Petition the Government." *William & Mary Bill of Rights Journal* 4, no. 2 (February 1, 1995): 736.

[53] Fair Political Practices Com. v. Superior Court, Supreme Court of California (1979).

[54] Luneburg, William V., Thomas M. Susman, and Rebecca H. Gordon. *The Lobbying Manual: A Complete Guide to Federal Lobbying Law and Practice.* American Bar Association, (2009) Footnote 2 Chapter 10.

[55] Holman, Craig. "Origins, Evolution and Structure of the Lobbying Disclosure Act." *Public Citizen*, May 11, 2006. http://www.citizen.org/documents/LDAorigins.pdf.

[56] Luneburg, William V., Thomas M. Susman, and Rebecca H. Gordon. *The Lobbying Manual: A Complete Guide to Federal Lobbying Law and Practice.* American Bar Association, (2009). P.253.

[57] "History of the Lobbying Disclosure Act," *Public Citizen: LobbyingInfo.org*, July 26, 2005, http://www.lobbyinginfo.org/laws/page.cfm?pageid=15#_edn11.

[58] Lobbying Registration and Disclosure: Before and After the Enactment of the Honest Leadership and Open Government Act of 2007, Jacob Straus, CRS (2011).

[59] Luneburg, William V., Thomas M. Susman, and Rebecca H. Gordon. *The Lobbying Manual: A Complete Guide to Federal Lobbying Law and Practice.* American Bar Association, 2009 (11).

[60] "United States V. Rumely - 345 U.S. 41 (1953)." *Justia US Supreme Court Center*. Accessed July 28, 2013. http://supreme.justia.com/cases/federal/us/345/41/.

[61] *Ibid.*

[62] "United States V. Harriss - 347 U.S. 612 (1954)." *Justia US Supreme Court Center*. Accessed July 28, 2013. http://supreme.justia.com/cases/federal/us/347/612/case.html.

[63] Holman, Craig. "Origins, Evolution and Structure of the Lobbying Disclosure Act." *Public Citizen*, May 11, 2006. http://www.citizen.org/documents/LDAorigins.pdf.

[64] Canady, Charles. *Lobbying Disclosure Act of 1995.* 104th Congress, 1st Session, House of Representatives, Committee of the Whole House on the State of the Union, November 14, 1994.

[65] Holman, Craig. "Origins, Evolution and Structure of the Lobbying Disclosure Act." *Public Citizen*, May 11, 2006. http://www.citizen.org/documents/LDAorigins.pdf.

[66] Luneburg, William V., Thomas M. Susman, and Rebecca H. Gordon. *The Lobbying Manual: A Complete Guide to Federal Lobbying Law and Practice.* American Bar Association, 2009 (276).

[67] *Limitation on Use of Appropriated Funds to Influence Certain Federal Contracting and Financial Transactions. 31USC1352.*

[68] *Ibid.*

[69] The Constitutionality of Lobby Reform: Implicating Associational Privacy and the Right to Petition the Government, Steven Browne, William & Mary Bill of Right Journal, Volume 4, Issue 2 (1995)

[70] "The Lobbying Game: Influence-brokers In D.c. How Representatives Of Foreign Interests Push Their Agendas Among Washington's Decision-makers." *Philly.com.* Accessed July 28, 2013. http://articles.philly.com/1996-09-17/news/25631817_1_trade-deficit-mfn-trading-status.

[71] Straus, Jacob R. *Lobbying Registration and Disclosure: The Role of the Clerk of the House and the Secretary of the Senate.* Congressional Research Service, June 20, 2013. http://www.fas.org/sgp/crs/misc/RL34377.pdf.

[72] Clinton, William J. "Remarks on Signing the Lobbying Disclosure Act of 1995 and an Exchange with Reporters." Roosevelt Room of the White House, December 19, 1995.

[73] Luneburg, William V., Thomas M. Susman, and Rebecca H. Gordon. *The Lobbying Manual: A Complete Guide to Federal Lobbying Law and Practice.* American Bar Association, 2009 (145).

[74] *Ibid, 147.*

[75] Luneburg, William V. "The Evolution of Federal Lobbying Regulation: Where We Are Now and Where We Should Be Going." *McGeorge Law Review* 41 (2009), 124.

[76] *Ibid, 89.*

[77] Babington, Charles. "Bush Signs Lobby-Ethics Bill." *The Washington Post,* September 15, 2007, sec. Nation. http://www.washingtonpost.com/wp-dyn/content/article/2007/09/15/AR2007091500589.html.

[78] *An Act to Provide Greater Transparency in the Legislative Process,* 2007.

[79] *Ibid, (Sec. 211)*

[80] *Ibid, (Sec. 101)*

[81] Straus, Jacob R. *Lobbying the Executive Branch: Current Practices and Options for Change.* DIANE Publishing, 2010.

[82] Citizens United v. Federal Election Commission (United States Supreme Court 2010).

[83] Carney, Timothy. "Why Lobbyists Dislike Citizens United | WashingtonExaminer.com." *Washington Examiner.* Accessed July 28, 2013. http://washingtonexaminer.com/article/2515086.

[84] "2012 Lobbying Disclosure: Observations on Lobbyists' Compliance with Disclosure Requirements." Accessed July 28, 2013. http://www.gao.gov/products/GAO-13-437?source=ra.

[85] *Ibid.*

[86] Levin, Robert M. *Lobbying Law in the Spotlight: Challenges and Proposed Improvements.* Report of the Task Force on Federal Lobbying Laws Section of

Administrative La w and Regulatory Practice American Bar Association, January 3, 2011.

[87] "Ethics: Contingency Fees for Lobbyists." *National Conference of State Legislatures*, March 2013. http://www.ncsl.org/legislatures-elections/ethicshome/50-state-chart-contingency-fees.aspx.

[88] Kirkpatrick, David D., and Charlie Savage. "Star Lobbyist Closes Shop Amid F.B.I. Inquiry." *The New York Times*, March 30, 2009, sec. U.S. / Politics. http://www.nytimes.com/2009/03/30/us/politics/30pma.html.

[89] "Annual Lobbying by PMA Group." *Open Secrets: Center for Responsive Politics*. Accessed August 4, 2013. http://www.opensecrets.org/lobby/firmsum.php?id=D000000501&year=2009.

[90] Eggen, Dan, and Maria Glod. "Ex-lobbyist Paul Magliocchetti Charged with Campaign-finance Fraud." *The Washington Post*, August 6, 2010, sec. Metro. http://www.washingtonpost.com/wp-dyn/content/article/2010/08/05/AR2010080504416.html.

[91] *Ibid.*

[92] "Paul Magliocchetti Pleads Guilty - John Bresnahan." *POLITICO*. Accessed August 4, 2013. http://www.politico.com/news/stories/0910/42690.html.

[93] Gardiner, Sean. "Lobbyist Gets Prison In Bribery Scandal." *Wall Street Journal*, September 29, 2012, sec. NY Politics. http://online.wsj.com/article/SB20000872396390443389604578024842514284034.html.

[94] Frankel, Tamar. *Trust and Honesty: America's Business Culture at a Crossroad*. New York: Oxford University Press, 2008 (31).

[95] Sean Gardiner, "Lobbyist Gets Prison In Bribery Scandal," *Wall Street Journal*, September 29, 2012, sec. Ny Politics, http://online.wsj.com/article/SB20000872396390443389604578024842514284034.html.

[96] Abramoff, Jack. *Capitol Punishment: The Hard Truth About Washington Corruption from America's Most Notorious Lobbyist*. Washington, D.C.; New York: WND Books ; distributed to the trade by Midpoint Trade Books, 2011 (233).

[97] *Ibid, 213.*

[98] *Ibid, 234.*

[99] *Ibid, 235.*

[100] *Ibid, 234.*

[101] John Emerich Edward Dalberg Acton, 1st Baron Acton (English Historian and Moralist) : Supplemental Information." *Encyclopaedia Britannica*. Accessed August 4, 2013. http://www.britannica.com/EBchecked/topic/4647/John-Emerich-Edward-Dalberg-Acton-1st-Baron-Acton/4647suppinfo/Supplemental-Information.

[102] The Psychology of Power Absolutely, The Economist, Jan 21, 2010.

[103] Woodstock Theological Center. *The Ethics of Lobbying: Organized Interests, Political Power, and the Common Good.* Washington, D.C.: Georgetown University Press, 2002 (29).

[104] Jones, Jeffrey M. "Lobbyists Debut at Bottom of Honesty and Ethics List." *Gallup*, December 10, 2007. http://www.gallup.com/poll/103123/lobbyists-debut-bottom-honesty-ethics-list.aspx.

[105] Saad, Lydia. "Americans Decry Power of Lobbyists, Corporations, Banks, Feds." *Gallup Politics*, April 11, 2011.

[106] "The Shadow Lobbyist." *Opinionator.* Accessed August 4, 2013. http://opinionator.blogs.nytimes.com/2013/04/25/the-shadow-lobbyist/.

[107] "Congress and the Public." Accessed August 4, 2013. http://www.gallup.com/poll/1600/Congress-Public.aspx#1.

[108] Woodstock Theological Center, *The Ethics of Lobbying: Organized Interests, Political Power, and the Common Good.* (Washington, D.C.: Georgetown University Press, 2002), 56.

[109] Abramoff, *Capitol Punishment*, 264.

[110] "Code of Ethics." American League of Lobbyists. Accessed July 6, 2013. http://www.alldc.org/ethicscode.cfm.

[111] *Ibid.*

[112] *Ibid.*

[113] *Ibid.*

[114] *Ibid.*

[115] Woodstock Theological Center, *The Ethics of Lobbying*, 2.

[116] Jack Abramoff, *Capitol Punishment: The Hard Truth about Washington Corruption from America's Most Notorious Lobbyist* (Washington, D.C.; New York: WND Books ; distributed to the trade by Midpoint Trade Books, 2011), 95.

[117] Woodstock Theological Center, *The Ethics of Lobbying*, 61.

[118] *Ibid, 84.*

[119] *Ibid, 31.*

[120] *Ibid, 89.*

[121] This concept was developed by Lindsey Parker, candidate for JD in 2013, in a final paper for Law and the Lobby at Boston University School of Law in 2013. The unpublished paper is available upon request.

[122] Lobbying Reform With Teeth: Incorporating Lobbying Into The American bar Association's Model Rules of Professional Conduct, Lindsey Parker, Unpublished paper for Law and the Lobby, Boston University School of Law, 2013.

[123] "Standards for Lawyer Sanctions." *The Florida Bar.* Accessed August 4, 2013. http://www.floridabar.org/tfb/TFBLawReg.nsf/9dad7bbda218afe885257002004833c5/ca758a1382421b60852574ba00649949.

[124] Standards for Lawyer Sanctions, The Florida Bar

[125] Hasen, Richard L. "Lobbying, Rent-Seeking, and the Constitution." *Stanford Law Review* 64, no. 1 (January 1, 2012): 191.

[126] *Ibid, 235.*

[127] Tamar Frankel, *Fiduciary Law* (Oxford; New York: Oxford University Press, 2011), http://site.ebrary.com/id/10476943.

[128] *Ibid, 29.*

[129] M. Thomas Arnold and Dan L. Goldwasser, *Accountants' Liability* (Practising Law Institute, 2013), 7–6.

[130] Ibid., 7–24.

[131] "About the Financial Industry Regulatory Authority." Accessed August 4, 2013. http://www.finra.org/AboutFINRA/.

[132] Jerry M. Burger et al., "The Norm of Reciprocity as an Internalized Social Norm: Returning Favors Even When No One Finds out," *Social Influence* 4, no. 1 (2009): 11–17, doi:10.1080/15534510802131004.

[133] Dennis Regan, "Effects of a Favor and Liking on Compliance," *Journal of Experimental Psychology* 7 (1971): 627–39.

[134] Burger et al., "The Norm of Reciprocity as an Internalized Social Norm."

[135] Benjamin A. Converse et al., "Reciprocity Is Not Give and Take, Asymmetric Reciprocity to Positive and Negative Acts," *Psychological Science* 19, no. 12 (2008).

[136] Robert B. Cialdini, *Influence: The Psychology of Persuasion, Revised Edition*, Revised edition (New York: Harper Business, 2006), 19.

[137] Petia K. Petrova, Robert B. Cialdini, and Stephen J. Sills, "Consistency-Based Compliance across Cultures," *Journal of Experimental Social Psychology* 43 (2007): 104–11.

[138] John Harwood, "Flip-Flops Are Looking Like a Hot Summer Trend," *The New York Times*, June 23, 2008, sec. U.S. / Politics, http://www.nytimes.com/2008/06/23/us/politics/23caucus.html.

[139] "Commitment," *Environmental Assistance and Customer Service - N.C. Department of Environment and Natural Resources*, accessed August 2, 2014, http://portal.ncdenr.org/web/deao/outreach/recycling-education-campaigns/social-marketing/strategies/commitment.

[140] Cialdini, *Influence*, 82.

[141] Petia K. Petrova, Robert B. Cialdini, and Stephen J. Sills, "Consistency-Based Compliance across Cultures," *Journal of Experimental Social Psychology* 43 (2007): 104–11.

[142] Sammy Said, "The Top Five Biggest Athlete Endorsement Deals," *TheRichest*, accessed August 2, 2014, http://www.therichest.com/expensive-

lifestyle/money/the-top-five-biggest-athlete-endorsement-deals/.

[143] Cialdini, *Influence*, 90.

[144] Ibid., 99.

[145] Daniel O'Keefe, "Persuasion Theory and Research," *Sage*, 1990, 106.

[146] "Seeds of Peace: Building Peace at Summer Camp Transcript" (United States Institute of Peace), accessed August 2, 2014, http://www.buildingpeace.org/teach-visit-us-and-learn/exhibits/witnesses-transcripts/seeds-peace.

[147] W. Sluckin, D.J. Hargreaves, and A.M. Colman, "Some Experimental Studies of Familiarity and Liking," *Bulletin of the British Psychological Society*, 1982, 194.

[148] Saul McLeod, "The Milgram Experiment," http://www.simplypsychology.org/milgram.html, *SimplyPsychology*, (2007).

[149] Mark Fagan and Tamar Frankel, *Trust and Honesty in the Real World*, 2 edition (Anchorage, AK: Fathom Publishing Company, 2009).

[150] Badkar, Mamta. "9 Wars That Were Really About Commodities." *Business Insider*. Aug 15,

2012. Accessed August 2, 2014. http://www.businessinsider.com/nine-wars-that-were-fought-over

commodities-2012-8.

[151] Carol Vogel, "'The Scream' Sells for Nearly $120 Million at Sotheby's Auction," *The New York Times*, May 2, 2012, sec. Arts / Art & Design, http://www.nytimes.com/2012/05/03/arts/design/the-scream-sells-for-nearly-120-million-at-sothebys-auction.html.

[152] Howard Gardner, *Changing Minds: The Art And Science of Changing Our Own And Other People's Minds*, First Trade Paper Edition edition (Boston, Mass.: Harvard Business Review Press, 2006), 16.

[153] John Stefano, "Body Language and Persuasion," *Litigation* 3 (1977 1976): 31–33, 54–55.

[154] Raasch, Janet, When Persuading, Body Language Beats Words Re: Persuasion and Negotiation in the Practice of Law, *The National Law Review*, 2014.

[155] John Stefano, "Body Language and Persuasion," *Litigation* 3 (1977 1976): 31–33, 54–55..

[156] Ibid., 31–33, 54–55.

[157] Jason Nazar, "The 21 Principles of Persuasion," *Forbes*, March 26, 2013, http://www.forbes.com/sites/jasonnazar/2013/03/26/the-21-principles-of-persuasion/.

[158] Steve Horn, "NY Assembly Passes Two-Year Fracking Moratorium, Senate Expected to Follow," *Huffington Post*, March 7, 2013, http://www.huffingtonpost.com/steve-horn/ny-assembly-fracking-

moratorium_b_2831272.html.

159 Steve Horn, "NY Assembly Passes Two-Year Fracking Moratorium, Senate Expected to Follow," *Huffington Post*, March 7, 2013, http://www.huffingtonpost.com/steve-horn/ny-assembly-fracking-moratorium_b_2831272.html.

160 "Campaign," *Merriam-Webster* (An Encyclopedia Britannica Company, n.d.), http://www.merriam-webster.com/dictionary/campaign.

161 Henry Mintzberg, "The Strategy Concept I: Five Ps For Strategy," *California Management Review* 30, no. 1 (Fall 1987): 11.

162 : Constantinos Costas Markides, "What Is Strategy and How Do You Know If You Have One?," 2004, doi:10.1111/j.0955-6419.2004.00306.x.

163 Smita, Nair. "Apple's Premium Pricing Strategy and Product Differentiation," *Yahoo Finance*, January 28, 2014, http://finance.yahoo.com/news/apple-premium-pricing-strategy-product-191247308.html.

164 Michael E. Porter, "What Is Strategy?" *Harvard Business Review*, accessed August 3, 2014, http://hbr.org/1996/11/what-is-strategy/ar/1.

165 Patrick Seitz, "Sorry, Cheapskates, Apple iPhones to Remain Pricey," *Investor's Business Daily*, February 26, 2014, http://news.investors.com/SiteAds/Sponsorship.aspx?page=/NewsAndAnalysis/Article.aspx&position=sponsorbtn1&identifier=click&tile=2&ord=7364171220064911.

166 Brad Tuttle, "Southwest Airlines: We're Not Really About Cheap Flights Anymore," *Time*, March 26, 2013, http://business.time.com/2013/03/26/southwest-airlines-were-not-really-about-cheap-flights-anymore/.

167 Frances X. Frei, "The Four Things a Service Business Must Get Right," *Harvard Business Review*, accessed August 3, 2014, http://hbr.org/2008/04/the-four-things-a-service-business-must-get-right/ar/1.

168 Ibid.

169 Martin Reeves, Claire Love, and Philipp Tillmanns, "Your Strategy Needs a Strategy," *Harvard Business Review*, accessed August 3, 2014, http://hbr.org/2012/09/your-strategy-needs-a-strategy/ar/1.

170 Ibid.

171 Dartmouth College, The Office of Human Resources, The Goal Setting Process, accessed May 22, 2014.

172 Jeffrey M. Berry et al., "Washington: The Real No-Spin Zone" (presented at the Prepared for delivery at the Annual Meeting of the American Political Science Association, Chicago, Illinois, 2007), 3.

[173] *Framing Public Issues* (Washington D.C.: FrameWorks Institute, April 2005), 1, http://www.frameworksinstitute.org/assets/files/PDF/FramingPublicIssuesfinal.pdf.

[174] *Framing Public Issues.*

[175] Christopher Neefus, "Sen. Inhofe's Family Builds Igloo for Global Warming Spokesman Al Gore in Snow-Laden D.C.," *CNS News*, February 9, 2010, http://www.cnsnews.com/news/article/sen-inhofe-s-family-builds-igloo-global-warming-spokesman-al-gore-snow-laden-dc.

[176] "Executive Order -- Minimum Wage for Contractors," *The White House: Office of the Press Secretary*, February 12, 2014, http://www.whitehouse.gov/the-press-office/2014/02/12/executive-order-minimum-wage-contractors.

[177] Marie Hojnacki et al., "Goals, Salience, and the Nature of Advocacy," *American Political Science Review*, August 31, 2006, 4, http://www.unc.edu/~fbaum/papers/APSA06_lobby.pdf.

[178] Ibid.

[179] Thomas T. Holyoke, "Choosing Battlegrounds: Interest Group Lobbying Across Multiple Venues," *Political Research Quarterly* 56, no. 3 (September 1, 2003): 325–36, doi:10.1177/106591290305600307.

[180] Brian O'Mahony, *Developing and Sustaining an Effective Lobbying Campaign* (Irish Haemophilia Society, 2006), http://www1.wfh.org/publication/files/pdf-1255.pdf.

[181] Ibid., 22.

[182] "Influence: Influence & Lobbying: Ranked Sectors," *OpenSecrets*, accessed May 27, 2014, http://www.opensecrets.org/lobby/top.php?showYear=2010&indexType=c.

[183] "State Legislators Guide to Repealing ObamaCare," *ALEC - American Legislative Exchange Council*, accessed August 3, 2014, http://www.alec.org/publications/the-state-legislators-guide-to-repealing-obamacare/.

[184] Ibid.

[185] Ibid.

[186] Ibid.

[187] Lauren Feeney, "ALEC's Attempts to Thwart Obamacare," *Moyers & Company*, accessed August 3, 2014, http://billmoyers.com/2013/08/13/alecs-attempts-to-thwart-obamacare/.

[188] Lisa Graves, "A CMD Special Report on ALEC's Funding and Spending, accessed August 23, 2014, http://www.prwatch.org/news/2011/07/10887/cmd-special-report-alecs-funding-and-spending.

[189] Ibid.

[190] "Foreign Assistance Fast Facts: FY2012," *U.S. Overseas Loans and Grants*, accessed August 3, 2014, http://gbk.eads.usaidallnet.gov/data/fast-facts.html.

[191] Anupama Narayanswamy, Luke Rosiak, and Jennifer LaFleur, "Adding It up: The Top Players in Foreign Agent Lobbying," *Sunlight Foundation*, accessed August 18, 2009, http://sunlightfoundation.com/blog/2009/08/18/adding-it-top-players-foreign-agent-lobbying/.; Anu Narayanswamy, "International Influence: Agents of Foreign Clients Report Thousands of Lobbying Contacts, Millions in Fees," *Sunlight Foundation*, December 2, 2010, http://sunlightfoundation.com/blog/2010/12/02/top-players-2009/.

[192] "Foreign Influence Explorer, Client Profile: Country of Peru," *Sunlight Foundation*, accessed August 3, 2014, http://foreign.influenceexplorer.com/client-profile/129990.

[193] Ibid.

[194] Ibid.

[195] "Foreign Influence Explorer: Government of the Kingdom of Morocco," *Sunlight Foundation*, accessed August 3, 2014, http://foreign.influenceexplorer.com/client-profile/129964.

[196] Narayanswamy, "International Influence."

[197] Narayanswamy, Rosiak, and LaFleur, "Adding It up."

[198] Ibid.

[199] Ibid.

[200] Lee Fang, "Demonstrations Test Turkey's Lobbying Clout in Washington," *The Nation*, June 5, 2013. http://www.thenation.com/blog/174672/demonstrations-test-turkeys-lobbying-clout-washington.

[201] Kishore Gawande, Pravin Krishna, and Michael J. Robbins, *Foreign Lobbies and US Trade Policy*, Working Paper (National Bureau of Economic Research, January 2004), http://www.nber.org/papers/w10205.

[202] Felicity Vabulas and Jon Pevehouse, *The Role of Informational Lobbying in US Foreign Aid: Is US Assistance for Sale?* (Charlottesville, VA: International Political Economy Society Conference, November 2012), https://ncgg.princeton.edu/IPES/2012/papers/S300_rm1.pdf.

[203] Ibid.

[204] Alexander Hamilton, "The Federalist Papers: No. 22," *The Avalon Project*, December 14, 1787, http://avalon.law.yale.edu/18th_century/fed22.asp.

[205] Gawande, Krishna, and Robbins, *Foreign Lobbies and US Trade Policy*.

[206] Jesse Helfrich, "Foreign governments lobbying hard in favor of immigration reform," *The Hill*, (February 7, 2013),

http://thehill.com/policy/international/281605-foreign-governments-lobby-hard-in-favor-of-immigration-reform.

[207] "Notes on 22 U.S.C. § 611 : US Code - Notes," *Findlaw*, accessed August 6, 2014, http://codes.lp.findlaw.com/uscode/22/11/II/611/notes.

[208] Jahad Atieh, "Foreign Agents: Updating FRA to Protect American Democracy," *University of Pennsylvania, Journal of International Law* 31, no. 4 (2010).

[209] "FARA - Enforcement," *The United States Department of Justice*, accessed August 6, 2014, http://www.fara.gov/enforcement.html.

[210] Atieh, "Foreign Agents: Updating FRA to Protect American Democracy," 1078.

[211] Ibid.

[212] Will Evans and Avni Patel, "Lobbyists for Foreign Governments Raise Money, Get Clinton, McCain Meetings," *ABC News*, February 1, 2008, http://abcnews.go.com/Blotter/story?id=4228113&page=1.

[213] Ibid.

[214] "2062 Foreign Agents Registration Act Enforcement," *United States Attorneys' Manual*, 1997, http://www.justice.gov/usao/eousa/foia_reading_room/usam/title9/crm02062.htm.

[215] Atieh, "Foreign Agents: Updating FRA to Protect American Democracy," 1062.

[216] "Justice and Law Enforcement: Effectiveness of the Foreign Agents Registration Act of 1938, as Amended, and Its Administration by the Department of Justice," March 13, 1974, http://www.gao.gov/products/B-177551.

[217] Narayanswamy, Rosiak, and LaFleur, "Adding It up."; Narayanswamy, "International Influence."

[218] New York Senator Wants to Halt Port Deal, NPR, February 22, 2006.

[219] "Sidley Austin Lobbying for Cayman Islands," *The Blog of LegalTimes*, March 25, 2010, http://legaltimes.typepad.com/blt/2010/05/sidley-austin-lobbying-for-cayman-islands.html.

[220] "Foreign Influence Explorer: Democratic Party of Albania," *Sunlight Foundation*, accessed August 6, 2014, http://foreign.influenceexplorer.com.

[222] Kevin Bogardus, "Justice amps up enforcement of law on foreign advocacy," *The Hill*, October 28, 2011. http://thehill.com/business-a-lobbying/190379-officials-turn-up-enforcement-of-foreign-lobby-law.

[223] Zachary Newkirk, "Tiny Towns Spend Big Bucks on Lobbyists to Reap Federal Government Riches," *OpenSecrets Blog*, May 4, 2011,

https://www.opensecrets.org/news/2011/05/tiny-towns-spend-big-on-lobbyists-to-reap-federal-government-riches/.

[224] Whaley, Sean. "Nevada Tops List On Federal Lobbyist Spending, Near Bottom On Returns," July 20, 2010, http://www.nevadanewsbureau.com/2010/07/20/nevada-tops-list-on-federal-lobbyist-spending-near-bottom-on-returns/.

[225] "Lobbying Database," *OpenSecrets.org Center for Responsive Politics*, n.d., https://www.opensecrets.org/lobby/.

[226] Ibid.

[227] "Lobbying Industry: Transportation," *OpenSecrets.org Center for Responsive Politics*, accessed August 6, 2014, https://www.opensecrets.org/lobby/background.php?id=M&year=2013.

[228] "Defense Base Closure and Realignment Commission," 2005, www.brac.gov.

[229] Kerr, William, Lincoln, William, Mishra, Prachi, "The Dynamics of Firm Lobbying, National Bureau of Economic Research, Working Paper 17577, November 2011.

[230] Fagan, Mark, Perez, Dante, Tighe, Patrick, Lobbying in Washington: What do Pennsylvania, Nevada, New York and Hawaii Know that the Other States Do Not?!, Mossavar Rahmani Center for Business and Government Seminar Presentation, Harvard Kennedy School, April 24, 2014, Soundcloud: https://soundcloud.com/harvard/sets/m-rcbg-podcasts .

[231] Matt Loftis and Jaclyn J. Kettler, "Lobbying from inside the System: Why Local Governments Pay for Representation," August 14, 2013,

[232] Tristan Hallman, "Cities, Counties Spend Millions to Lobby in D.C.," *Texas Tribune*, November 11, 2010.

[233] Ibid.

[234] Loftis and Kettler, "Lobbying from inside the System," 3.

[235] Hallman, "Cities, Counties Spend Millions to Lobby in D.C."

[236] Ron Nixon, "In the Post-Earmarks Era, Small Cities Struggle for Federal Grants," *The New York Times*, February 2, 2012, sec. U.S., http://www.nytimes.com/2012/02/03/us/in-the-post-earmarks-era-small-cities-struggle-for-federal-grants.html.

[237] Newkirk, "Tiny Towns Spend Big Bucks on Lobbyists to Reap Federal Government Riches."

[238] "Charities & Non-Profits," *Internal Revenue Service*, accessed August 7, 2014, http://www.irs.gov/Charities-&-Non-Profits.

[239] Pamela O'Kane Foter, Looking on the Internet and the Internal Revenue Code's Regulation of Charitable Organizations, 43 N.Y.L. SCH. L. REV. 567 (1999).

[240] "Charities & Non-Profits."

241 Ibid.

242 William V. Luneburg, Thomas M. Susman, and Rebecca H. Gordon, *The Lobbying Manual: A Complete Guide to Federal Lobbying Law and Practice* (American Bar Association, 2009), 329.

243 "Christian Echoes National Ministry, Inc. v. United States," *United States Court of Appeals Tenth Circuit* F2d, no. 470 (December 18, 1972), http://openjurist.org/470/f2d/849/christian-echoes-national-ministry-inc-v-united-states.

244 "Charities & Non-Profits."

245 Cammarano v. United States, 358 U.S. 498 (U.S. Supreme Court 1959).

246 Regan v. Taxation With Representation, 461 U.S. 540 (U.S. Supreme Court 1983).

247 Ibid.

248 Beth L. Leech, *Lobbyists at Work*, 1 edition (Berkeley, CA; New York: Apress, 2013), 47–48.

249 Lester M. Salamon, Stephanie Lessans Geller, and Susan C. Lorentz, *Nonprofit America: A Force for Democracy* (Johns Hopkins University: Center for Civil Society Studies Institute for Policy Studies, 2008).

250 Jeffrey M. Berry, "Nonprofit Groups Shouldn't Be Afraid to Lobby," *The Chronicle of Philanthropy*, November 27, 2003, http://philanthropy.com/article/Nonprofit-Groups-Shouldnt-Be/61998/.

251 Ibid.

252 Jocelyn D. Taliaferro and Nicole Ruggiano, "The 'L' Word: Nonprofits, Language, and Lobbying," *Journal of Sociology & Social Welfare* XL (June 2013).

253 Lester M. Salamon, Stephanie Lessans Geller, and Susan C. Lorentz, *Nonprofit America: A Force for Democracy* (Johns Hopkins University: Center for Civil Society Studies Institute for Policy Studies, 2008).

254 Taliaferro and Ruggiano, "The 'L' Word: Nonprofits, Language, and Lobbying."

255 Salamon, Geller, and Lorentz, *Nonprofit America: A Force for Democracy*.

256 Announcement 2000-84: Internal Revenue Service. *Request for Comments Regarding Need for Guidance Clarifying Application of the Internal Revenue Code to Use of the Internet by Exempt Organizations* (October 16, 2000).

257 Elizabeth Kingsley et al., "E-Advocacy: Using the Internet for Lobbying and Other Political Activities," *The Grantsmanship Center*, 2001, http://www.tgci.com/sites/default/files/pdf/E%20advocacy_0.pdf.

258 Ibid.

259 Kristina Charrad, "Lobbying the European Union," *Westfälische Wilhelms-Universität Münster Nachwuchsgruppe „Europäische Zivilgesellschaft Und Multilevel Governance*, n.d.

260 Claims that 80 per cent of laws adopted in the EU Member States originate in Brussels actually tell us very little about the impact of EU policy-making, Annette Elisabeth Toeller, blogs.lse.ac.uk, 6/13/2012.

261 Annette Toeller, "Claims That 80 per Cent of Laws Adopted in the EU Member States Originate in Brussels Actually Tell Us Very Little about the Impact of EU Policy-Making," *EUROPP*, accessed August 11, 2014, http://blogs.lse.ac.uk/europpblog/2012/06/13/europeanization-of-public-policy/.

262 "Financial Programming and Budget," *European Commission*, accessed August 14, 2014, http://ec.europa.eu/budget/index_en.cfm.

263 Charrad, "Lobbying the European Union."

263 Alex Warleigh and Jenny Fairbrass, *Influence and Interests in the European Union: The New Politics of Persuasion and Advocacy* (Europa Publications, 2002).

264 David Coen, *Lobbying in the European Union* (Directorate General Internal Policies of the Union, November 2007).

265 David Coen and Jeremy Richardson, eds., *Lobbying the European Union: Institutions, Actors, and Issues* (Also available as: eBook, 2009), 75–78.

266 Author analysis of European Commission Consultations webpages.

268 Kevin J. O'brien, "Silicon Valley Companies Lobbying Against Europe's Privacy Proposals," *The New York Times*, January 25, 2013, sec. Technology, http://www.nytimes.com/2013/01/26/technology/eu-privacy-proposal-lays-bare-differences-with-us.html.

269Coen, *Lobbying in the European Union.*

270 *Transparency Register: Frequently Asked Questions* (Joint Transparency Register Secretariat, October 4, 2012).

271 "Rescue the Register! How to Make EU Lobby Transparency Credible and Reliable," *ALTER-EU: Europe's Campaign for Lobbying Transparency*, June 20, 2013, 6, http://www.alter-eu.org/documents/2013/06/rescue-the-register.

272 Christian Thu, "EU Lobbying Top 100 Biggest Spending Organizations," *Association of Accredited Public Policy Advocates to the European Union*, September 26, 2013, http://www.aalep.eu/eu-lobbying-top-100-biggest-spending-organisations.

274 Pieter Bouwen, "Exchanging Access Goods for Access: A Comparative Study of Business Lobbying in the European Union Institutions," *European Journal of Political Research*, no. 43 (2004): 337–69.

[275] Ibid., 339.

[276] Justin Greenwood, *Interest Representation in the European Union* (Palgrave Macmillan, 2003).

[277] Bouwen, "Exchanging Access Goods for Access: A Comparative Study of Business Lobbying in the European Union Institutions," 358.

[278] Bouwen, "Corporate Lobbying in the European Union: The Logic of Access," *Journal of European Policy* 9:3 June 2002.

[279] Pieter Bouwen and Margaret Mccown, "Lobbying versus Litigation: Political and Legal Strategies of Interest Representation in the European Union," *Journal of European Public Policy* 14, no. 3 (n.d.): 429, doi:10.1080/13501760701243798.

[280] Pieter Bouwen and Margaret Mccown, "Lobbying versus Litigation: Political and Legal Strategies of Interest Representation in the European Union," *Journal of European Public Policy* 14, no. 3 (n.d.): 429, doi:10.1080/13501760701243798.

[281] John O'Donnell, "Special Report - How Lobbyists Rewrite Europe's Laws," *Reuters*, March 18, 2011.

[282] "Worst EU Lobbying Awards 2010," accessed August 11, 2014, http://www.worstlobby.eu/.

[283] Eric Lipton and Danny Hakim, "Lobbying Bonanza as Firms Try to Influence European Union," *The New York Times*, October 18, 2013, sec. World / Europe, http://www.nytimes.com/2013/10/19/world/europe/lobbying-bonanza-as-firms-try-to-influence-european-union.html.

[284] Teri Schultz, "Lobbying Scandal Shocks Europe; Members of the European Parliament Resign (VIDEO)," *GlobalPost*, accessed August 11, 2014, http://www.globalpost.com/dispatch/news/regions/europe/110407/european-parliament-lobbying-scandal.

[285] "Ex-Austrian MEP Imprisoned in Lobbying Scandal," *EurActiv*, (January 15, 2013), http://www.euractiv.com/future-eu/lobbying-scandal-sends-mep-jail-news-517055.

[286] Laurence Peter, "Fourth Euro MP in Lobbying Probe," *BBC News*, March 28, 2011, http://www.bbc.com/news/world-europe-12880701.

[287] "ALTER-EU Reacts to MEP Lobbying Scandal," *Corporate Europe Observatory*, August 11, 2014, http://corporateeurope.org/2011/03/alter-eu-reacts-mep-lobbying-scandal.

[288] Henry Hauser, "European Union Lobbying Post-Lisbon: An Economic Analysis," *Berkeley Journal of International Law* 29, no. 2 (2011): 687.

[289] Qiang Yan, "Bandwagoning, Balancing, and the Unification of Seven Countries in China," n.d.

[290] Scott Kennedy, *The Business of Lobbying in China*, First Edition edition (Cambridge, Mass.; London: Harvard University Press, 2008), 3.

[291] Ibid., 55.

[292] Ellen D. Friedman, "Complicity, Campaigns, Collaboration, and Corruption: Strategies and Responses to European Corporations and Lobbyists in China," *Globalization Monitor Limited*, November 29, 2010, 37, http://www.amrc.org.hk/node/1030/print.

[293] Ibid., 45.

[294] Ibid., 25.

[295] Kennedy, *The Business of Lobbying in China*.

[296] Friedman, "Complicity, Campaigns, Collaboration, and Corruption: Strategies and Responses to European Corporations and Lobbyists in China," 66.

ISBN: 978-1-60042-228-7, August 2014, Hardcover, 740 pages, $ 89.95

[297] Gordon G. Chang, "How To Lobby Beijing," *Forbes*, May 6, 2010, http://www.forbes.com/2010/05/06/china-business-government-opinions-columnists-gordon-chang.html.

[298] Kennedy, *The Business of Lobbying in China*, 215.

[299] Deng Guosheng and Kennedy, Scott, "Big Business and Industry Association Lobbying in China: The Paradox of Contrasting Styles" (Indiana University, Indianapolis and Bloomington, Indiana, 2009), 15.

[300] "Public Anti-Corruption Initiatives," *Business Anti-Corruption Portal: Global Advice Network*, accessed August 11, 2014, http://www.business-anti-corruption.com/country-profiles/east-asia-the-pacific/china/initiatives/public-anti-corruption-initiatives.aspx.

[301] Friedman, "Complicity, Campaigns, Collaboration, and Corruption: Strategies and Responses to European Corporations and Lobbyists in China."

[302] "The State Council," *The Central People's Government of the People's Republic of China*, accessed August 11, 2014, www.gov.cn.

[303] Michael Bristow, "How China Is Ruled: National People's Congress," *BBC News*, March 4, 2009, http://www.bbc.co.uk/news/world-asia-pacific-13908155.

[304] Ibid.

[305] Friedman, "Complicity, Campaigns, Collaboration, and Corruption: Strategies and Responses to European Corporations and Lobbyists in China," 88.

[306] Ibid., 46.

[307] Guosheng and Kennedy, Scott, "Big Business and Industry Association Lobbying in China: The Paradox of Contrasting Styles," Table 5.

[308] Scott Kennedy, "Comparing Formal and Informal Lobbying Practices in China The Capital's Ambivalent Embrace of Capitalists," *China Information* 23, no. 2 (July 1, 2009): 214, doi:10.1177/0920203X09105125.

[309] "Constitucion Politica de Los Estados Unidos Mexicanos: Articulos 5,6,7," February 5, 1917, http://www.diputados.gob.mx/LeyesBiblio/htm/1.htm.

[310] Galaviz, Elias Ephrem, Legislative Lobbying and Regulation, ISBN 970-32-3921-8.

[311] Erika Ramirez, "En Las Cámaras, 250 Grupos de Cabilderos Al Servicio de Trasnacionales," *Contralinea*, July 2, 2013.

[312] Susana Gonzalez, "Fortalecer El Cabildeo, Pide Directivo de Grupo Salinas," *La Jornada*, July 5, 2010.

[313] *PROCAB: Codigo de Etica*, accessed August 11, 2014, http://www.procab.org.mx/etica.aspx.

[314] Ramirez, "En Las Cámaras, 250 Grupos de Cabilderos Al Servicio de Trasnacionales."

[315] Diane E. Johnson, "Continuity and Change in Argentine Interest Group Activity and Lobbying Practices," *Journal of Public Affairs* 8, no. 1–2 (February 1, 2008): 82, doi:10.1002/pa.282.

[316] Ibid., 91.

[317] Ibid.

INDEX

M:

Marshall v. Baltimore and Ohio RR: 49, 50
    citations: 74
    endnotes: p221 (#49)
Medicare/Medicaid: 23, 27, 28, 31, 138, 158, 159
Mexico: 147, 184, 204, 207
    citations: 209
    endnotes: p237 (#309)
Mintzberg, Henry: 117, 118
    citations: 142
    endnotes: p228 (#161)
Multiple Intelligences: 107, 113

O:

Open Secrets: 14, 15, 22, 25, 26, 31, 32, 39, 45, 48, 63, 75, 160, 161, 162, 163, 174, 175, 176
    citations: 20, 91, 142, 168
    endnotes: p220 (#28), p224 (#89), p229 (#182), p231 (#223), p232 (#225, 227)

P:

Podesta: 27, 31, 32, 146, 159
Porter, Michael: 118-120, 124, 140
    citations: 143
    endnotes: p228 (#164)

R:

Reciprocity:
Regan v. Taxation with Representation : 49
    citations: 74
    endnotes: p221 (#45), p233 (#246)
Revolving Door: 34, 63-66, 81, 82

S:

Sunlight Foundation: 39, 41, 43, 45, 52, 114, 149, 151, 152
    citations: 47, 156, 157
    endnotes: p221 (#s 37, 42), p230 (#s 191, 192, 195), p231 (#220

T:

Taxation: 23, 25, 45, 187
Tool Company v. Norris: 3, 4, 49
    citations: 20
    endnotes: p219 (#8)
Trade: 11, 23, 26, 45, 52, 141, 144, 144, 146, 147, 153, 155, 187, 212
    associations/groups/organizations/unions: 25, 28-30, 42, 45, 139, 188, 190
    industry: 52, 68

CPSIA information can be obtained at www.ICGtesting.com
Printed in the USA
BVOW08s0453020415

394383BV00005B/30/P